GN01090994

17 APR 2008

HUSSERL AND HEIDEGGER ON HUMAN EXPERIENCE

In this book, Pierre Keller examines the distinctive contributions, and the respective limitations, of Husserl's and Heidegger's approach to fundamental elements of human experience. In a clear, detailed, and non-partisan analysis, he shows how their accounts of time, meaning, and personal identity are embedded in important alternative conceptions of how experience may be significant for us, and discusses both how these conceptions are related to each other and how they fit into a wider philosophical context. His sophisticated and accessible account of the phenomenological philosophy of Husserl and the existential phenomenology of Heidegger will be of wide interest to students and specialists in these areas, while analytic philosophers of mind will be interested by the detailed parallels which he draws with a number of concerns of the analytic philosophical tradition.

Pierre Keller is Associate Professor of Philosophy at the University of California, Riverside, and the author of *Kant and the Demands of Self-Consciousness* (Cambridge University Press, 1998).

HUSSERL AND HEIDEGGER ON HUMAN EXPERIENCE

PIERRE KELLER

University of California, Riverside

CAMBRIDGE
UNIVERSITY PRESS

PUBLISHED BY THE PRESS SYNDICATE OF THE UNIVERSITY OF CAMBRIDGE
The Pitt Building, Trumpington Street, Cambridge, United Kingdom

CAMBRIDGE UNIVERSITY PRESS
The Edinburgh Building, Cambridge, CB2 2RU, UK
www.cup.cam.ac.uk
40 West 20th Street, New York, NY 10011–4211, USA
www.cup.org
10 Stamford Road, Oakleigh, Melbourne 3166, Australia
Ruiz de Alarcón 13, 28014 Madrid, Spain

© Pierre Keller 1999

First published 1999

Printed in the United Kingdom at the University Press, Cambridge

Typeset in Baskerville 11/12.5pt [CE]

A catalogue record for this book is available from the British Library

Library of Congress Cataloguing in Publication data
Keller, Pierre, 1956–
Husserl and Heidegger on human experience / Pierre Keller.
p.   cm.
Includes bibliographical references and index.
ISBN 0 521 63342 7 (hardback)
1. Husserl, Edmund, 1859–1938 – Contributions in philosophy of experience.
2. Heidegger, Martin, 1889–1976 – Contributions in philosophy of experience.
3. Experience – History.   I. Title.
B3279.H94K38   1999
128′.4′0922 – dc21   98–11678   CIP

ISBN 0 521 63342 7 hardback

Contents

Introduction   *page* 1

1   Experience and intentionality   15

2   Husserl's methodologically solipsistic perspective   39

3   Husserl's theory of time-consciousness   59

4   Between Husserl, Kierkegaard, and Aristotle   84

5   Heidegger's critique of Husserl's methodological solipsism   111

6   Heidegger on the nature of significance   132

7   Temporality as the source of intelligibility   156

8   Heidegger's theory of time   184

9   Spatiality and human identity   207

10   "Dasein" and the forensic notion of a person   227

Select bibliography   242
Index   258

Introduction

In this book, I explore the account of experience developed by Edmund Husserl and critically modified and transformed by Martin Heidegger. I develop the nature of the relation between our awareness of the world and the temporal structure of our experience as it is articulated by Husserl in his phenomenology and then transformed by Heidegger in his own existential conception of phenomenology. The connection between our capacity to come to terms with our environment, the directedness of our consciousness and behavior at items in our environment, and the temporal character of our experience is an intimate one. It is the merit of both Husserl and Heidegger to have explored this connection to a degree not easy to find elsewhere in the history of philosophy, and at the same time to have developed fundamentally different accounts of how the connection in question is to be understood.

GENERAL REMARKS

The concept of a private experience ("Erlebnis") provides the methodological starting-point for Husserl's investigation of the different kinds of objects that populate our shared, public and objective world and the structures that allow us to understand that world. Heidegger rejects the notion of a private experience, indeed the very notion of *Erlebnis*, that has its heyday at the end of the nineteenth century and in the early twentieth century.[1] However, Heidegger continues to give central importance to the other

---

[1] There is an interesting philosophical history of the term "Erlebnis" in Hans-Georg Gadamer, *Truth and Method* (New York: Continuum, 1989), pp. 60–70. Gadamer follows his former teacher Heidegger in connecting the later nineteenth-century subjectivization of experience in general, and aesthetic experience in particular, to the rise of the notion of "Erlebnis."

German term for experience, *Erfahrung*. This notion of experience lacks the connotation of private, subjective experience that is characteristic of the notion of *Erlebnis*.

Husserl introduces the term "intentionality" to describe the capacity that human beings have to direct themselves at objects. Intentionality consists in our awareness of objects and of the contextual features of our environment involved in any awareness on our part of objects. For Husserl, intentionality is a basic, irreducible, and constitutive feature of consciousness that can never be exhaustively understood in terms of any structural features that are characteristic of natural events. As such, intentionality is for him the key to understanding human experience.

Husserl insists that there are various levels to intentionality. These levels of intentionality make up the different levels of human experience. Intentionality reaches down into the most basic forms of perception. At first, however, Husserl excludes immediate sensory awareness, sensation, from intentionality. Unlike perception, sensation does not involve the experience of objects distinct from the having of a certain experience. However, he eventually argues that intentionality is a feature of all consciousness of time. Since he reasonably assumes that all consciousness involves some consciousness of time, this leads him to maintain that even our most basic sensory awareness, such as our awareness of pleasure and pain, involves a kind of intentionality. Unlike perceptions, these sensations do not even have objects that are logically distinguishable from the having of the sensory experiences themselves. Thus, intentionality is involved in a certain way in what seem to be logically private experiences that cannot be shared by different individuals. But intentionality also extends upwards to the most sophisticated forms of human experience and cultural involvement. For it is because we have the capacity for intentionality that we are able to reason about objects in the world and to communicate with other persons.

While Husserl thinks that one can analyze experience in abstraction from the actual environment in which an individual might find him- or herself, he also emphasizes the importance of the environmental aspect of experience. He maintains that experience is always based on some awareness of an individual's perceptual environment. However, in principle, this perceptual environment is something that is, and can be, privately experienced by each individual. The public, shared environment of a common world is a construct from private individually experienced environments. Thoughts endowed with abstract meaning are required in order to underwrite the possibility of communication between different private worlds of experience.

Such meanings are themselves independent of individual experience, indeed they are quasi-Platonic objects. They are really abstract types of functional roles, where such functional roles consist in the differential contribution that bearers of meaning such as words and sentences make to the truth or falsity of judgment and inferences. These meanings cannot be understood in isolation from each other, but they are accessible to the individual in a way that involves no recourse to the actual environment in which the individual finds him- or herself. The environment of the individual as it is meant by the individual is the notional environment of the individual. This notional environment, in principle, can be quite different from the individual's actual environment. What the actual environment is, is a matter of the extent to which the world as it is meant by the individual corresponds to the world as it is independently of how it is meant by the individual. This, in turn, depends on the extent to which an individual's beliefs are true.

Husserl treats intentionality as a person's intention to refer to objects that may be either inside or outside of consciousness. For Husserl, it is therefore always an open question as to whether an individual is referring to objects that are outside of his consciousness. It is even possible that all of our beliefs about the external world and about the existence of other minds might turn out to be false. Heidegger claims that thinking of intentionality as allowing even the possibility of a completely private experience is based on a misunderstanding of the self-transcendent nature of intentionality. The mistake arises from failing to see that there cannot be a private experience that is not itself parasitic on public experience of the external world. To avoid this mistake, Heidegger suggests that the notion of intentionality be interpreted in terms of the notion of transcendence. It is then no longer a question of whether our beliefs are about anything in the world at all, but rather a question of whether they are true of what is in the world.

Heidegger argues that we have no intelligible conception of an individual human being who experiences a completely private environment. For the very notion of private experience is logically dependent on the existence of a publicly accessible domain of entities. He maintains that, once one gives up on a conception of mind that is based on occurrent, in principle private, mental episodes, one will not need to appeal to abstract structures to underwrite communication. To think of communication as something that is underwritten by abstract structures is to misunderstand the very nature of human existence and intentionality. We are able to understand ourselves because to be a human being is to already be in relation to other human beings and other things in a shared world. The possibility of communication is to be understood in terms of the fact that what we initially take to be an independent private sphere of experience is, in fact, parasitic on the social and natural environment in which we form the conception of our own distinctive self.

In exploring the nature of human existence, Heidegger, like Husserl, is centrally concerned with very general structures of human experience. Heidegger argues, as does Husserl, that individual experience is unintelligible when taken in abstraction from such general structures of experience. However, this means something quite different for Heidegger than it does for Husserl. For Husserl, the general structures of experience are a priori, that is, necessary and universal, features of consciousness. For Heidegger, by contrast, general structures of experiences are not universal forms to be instanced in different individual experiences, but rather particular concrete aspects of the manner in which concrete, historical human existence expresses itself. This leads Heidegger to argue, again against Husserl, that general structures of experience are unintelligible when taken in abstraction from the particular experience of an individual human being. Heidegger maintains that the very notion of consciousness with which Husserl works is ultimately an unintelligible abstraction from a human being's interaction with his or her actual environment.

Now Heidegger agrees with Husserl that the most basic and pervasive feature of our intentional relation to the world and entities within the world is the temporal structure of intentionality. Indeed, Heidegger argues that the a priori should be understood in terms of the originating temporal structure of intentionality. However, Heidegger argues that Husserl's idea that all experience has a foundation in private perceptual experience ("Erlebnisse") prevents Husserl from fully understanding and hence from properly explicating and exploiting the temporal structure of experience.

Husserl has an extremely sophisticated model of how past,

present, and future episodes of consciousness might be linked together in a "stream of consciousness." However, from Heidegger's point of view, this analysis has serious flaws to it. First of all, it works with the assumption that the basic stratum of human experience consists of private sensations. And even if one waives worries about the existence of sensations, Heidegger insists that thinking of experience in terms of a series of successively occurrent episodes of experience is a mistake.

In the course of thinking about the nature of time and of our experience of time, Husserl becomes aware of the limitations of any attempt to understand experience in terms of a "stream of consciousness." This leads him to embed our experience of past, present, and future in a tenseless, but nevertheless still, in some sense, temporal account of mental episodes. Husserl also comes to question the primacy of sensation in an understanding of temporal experience, but never succeeds in developing an alternative account.

In some respects, Husserl also begins to see the limitations of the occurrent state conception of human experience. In the course of his work, another conception of mental and physical events begins to emerge. According to this conception of the mental and the physical, mental and physical states are different in that mental states are not subject to strict causal laws, while physical states are subject to such laws. However, mental and physical states have something important in common. They are inherently dispositional. That is, they can only be understood in terms of the way in which persons and physical objects would react to certain circumstances in their environment. For Husserl, this dispositional account of states and properties applies to all "real" things, and thus to minds as well as bodies. However, Husserl stops short of conceiving the basic level of all experience, which for him, is also the basic level of all being, in terms of entities whose nature is defined in terms of a complex of dispositions to interact with the environment. At the most basic level of experience, Husserl sustains a commitment to the idea of a sequence of successively occurrent mental episodes. It is from the vantage-point of this "living present" that Husserl wishes ultimately to reconstruct all of experience.

Heidegger appropriates the complex analysis of the inter-dependence of past, present, and future developed by Husserl on the basis of our experience of tense, while rejecting Husserl's tendency to think of our experience as a stream of successively occurrent private mental episodes. Heidegger provides an alternative account of temporality that gives up the idea of a "stream of consciousness" or a "stream of time" while still holding on to the primacy of past, present, and future (tense) in our understanding of time.

Heidegger links his alternative conception of temporality with a conception of human experience as a set of abilities to respond to the world that can never be understood purely in terms of occurrent states. In his endeavor to distinguish his position from Husserl's mixed disposition-occurrent state account of experience, Heidegger actually goes to the extreme of denying that there are any occurrent episodes of experience at all. But his analysis is different from the traditional behaviorist analysis of experience. Behaviorists are committed to being able to demonstrate that there is a one-to-one correlation between mental states and behavioral properties. This allows the behaviorist to claim that mental states are nothing but behavioral dispositions. The problem with such behaviorism is that mental states cause behavior by virtue of their connections to other mental states. A person's beliefs, emotions, and desires are all required in order to make sense of that person's behavior. It is thus arguable that the totality of a person's mental states is relevant to how the person would behave relative to any specific situation.

Heidegger accepts a holistic account of behavioral dispositions. Such dispositions are, for him, differential capacities that we have for disclosing the world as a whole. And, unlike behaviorists, he allows for behavior that cannot be observed by other persons. Where the behaviorist demands an exclusively third-personal account of experience in terms of behavior that can be observed by other persons, Heidegger treats the capacities that constitute our experience in essentially first-personal terms. He avoids problems of privacy by thinking of what each of us individually experiences as parasitic not only on what we can do together, but on our whole shared experience of the world. This shared experience of the world is, in turn, grounded in the very general conditions of human existence that make us all experience the world in the same basic ways.

For Heidegger, the essence of being human is a process of coming to terms with the entities in the world. In this process, a human being develops the capacities that it has. These abilities make each human being who he or she is. For it is of the essence of human life that in it the world is disclosed to one or has some truth for one. The world is disclosed to one on the basis of the general conditions governing human existence. These most general conditions include, but are not exhausted by, moods and the ability spatially and temporally to find one's way about the world. These general conditions, in turn, put us in a position to occupy social roles, to work with tools and to use language as a tool for communication.

Heidegger is sympathetic to the idea that the meaning of expressions in language, and, more generally, the meaning of different forms of human behavior, have to do with the distinctive normative roles that expressions play in language and that forms of behavior play in different communities. However, he is critical of the algorithmic conception of understanding suggested by neo-Kantian interpretations of meaning as function (for instance, Ernst Cassirer's idea that the development of modern science is characterized by the dissolution of substance into functional and relational notions).[2] This rejection of a formal interpretation of function dovetails with Heidegger's rejection of the Platonism that characterizes Husserl's interpretation of functional role as meaning species. In reinterpreting Husserl's notion of meaning as the functional role that expressions, and also other non-linguistic objects and activities, may play in contributing to the truth and hence also the falsity, of inferences and other norm-guided behavior, Heidegger agrees with Husserl that meanings are constituted by the differential contribution that bearers of meaning make to the potential truth of our understanding of the world. But he argues that meaning is constituted in a use that cannot be understood independently of our capacities to respond differentially to our environment.

Heidegger shares Husserl's rejection of a psychologistic theory of meaning, acccording to which what a person means would be determined by the psychological state a person happened to be in.

[2] Ernst Cassirer, *Substance and Function and Einstein's Theory of Relativity*, W. and Marie Swabey trans. (New York: Dover, 1923), pp. 3ff. In the Davos Disputation between Heidegger and Cassirer, Cassirer succinctly summarizes his position: "The being of the old metaphysics was substance, the one substrate. The being in the new metaphysics is in my language no longer the being of a substance, but being that derives from a manifold of functional determinations and meanings. And therein seems to be the essential point of difference of my position relative to Heidegger." The disputation is published as an addendum to M. Heidegger, *Kant and the Problem of Metaphysics*, Richard Taft trans. (Bloomington: Indiana University Press, 1990), original in: *Martin Heidegger: Gesamtausgabe* (Frankfurt: Vittorio Klostermann, 1991), p. 294. For convenience, my citations are henceforth from the *Gesamtausgabe* abbreviated as *GA* with volume and page numbers. The pagination of the *GA* is reproduced in the available English translations. The translations are, however, mine throughout the book.

But, since he rejects the standard notion of a psychological state, he disagrees with Husserl that the only alternative to psychologism is Platonism. From Heidegger's standpoint, such Platonism is only necessary if one understands experience itself on the model of psychological states. Rather than thinking of experience in terms of psychological states, Heidegger proposes to think of experience and meaning in terms of the way the world differentially displays itself to different human beings from different standpoints in the world.

OUTLINE OF THE ARGUMENT

First, in chapter one, I articulate the notion of intentionality and its historical role in providing us with a conception of human experience. Here I emphasize the importance of Aristotle's "psychology" in the development of the notion of intentionality that has now become so central to the philosophy of mind through the influence of Husserl's teacher, Franz Brentano, and those who have been influenced by Husserl and Brentano.

The analysis that Husserl provides of the internal temporal structure of experiences leads him to argue that experiences must be connected together in a transcendental ego that gives those experiences their unity. It also encourages him to argue that there must be a unity in what is experienced that cannot be understood only in terms of a bundle of appearances or senses. The discovery of an intrinsic unity in the subject of experience that is mirrored in the abstract object of experience suggests that an account of the content of experience can be given that completely abstracts from the real psychological content of experience and from any real objects to which one may be referring. Husserl now comes to focus on a "Cartesian" investigation of the content of mental states. Such a "Cartesian" investigation of content requires the possibility of an inquiry into their structure independently of the actual objects to which they apply. Such an investigation, as Husserl understands it, is not a psychological investigation of content (in this respect it seems to dovetail with the intentions of the historical Descartes), but an analysis of the meaning which representational states have that appeals to abstract structures compared by Husserl to Platonic ideas.

Husserl's position is internalist because it is committed to the idea that one can understand experience in a manner that is methodologically solipsistic. One can understand experience in a manner that abstracts from the existence of other persons and of the external world in general. The possibility of understanding experience in a methodologically solipsistic manner is a result of Husserl's conception of intentionality as something that is to be analyzed in terms of abstract or ideal objects that, in principle, are available to one regardless of whether one has any knowledge of the world or not. This does not mean that Husserl neglects the existence of other minds or the existence of the external world any more than Descartes does. But it does mean that he thinks we must reconstruct the existence of other minds and the external world from the vantage-point of how the existence of the external world modifies individual experience. Such a reconstruction is based on what Husserl calls the transcendence of what we experience immanently in consciousness in the immanence of consciousness.

After developing Husserl's account of the abstract structure of intentionality, and the meaning conferring activities in terms of which individual experiences can be connected together in one shared experience, I turn to the most fundamental structure of experience, and explore the kind of intentionality that is constitutive of any experiences as such. I discuss Husserl's theory of temporality and its role in constituting the most basic level of experience. I show how Husserl discovers a new form of intentionality in the kind of temporal experience involved even in sensations that have no object that is distinct from the having of the experience in question (for instance, a pain). This intentionality connects the present to the past and future.

I argue that Husserl gets into difficulties and is forced to make implausible assumptions about what we can experience because he wants to find a place for punctual experiences in a basically duration-based account of time. At the most fundamental level of intentionality, which Husserl refers to as absolute subjectivity, the successiveness of time-consciousness gives way to what amounts to a tenseless ordering of the episodes of experience according to relations of earlier, later, and simultaneous. One can no longer say that the basic states of intentionality are in time, for they constitute time itself.

I confront Husserl's internalist account of experience with Heidegger's critique. Heidegger signals his rejection of the "Cartesianism" that is explicit in Husserl's philosophical position by emphasizing the transcendence of all experience against Husserl's idea that all experience is immanent, or rather, as Husserl would say, transcendent in immanence. Husserl claims that all experience is describable in terms that do not require the actual existence of the external world, even though such experience is by and large directed at the external world. Heidegger argues, by contrast, that we cannot even make sense of inner experience (and hence any notion of immanence at all) except by recourse to relations that our experiences have to what is temporally and spatially outside of them. He refers to this transcendence that characterizes our temporal and spatial experience as the ecstatic character of temporality and spatiality.

I then show how Heidegger's reinterpretation of the relation between existence and essence is the basis for a powerful critique of Husserl's internalism. Instead of thinking of the intentional as a relation between ideal, atemporal structures of meaning and their temporal instantiations in experience, Heidegger argues that the whole relation between the ideal and the real must be reinterpreted in light of the proper understanding of human existence which is for it to be its own possibilities or to have the way it exists as its very essence. Heidegger articulates this conception of human existence as constituting the essence of what it is to exist into a conception of intentionality and human experience in general that is no longer based on the idea of mental episodes.

I show how Heidegger develops his own modified non-mentalistic conception of experience and ontology out of the Husserlian account by appropriating key features of Husserl's analysis of abstract reference and truth, while rejecting the Platonism that underlies Husserl's theory of truth and meaning. For Heidegger, human existence as a whole becomes a process of disclosure, but also of hiding things from oneself. Truth, so conceived, is not an abstract atemporal structure with an eternal essence to it, as Husserl conceives it, but something whose very nature can only be understood by living through a life. It is only in living one's life that things and sentences have truth for one. Since truth is understood as the condition for the possibility of the very process that is constitutive of human existence, all aspects of human existence are to be thought of as expressions of the truth that makes human existence what it is. This leads to a holistic conception of truth as what gives intrinsic unity, or authenticity, to one's life.

The conception of truth as disclosure underwrites Heidegger's distinctive, holistic conception of meaning. Heidegger refers to this holistic conception of meaning as significance. This theory of significance is a critical development out of Husserl's thesis that all meaning is essentially perspectival and horizonal because it is constituted by the differential contribution it makes to the understanding of perceptual experience. Meaning has an indeterminate fringe of background meaning (its horizon) that is a function of the way in which it structures our intentional relations to the world.

Like Husserl, Heidegger finds the initial basis for meaning in something like the functional role that expressions and other items in the world have in virtue of their systematically differential contribution to the understanding of experience. However, unlike Husserl, Heidegger argues that the functional roles of terms in a language, or of tools in a work-place, or of individuals in a social setting cannot be understood in terms of abstract objects or types. Indeed, he argues that there is no standpoint available to us from which we could come to grasp such types as anything but generalizations from experience that have a certain truth to them within a certain context.

The importance of the anonymous role that a certain term or job has in one's existence has encouraged a reading of Heidegger that gives almost exclusive importance to the way in which our anonymous social roles constitute meaning for us. I do not wish to reject the importance of anonymous social roles in language and human interaction, but I do wish to argue that the anonymity of what anyone does (Heidegger's conception of what "das Man" does) is not the ultimate source of meaning or of significance.

Heidegger argues that truth, intentionality, and meaning, key notions for an understanding of human experience, have a common source in the temporality of human existence. So, while granting the significance of anonymous social practices for Heidegger in making sense of our ability to understand each other, I argue that temporality is what gives unity to the different structures of human existence, including language, and other human practices. This temporality is linked to the dispositional nature of human existence. Human existence is always a differential response to what has happened, and would have or might have happened, or might yet happen.

I reject both solipsistic ("existentialist") and pragmatist conceptions of the source of such significance, arguing that significance is based on the complicated structures of existentials, or conditions for the possibility of existence, that are constituted by human temporality, but is in no interesting sense reducible to temporality. These existentials are best understood as the set of underlying dispositions that allow human beings to form more specific dispositions as they react to what is past, present, and future for them.

Husserl pushes time-consciousness back to a source in experience in which the very distinction between past, present, and future breaks down, and in which one cannot properly talk of object-directedness at all. But Husserl nowhere indicates any tendency to think of temporality as a structure that would help us understand the very nature of the object-directedness involved in intentionality. Heidegger radicalizes Husserl's account of the dependence of intentionality on temporality by arguing that we can understand the nature of the intentionality of behavior by understanding the transcendence involved in all temporality. In the process, Heidegger uses the broader notion of intentionality that Husserl had discovered in the temporal structure of sensory experience to reconstruct behavioral dispositions such as moods that are not properly regarded as object-directed at all. This reconstructive job ultimately has its justification in the idea that intentionality itself is best understood as a specific kind of dispositional response to the world that is based on the capacity that human beings have to relate to things as past, present, and future.

Husserl already regards temporality as constituted by a relation of the present to the past and the future. In this sense, Husserl's own conception of temporality is already ecstatic. What Heidegger brings to the Husserlian notion that the present is always already outside of itself in relating to the past and the future is the further idea that we have no coherent idea of experiences that exist in (immanent to) consciousness without having a necessary relation to an environment that is outside of consciousness. I argue that Heidegger does not really attempt to reduce all forms of transcendence to a distinctively temporal form of transcendence. Such an attempt would be doomed to failure. However, there is some plausibility in thinking of the transcendence involved in temporality as the basis for the unity of an experience that has a manifold of other distinctive forms of transcendence towards the environment, that is, ways in which it depends on the environment. A proper understanding of the transcendence involved in temporality can then lead one to understand the way in which objects are presented to consciousness as a special derivative form of the temporality that is constitutive of all human existence.

After arguing that, for Heidegger, all intelligibility is ultimately based on temporality, albeit not reducible to temporality, my next step is to develop Heidegger's conception of temporality in more detail. I show how it provides an interesting alternative understanding of both time and time-consciousness to that to be found in either contemporary discussion of tense or of physical time. In contrast to most conceptions of tense, Heidegger argues against the primacy of temporal passage (succession), and against most conceptions of either tense or physical time; he argues that time is not to be understood fundamentally in terms of the notion of sequence.

I turn to Heidegger's account of the self and its relationship to human existence ("Dasein"). Here, I show how Heidegger's conception of self-identity is embedded in an essentially spatio-temporal conception of human existence. First, I discuss the way in which Heidegger argues for a conception of the self that is essentially spatial, and confront this conception with contemporary conceptions of personal identity. I show how Heidegger develops his conception of self out of an almost neo-Kantian reconstruction of Aristotle's idea that the soul is the form through which the life of the body is organized. Heidegger agrees with Aristotle and Husserl that we can understand the human body as a set of capacities, and that such dispositions are organized by an overall end of living well. This end of living well can be described as that for the sake of which human beings exist.

However, Heidegger rejects Aristotle's and Husserl's view that there is a fixed form that prescribes how such a life is to be lived, in favor of the idea that there is nothing more basic than the capacities that human beings have. Unlike the Kantian notion of the self as an end in itself and the Aristotelian notion of the self as a purpose (a "hou heneka," or that for the sake of which), Heidegger insists with Kierkegaard that the very being or existence of the self is its essence. The self thus has no essence that is independent of the ends that it chooses for itself.

This picture of what it is to be a self leads to a forensic conception of self. The forensic notion of self is the notion of self as the bearer of responsibility for actions. I argue, however, that Heidegger's conception of self is not exhausted by its forensic role, I show that the functional dimension of his conception of human existence leads him to ground responsibility for self and for its actions in the unity of a human existence over time and space. In the process of developing Heidegger's exploration of the limits of the forensic notion of self, I take up the distinctive future-oriented and eschatological conception of time that Heidegger takes over from the interpretation of early Christian existence sketched by the young Luther. I show that this eschatological (and indeed death-oriented) conception of human time is based on his forensic conception of the self.

Experience and intentionality

In this chapter, I concern myself with developments in the theory of intentionality from Aristotle to the present. These developments provide the background against which Husserl's and Heidegger's accounts of experience may be understood. My intention is to flesh out competing pulls in the notion of intentionality that provide the basis for fundamental disagreements about the nature and the status of intentionality and the role of intentionality in understanding human experience. The competing pulls inherent in the notion of intentionality are crucial to understanding Husserl's account of intentionality in his *Logical Investigations*[1] and more generally to understanding what is at issue between Husserl and Heidegger when it comes to understanding the fundamental nature of experience.

Both Husserl and Heidegger come to an understanding of experience from the role of intentionality in experience. Husserl makes important modifications in Brentano's account of intentionality which determine the character of his conception of experience. Heidegger later reaches back behind Brentano's appropriation of Aristotle's conception of intentionality and attempts to provide a radically new account of intentionality which undermines the subjectivist tendency implicit in both Brentano's and Husserl's account of experience.

The notion of intentionality has its source in the Aristotelian conception of soul as a source of life and cognition. For Aristotle, the

---

[1] Edmund Husserl, *Logical Investigations*, J. N. Findlay trans. (New York: Humanities Press, 1970), *Hua* 19. *Husserliana: Edmund Husserls Gesammelte Werk* is abbreviated as *Hua*. I abbreviate the *Logical Investigations* as *Investigations* and *LU* for ease of citation and I cite it along with other works of Husserl by paragraphs, where available, for ease in moving between the original texts and translations.

soul is a functional unity that is characterized in the case of animals and human beings by a capacity for experience and cognition. This capacity for experience and cognition is, in turn, based on more specific functional subsystems of the functional unity that is the soul. These subsystems are ones that allow the soul (as functional unity of the capacities inherent in a certain body) to relate to individuals in the environment outside of it even when those individuals are not physically present. The capacity for the soul to discriminate physical individuals outside of it when those objects are present and relate to them even when they are absent is based on the fact that its function is governed by an underlying structure or form. It is this form that is then capable of yielding an experience of the physical object without that physical object being physically present in the individual that is having the experience. Such forms in Aristotle are the historical and etymological source of the concept of intentionality.

In Aristotle, experience is not identified with consciousness. This does not mean that Aristotle does not take experience to involve forms of dispositional and occurrent awareness. However, the awareness that an individual has of him- or herself is taken to be a function of the operation of his or her organism (the soul). In the modern period, intentionality has been revived in the context of a theory of consciousness.

The modern theory of intentionality as a theory of consciousness allows for a direct realist reading of the notion that a state of consciousness is directed at an object. In this case, the state of consciousness directly grasps the object that it is directed at. Alternatively, the state of consciousness may be thought to be directed at an object by means of a representation of that object. Such a representation then serves as a psychic intermediary between the state of consciousness and the object at which it is directed. Pulls in these two competing directions have been a hallmark of the notion of intentionality throughout its history, since they antedate the modern notion of consciousness and can be discerned in Aristotle's own conception of intentionality.

In exploring the competing pulls in the notion of intentionality, I look first at the role of intentionality in the contemporary philosophy of mind. Then I explore the historical origins of our conception of intentionality. Then I probe Husserl's critique of both Brentano's immanentist or internalist conception of intentionality as intentional inexistence, as well as his critique of the transcendent or externalist conception of intentionality. Husserl's argument against the object theory of intentionality in either its internalist or its externalist forms leads him to opt for a theory of intentionality based on acts of consciousness that need have no object at all.

In arguing that acts of consciousness have meaning only in virtue of functional role types that they exemplify, Husserl reappropriates the Aristotelian notion of an intention as a form (species) existing in the mind without the psychological and indeed psychologistic implications of Brentano's understanding of intentional inexistence. Husserl rejects the idea that the object-directedness of experience is based solely on a functional relation between psychological or eventually of material states. In this respect he can rightly be regarded as an early critic of functionalism in the philosophy of mind. However, he does argue that the kind of object-directedness involved in intentionality must be understood in terms of the differential functional role that words, statements, and types of mental states can play in reasoning and inference. And he wishes ultimately to argue that these roles cannot be understood completely independently of an account of the functioning of the mind.

INTENTIONALITY AND NATURALISM

The philosophy of mind now pays increasing attention to the thesis that consciousness, in particular, and human experience, in general, are characterized by intentionality. Philosophers of mind distinguish referential intentionality, the directedness of representations at objects, from content intentionality, the possession by representations such as intentions, perceptions, and beliefs of a distinctive meaning or content, in virtue of which they are able to represent things. In contrast to referential intentionality, content intentionality need not involve a directedness at a specific object. A belief, such as the belief that no one is in the room, has a content even if it has no specific object at which it is directed. By contrast, when an individual fears some thing, a lion for instance, or has a belief of a lion that it is something to be feared, then that person is in a state involving referential intentionality.

The relatively recent rehabilitation of the notion that thoughts exhibit intentionality and that sensations and other qualitative states have a distinctive phenomenal content is due largely to difficulties encountered by attempts to provide reductive analyses of the mental.[2] It is difficult to see how the propositional attitudes of what is often called folk psychology can be reconstructed in purely material terms. Common-sense psychological terms such as "believe," "feel," "imagine," "fear," "desire," "think" are crucial to our everyday dealings with one another. They have complex systematic relations to each other which allow us to form interesting generalizations about our experience. These empirical generalizations about psychological states resist formulation in terms of neurophysiological theories. It is difficult to envision how the systematic connections between propositional attitudes could be mirrored in any interesting way in neurophysiological laws.

It is also quite difficult to see how qualitative experiences, such as the experiencing of the color red or the experiencing of pain, can be given a purely physical characterization. Any attempt to characterize such qualitative experiences in terms of their causal and dispositional relations to perceptual inputs and behavioral outputs faces the problem that the existence of such causal functional relations seems to be consistent with the absence of the qualitative experiences in

---

[2] Perhaps the most prominent proponent of intentionality in contemporary philosophy of mind has been John R. Searle, *Intentionality* (New York: Cambridge University Press, 1983). However, the influence of Roderick Chisholm on the contemporary debate should also not be underestimated. Chisholm, who is also the most distinguished contemporary interpreter of Brentano's philosophy, has countered early behaviorist and particularly functionalist models of the mind with the thesis of the irreducibility of the intentional, see Roderick M. Chisholm, *Perceiving: A Philosophical Study* (Ithaca, N.Y.: Cornell University Press, 1957), pp. 168–185. There is a famous defense by Chisholm of the irreducibility of the intentionality of the mental against Wilfrid Sellars's functionalist account of the mind in R. M. Chisholm and Wilfried Sellars, "Intentionality and the Mental," in H. Feigl, M. Scriven, and G. Maxwell (eds.), *Concepts, Theories, and the Mind–Body Problem* (Minneapolis, Minn.: University of Minnesota Press, 1958), pp. 507–539. A more Aristotelian and neo-scholastic approach to intentionality has been defended by P. T. Geach, *Mental Acts* (London: Routledge and Kegan Paul, 1957), and, *Logic Matters* (Oxford: Blackwell, 1972); Elizabeth Anscombe, "The Intentionality of Sensation: A Grammatical Feature," in R. J. Butler (ed.), *Analytical Philosophy*, second series (Oxford: Blackwell, 1965), pp. 158–180, idem, *Intention* (Oxford: Blackwell, 1957), and Anthony Kenny, *Action, Emotion, and the Will* (London: Routledge and Kegan Paul, 1963). The influence of Wittgenstein encourages Geach, Anscombe, and Kenny to interpret the notion of intentionality in a strikingly anti-internalist fashion as a way in which we relate to objects that are outside of the mind. Their interpretation of intentionality is thus more in harmony with that of Martin Heidegger than it is with Brentano or Husserl, interpreted in a subjectivist way. A more recent application of the synthesis of Aristotle and Wittgenstein to the problem of intentionality may be found in John McDowell, "Intentionality *De Re*," in E. LePore and R. van Gulick (eds.), *John Searle And His Critics* (Oxford: Blackwell, 1991), pp. 215–226. According to McDowell, thoughts about particular objects are only thinkable if the objects that they are about actually exist.

question. And, what is more, in trying to reduce the first-person experience of pain to causal and dispositional relations that are objective and available to the third-person point of view, we seem to leave out precisely what is distinctive about having the pain.

The recalcitrance of commonsense psychological explanation to explanation in narrowly naturalistic terms has led to two alternative approaches. Reductive materialists have argued that we need to wait for the resources of physical theory to develop further before we will be able to effect a reduction of psychological to physical idiom, but maintain that, in principle, such a reduction is possible. Philosophical behaviorists and eliminative materialists have argued that propositional attitudes do not really exist. Talk in the idiom of folk psychology should ultimately be replaced by a more perspicuous form of scientific discourse rather than reduced to underlying physical structure.[3] We seem to face the choice of believing that a sophisticated reduction of qualitative states and propositional attitudes to physical states may ultimately be possible, or of taking a purely instrumental approach to qualitative states and/or propositional attitudes. In either case, even if one accepts the validity of these points of view, there is some place, at least during the transition period while we are waiting for a more complete neuroscience, for an analysis of the relations between the propositional attitudes and qualitative states that make up folk psychology.

The contemporary difficulties in implementing reductive or eliminative materialism that have encouraged interest in consciousness and intentionality parallel those difficulties in late nineteenth-century naturalistic psychology that led Franz Brentano and Wilhelm Dilthey to develop a descriptive psychology as a companion to a genetic psychology. Descriptive psychology is based on the idea that many objects of psychological investigation can only be understood in first-personal terms. In this respect, such objects are distinct from objects that are fit for explanation in the impersonal terms of

[3] A classic defense of the position that folk psychology must ultimately give way to talk about ourselves in the more perspicuous scientific vocabulary of cognitive science may be found in Stephen Stich, *From Folk Psychology to Cognitive Science: The Case Against Belief* (Cambridge, Mass.: MIT Press, 1983). More recently, in *Deconstructing the Mind* (New York: Oxford University Press, 1996), Stich has become critical of the eliminativist conclusion that folk psychological states do not exist, while continuing to maintain that folk psychology will be abandoned by a mature science of the mind/brain. Stich now no longer regards attempts to naturalize intentionality as successful, nor does he think that the naturalization of intentionality is necessary in order to demonstrate that there is such a thing as intentionality.

theoretical physics or even of neurophysiology. Thus, descriptive psychology is to be distinguished from the naturalistic discipline of genetic psychology which, in principle, would ultimately link up to neurophysiology.

Brentano introduces the notion of "intentional inexistence" in 1874 in order to characterize the ability of mental states, thoughts, beliefs, emotions, and desires, to direct themselves at objects that do not actually exist.[4] He thinks that the ability of intentional attitudes to direct themselves at objects is the distinguishing mark of the mental and the key to understanding the generalizations involved in folk psychology. He maintains that this ability of the mind to direct itself at objects cannot be accounted for in terms of the causal relations between inputs and outputs in the brain or in terms of dispositions to respond to stimuli. Thus it is not an accident that the most influential aspect in Brentano's notion of intentional existence has been the idea that the mind might have a property of being directed at objects that cannot be reduced to other mental or physical phenomena. This aspect of intentionality, its object-directedness, has rightly almost completely overshadowed another dimension that has often been discerned in Brentano's conception of intentionality. This is the idea that intentional inexistence entails the immanent existence of represented objects in the mind. This idea promises an explanation of how something can be represented even if it does not exist.

THE ARISTOTELIAN LEGACY OF INTENTIONALITY

The notion of intentionality derives from the Latin term "intentio" ("intention"). The term "intention" has a prevailing meaning that is specifically practical. The Latin term from which the term "intention" is derived, "intentio," had the prevailing practical meaning until the beginning of the high scholastic period. The source of our term "intention" is, in fact, the scholastic Latin translation "intentio" for the terms "mana" and "maqul" that are used by the medieval philosopher Avicenna (or, more accurately, Ibn Sina) to

---

[4] Franz Brentano, *Psychology from an Empirical Standpoint*, L. L. McAlister trans. (London: Routledge and Kegan Paul, 1973), p. 88, and also "The distinction between mental and physical phenomena," in R. M. Chisholm (ed.), *Realism and the Background of Phenomenology* (Atascadero, Calif.: Ridgeview Publishing, 1960).

refer to (Aristotelian) forms as they exist without matter in the soul.[5] Brentano and philosophers who have been influenced by him turn to the wider usage of intention to refer to the way the soul is directed at entities, while regarding intentions in the more narrow practical sense familiar from ordinary language and the philosophy of action as a special case of this broader meaning of intention. In introducing the idea of the intentional inexistence of an object, Brentano not only refers to scholasticism, and particularly to Anselm and Thomas Aquinas, but also to Aristotle's *De Anima* (*On the Soul*):

Aristotle already speaks of this psychic inhabitation. In his books on the soul he says that what is sensed is in the individual who senses as sensed, sense takes up what is sensed without matter, what is thought is in the thinking understanding . . . Augustine touches on the same fact in his theory of *verbum mentis* and its internal origin. Anselm does so in his well-known ontological argument . . . Thomas Aquinas teaches that what is thought is intentionally in the one thinking, the object of love [is intentionally] in the person loving, what is desired [is intentionally] in the person desiring, and uses this for theological purposes.[6]

The received interpretation of both the Aristotelian and scholastic conception of the forms without matter, or intentions, in terms of which we are able to perceive objects outside of the "soul," is that such forms are not mental intermediaries between the soul and what the soul experiences, but rather the vehicles in terms of which we directly experience the things outside of the soul. But there are passages in Aristotle that seem to support the idea that forms in the soul are the direct objects of experience, rather than forms by means of which we directly experience things. After noting that only the form of the stone exists in the soul, and not the actual stone, Aristotle argues in *De Anima* that even mathematical knowledge involves objects of thought ("noeta") that reside in sensible forms:

---

[5] The connection between Ibn Sina and the non-specifically practical notion of intentionality has been widely discussed, see Überweg-Geyer, *Geschichte der Philosophie*, vol. 2 (1928), 343; "'Intention' and 'Intentionality' in the Scholastics, Brentano, and Husserl," L. McAlister and M. Schättle trans., in L. McAlister (ed.), *The Philosophy of Brentano* (London: Duckworth, 1976), p. 110; William Kneale and Martha Kneale, *The Development of Logic* (Oxford University Press, 1966), p. 229; and also especially William Kneale, "Intentionality and Intensionality," *Aristotelian Society Supplementary Volume* 42 (1968), 73–90.

[6] Brentano, *Psychology from an Empirical Standpoint*, p. 88n. Brentano develops his interpretation of Aristotle's theory of perception and thought in more detail in his earlier work, *The Psychology of Aristotle*, Rolf George trans. (Berkeley: University of California Press, 1977), pp. 54ff., where he already argues that the object of sense-perception is present in perception as object of perception. Husserl already displays familiarity with both of these works in his first book, *The Philosophy of Arithmetic* (1891), *Hua* 12, pp. 66n and 85n.

And for this reason no one could ever learn or understand anything without perceiving, so that even when we engage in theoretical contemplation, we must have some phantasm that we contemplate; for phantasms are like objects of perception except without matter. (432a8ff.)

It is very tempting to interpret such phantasms as mental images. For such phantasms are present according to Aristotle in non-veridical perception, memories, and dreams, in which the thing itself is absent. This might seem to suggest that Aristotle thinks of phantasms as psychic intermediaries that represent objects outside of the soul. However, one need not think of phantasms as mental images, since one can experience an absent object as present without having a mental image of the object in question. If phantasms were mental images, one would expect them to be involved in veridical perception, that is, in the perception of objects that are actually there and present themselves to us as they are. But Aristotle claims that in thought and perception the mind in some sense becomes its objects. He insists that "actual knowledge is identical with its object" (*De Anima*: 431a). He also notes that "within the soul the faculties of knowledge and sensation are *potentially* these objects, the one what is knowable, the other what is sensible. They must be either the things themselves or their forms. The former alternative is of course impossible: it is not the stone which is present in the soul, but its form" (*De Anima*: 431b27ff.). In the case of intellectual objects, an identity of the form in the mind and the object is possible, since the object is itself a form. But in the case of sensible objects such an identity must remain an unactualized possibility, since the object has not only a characteristic form, but one that is instanced in matter.

For Aristotle, there are undeniably vehicles, which he refers to as forms without matter or stuff, by means of which we are able to perceive and also to think things. He compares the way sense receives form without matter to "the way in which a piece of wax takes on the impress of a signet ring without the iron or gold" (*De Anima*: 424a19–20). However, there is no suggestion that these immaterial forms somehow exist only in the mind or soul or even have objects that exist only in the mind or soul. So there is no reason to think of Aristotle's view as genuinely supporting a representation-alist conception of experience, even if it can be interpreted in that fashion.

Aristotle's metaphor of form impressing matter like a signet ring impresses wax has suggested a materialist reading to some according to which the forms that are received by the senses are in fact physical information, while the somewhat more prevalent view has been that these forms are already immaterial in character. Thus the extent to which Aristotle's notion of a form in the soul without matter is itself genuinely immaterial is controversial.[7] According to Richard Sorabji, Arabic writers such as Ibn Sina still interpret the material states caused by the effect of sense objects on our senses as information or as a sign of their causes. This notion of intention is then interpreted by Thomas Aquinas as non-physical information that is physically housed, but does not of necessity involve an awareness of anything. Brentano then finally gives the notion of an intention an irredeemably "Cartesian" interpretation as something necessarily involving mental awareness.

The connection that Brentano draws between the form in intention and consciousness is apparent in his interpretation of Aristotle. Brentano argues that, when Aristotle says that the eye receives a certain color from some other object of sense, he means that the eye becomes aware of the color in question. From Sorabji's perspective, Brentano's interpretation of Aristotle's notion of perceptual form without matter as consciousness's directedness at objects involves serious distortion. Brentano has been defended, however, by Myles Burnyeat. Burnyeat argues plausibly that the effect that a certain object of sense has on an organ is itself for Aristotle a perceiving and thus a form of awareness.[8] Such an awareness seems already to involve a qualitative phenomenal experience of the kind that functionalists try to explain in terms of causal functional relations.

One need not, however, endorse Burnyeat's more robust claim that the relation between matter and form is essential in Aristotle in the case of beings that are essentially alive and sentient. This claim is

---

[7] Richard Sorabji tells the story of the history of the concept of intentionality as a shift from an initially physical notion to a progressively more mentalistic one, in Richard Sorabji, "From Aristotle to Brentano: The Development of the Concept of Intentionality," *Oxford Studies in Ancient Philosophy*, Supplementary Volume 9 (1991), 227–259, and also his paper "Intentionality and Physiological Processes," in Martha Nussbaum and Amélie Rorty (eds.), *Essays on Aristotle's De Anima* (New York: Oxford University Press, 1992), pp. 195–225. Sorabji interprets Aristotle as a proto-functionalist in the philosophy of mind. Sorabji argues rather contentiously that when Aristotle claims that the sense organ receives form without matter and becomes like the sensed object he means that the inner organ takes on physical sounds, odours, flavors, etc. The eye-jelly turns red, and the nose actually becomes smelly.

[8] Myles Burnyeat, "Is Aristotelian Philosophy of Mind Still Credible? A Draft," in Martha Nussbaum and Amélie Rorty, *Essays on Aristotle's De Anima*, pp. 15–26.

directed against functionalist interpretations of Aristotle such as that
defended by Sorabji that require multiple possible physical instantiations of mental states. Yet, even if one does not accept Burnyeat's
more robust claim, one need not endorse a functionalist interpretation. It is true that Aristotle's distinction between matter and form
(function) anticipates the claim that certain functionalists have made
against the identification of physical structure with function pro-
posed by advocates of a materialist identity theory of mind. But
seeing that Aristotle distinguishes physical structure and function
and then relates function to physical structure hardly constitutes a
sufficient reason for ascribing to Aristotle the substantive thesis of
functionalism. This is the claim that psychic (mental) states can be
individuated into types on the basis of the causal functional relations
that they bear to one another and to the inputs and outputs of the
system to which they belong.

Turning now to Thomas Aquinas, again the standard reading of
Thomas, as Sorabji concedes, assigns to intention a necessary
awareness component.[9] Thomas reconstructs Aristotle's theory of
perception in the following way:

> But the sensible image is not what is perceived, but rather that by which
> the sense perceives. Therefore the intelligible species is not what is
> understood, but that by which the intellect understands ... Since the
> intellect reflects upon itself, by this very reflection it understands both its
> own understanding and the species by which it understands. And thus the
> intelligible species is in a secondary sense that which is understood. But
> that which is understood in a primary sense is the thing of which the
> intelligible species is the likeness.[10]

Thomas rejects the idea that the objects that we experience are the
species or epistemic intermediaries in terms of which we experience
external objects. We directly perceive or think objects by means of
species (forms), but the objects that we experience are objects
external to the soul or mind. However, in a secondary sense, we also
have a consciousness of ourselves as perceiving or thinking those
objects through species.

---

[9] The standard reading of Thomas on intentionality may be found defended by Sheldon M.
Cohen, "Thomas Aquinas on the Immaterial Reception of Sensible Forms," *Philosophical
Review* 91 (1982), 193–209.

[10] Thomas Aquinas, *Summa Theologica* (New York: Benzinger Brothers, 1952), I, 85, 2.

BRENTANO AND INTENTIONAL INEXISTENCE

Brentano takes over the Aristotelian idea that we have a secondary awareness of ourselves perceiving or thinking whenever we think of or perceive some object, but, like Descartes, he seems to combine this doctrine with the non-Aristotelian idea that real external objects are not themselves characterized by the sensible qualities that we directly perceive in external perception. This leads to what is widely thought to be Brentano's "Cartesian" doctrine of the immanence of the mental.

Punning on the German word for perception, *Wahrnehmen,* Brentano argues that inner perception is the only form of perception that genuinely grasps what is true ("wahr-nimmt"). In inner perception, we immediately experience the objects of our representations, mental phenomena, since those objects are themselves representations. In outer perception, we perceive sensory qualities: colors, sounds, smells, warmth, cold, but these secondary qualities are qualities of physical objects only insofar as those objects are physical phenomena.

This suggests that the existence in the mind of forms (ideas) is based on a form of representational realism in which the forms (ideas) that we know are stand-ins or representatives of the things that we know through them. On the face of it, such representational realism seems alien to the spirit of Aristotle's conception of perception, which is more generally understood as a form of direct realism in which forms serve as the vehicles for perceptual awareness but are not themselves the actual objects of perception.

According to this widely held "Cartesian" interpretation of Brentano's earlier views, in 1904 Brentano then forsakes the idea of intentional inexistence in favor of the idea that we can only represent things, real objects, by which he means the accidents of substances. Brentano now rejects all existence claims concerning non-real entities. He then maintains that only substances and their accidents are real and representable; all other entities are linguistic fictions. This shift to reism has sometimes been referred to as Brentano's Copernican revolution.[11] Brentano's key argument for the primacy of things is that representation or thought is a univocal notion, and,

---

[11] Oskar Kraus, "Die 'kopernikanische Wendung,' in Brentanos Erkenntnis- und Wertlehre," *Philosophische Hefte* 3 (1929).

since representation is always representation of something, that something must also be univocal:

The expression "to represent" <*vorstellen*> is univocal. To represent is always to represent *something*. Since "to represent" is univocal, the term "something" must also be univocal. But there is no generic concept that can be common both to things and to non-things. Hence if "something" denotes a thing at one time, it cannot denote a non-thing – an impossibility, say – at another time.[12]

One conclusion that one might be tempted to draw from Brentano's argument is that it is impossible to represent non-existent things at all. This would be a rather implausible return to the position of the pre-socratic philosopher Parmenides. While Brentano thinks that we can represent things, real objects, that do not exist, he thinks that all "irreal" objects, by which he means all objects that are not actual or possible substances, or at least possible or actual accidents of substances, are mere linguistic fictions. Thus, all talk of non-real objects should be eliminable in favor of talk of real things, that is actual or possible things. Brentano's argument for his nominalistic ontology is not altogether convincing, since it relies on the rather dubious assumption that there is only one sense in which one can represent anything. However, it is significant that the constant in his thought is not the idea that objects of thought must literally exist in the mind, but the idea that thought involves the ability to direct itself at its objects. This is in keeping with the original Aristotelian inspiration of his thought.

Indeed, the Cartesian interpretation of Brentano's initial conception of the intentional has been challenged by the later Brentano and by other interpreters of his work. Such interpreters argue that Brentano never holds the view that intentional objects literally exist in the mind. Thus Richard Aquila argues that "Brentano never did argue, even during his early period, that whenever somebody thinks about centaurs, there is a centaur which is thought about"; Aquila insists that "the notion of an 'immanent object' was not intended by Brentano to suggest that some object is 'in' the mind, but only to suggest that it is an *object* for the mind."[13]

---

[12] Franz Brentano, *The True and the Evident*, R. Chisholm and E. Politzer trans. (London: Routledge and Kegan Paul, 1966), p. 108.

[13] Richard Aquila, *Intentionality: A Study of Mental Acts* (University Park: Pennsylvania State University Press, 1977), p. 100. The ontological view of the intentional is also challenged by Linda McAlister, "Chisholm and Brentano on Intentionality," *The Review of Metaphysics* 28

This direct realist interpretation is more in harmony with the Aristotelian views that Brentano thought he was reconstructing. Instead of thinking of intentional inexistence as the literal existence of objects in the mind, it is possible to understand intentional inexistence as a particular kind of relational feature of the mental. On this view, mental phenomena are just the way in which things that are independent of the mind appear to the mind. Unlike the more "Cartesian" interpretation of intentional inexistence, the primary objects of perception are taken to be things that are external to the mental acts in which they are thought; it is only the secondary objects of perception that are internal to the mind: "The primary object of such [mental] acts is transcendent simply because this realization of the form of the object, this mental act, is not itself an object save secondarily, in inner perception."[14]

The merit of the direct realist interpretation of Brentano over the representational realist interpretation is threefold: it allows one to see how the early Brentano is influenced by Aristotle and, in turn, inspires the Aristotelian direct realism of Husserl, Twardowski, and Meinong; it makes for a greater continuity in Brentano's own thought; and it conforms to Brentano's own interpretation of the relation between his earlier and later views. For Brentano later argues that the subjectivist interpretation of his early work is mistaken. He maintains that the term "immanent object" in his earlier writings refers to the fact that there might not be an object in the external world corresponding to the object in question:

But it *was not my opinion that the immanent object* = *"represented object."* The representation does not have "represented object," but "the thing," therefore for instance, the representation of a horse, not "represented Horser," *but rather* "horse" as (immanent, i.e. sole object authentically to be called) object. This object *however is not.* The representer has something as an object, *without it therefore being.*[15]

On the more Aristotelian interpretation, Brentano does not later reject his earlier notion of intentional inexistence, he merely insists more forcefully on the ontological primacy of things relative to

(1978), 328–338, and by Robert Richardson, "Brentano on Intentional Inexistence and the Distinction Between Mental and Physical Phenomena," *Archiv für Geschichte der Philosophie* 65 (1983), 250–282.

[14] *Ibid.*, p. 279.

[15] Brentano Letter to Anton Marty, March 17, 1905 in Franz Brentano, *Abkehr vom Nichtrealen* (Hamburg: Meiner Verlag, 1966), pp. 119–120.

properties and abstract objects.[16] Still, some account is needed of what it means for something to be a non-existent object. For intentionality seems only to be comprehensible to the extent that one can make sense of the possibility of a kind of quasi-relation between something real and a non-existent object. This raises the question of how one could relate to something that does not exist.

NON-EXISTENT OBJECTS IN THE BRENTANO SCHOOL

Brentano's early students, Twardowski, Meinong, and Husserl attempt to provide an answer to how something can be an object without actually existing. In response to this problem, Twardowski develops the object theory of intentionality in 1894, according to which all intentional acts have objects, but these objects may be either internal to or external to consciousness, and either existent or non-existent objects:

> The expression "objectless representation" <*Vorstellung*> is such that it contains a contradiction; for there is no representation which does not represent something as an object; there can be no such representation. But there are many representations whose objects do not exist, either because the objects combine contradictory determinations and hence cannot exist, or because they simply do in fact not exist.[17]

Twardowski distinguishes between the act of representing, the content of representation, and the object represented. The content of the representation constitutes the meaning or significance of the representation. The content of the representation is what is immanent to consciousness, while in most cases the object represented is not. Every representation consists of act, content, and object.

Husserl objects to the scheme developed by Twardowski on two separate grounds, one having to do with Twardowski's understanding of the notion of content and the second having to do with his understanding of what it is to be an object. First, Husserl argues that it is a mistake to identify the meaning or significance of a representation with its psychological content:

---

[16] Brentano regards accidents as the wholes of which the substances to which they belong are parts, see Franz Brentano, *Kategorienlehre*, Alfred Kastil (ed.) (Hamburg: Meiner Verlag, 1933), pp. 151ff.

[17] Kasimir Twardowski, *On the Content and Object of Presentations*, R. Grossman trans. (The Hague: Martinus Nijhoff, 1977), p. 26.

That each significant expression must in its normal function carry along with it, in addition to those changing contents, certain contents that are constant in all cases, without which understanding would not be possible, which could therefore be understood as *the* "content" of the respective representation in a more pregnant sense – all of this I hold to be psychological fiction ... The content resides in the representation as a real constituent, but the signification does so only functionally.[18]

Husserl argues persuasively that there is just no precisely identical psychological content in the mind of different persons who mean the same thing which would permit identification of meaning with psychological content. From this lack of any identical psychological content in different persons who share the same thought, he infers that meaning or signification is something ideal or abstract, rather than some real content. Of course, thinking of meaning as an abstract psychological content that is instanced in different individuals will not do either. There is not enough that the psychological states of different individuals have in common when those individuals mean the same thing. Husserl proposes instead that the identity of signification (meaning) depends on the way different expressions and psychological states may perform the same functional role in the way those individuals use language and reason.

Against Twardowski's object theory of intentionality, Husserl maintains that there can be objectless representations, such as "a round square" or "the present King of France." Twardowski maintains that we can distinguish between the non-existence of an object that is represented by us and its not being represented. Even if the object does not exist, it can still be represented by us. Husserl first argues that it is a consequence of Twardowski's view that an object of representation actually exists that is genuinely immanent in that representation. At least the object of representation exists as a represented object.[19] But if we are willing to countenance the existence of a round square as an object that is immanent in our representations, then we ought to countenance the existence of contradictory objects.

[18] Edmund Husserl, "Critical Discussion of K. Twardowski, *Zur Lehre vom Inhalt und Gegenstand der Vorstellungen. Eine Psychologische Untersuchung* (Vienna 1894)," *Hua* 22, p. 350n. There is an English translation in D. Willard (ed.), *Edmund Husserl: Early Writings in the Philosophy of Logic and Mathematics* (Dordrecht: Kluwer, 1994). The Willard translation reproduces the *Hua* pagination in the margins.

[19] The argument in question is to be found in a long unpublished paper "Intentional Objects," written between 1894 and 1898, but first published in *Hua* 22, pp. 303– 348, see esp. p. 352, also in D. Willard (ed.), *Edmund Husserl: Early Writings in the Philosophy of Logic and Mathematics.*

In fact, Meinong pursues this line of thought. Meinong argues that representations may have an intentional relation to existent or non-existent objects of different kinds, but that whenever there is an intentional relation there is some kind of object to which one is directed. He contends that one can talk of the being-such ("Sosein") even of contradictory objects. A whole realm of non-existent objects opens up which have what Meinong calls *Sosein*.[20] The object theory of intentionality is for this reason most closely associated with the work of Meinong.

Instead of pursuing the object theory route, Husserl argues that not every representation has an object in the authentic sense. Being an object in the authentic sense is equivalent to being an existing, true object of representation. This is only going to be satisfactory if some account can be provided of how an object can be given in an inauthentic sense. Husserl needs to account for our ability to talk about non-existent objects, such as Zeus. What does it mean to intend to refer to Zeus, in many cases under different descriptions, even though there is no such object? Husserl's suggestion is that we treat Zeus as if he were an object: "But our judging is then a 'modified' one, a judging which seems to be about the represented objects, insofar as we place ourselves on (phantasizing our way into, etc.) the grounds of the existence of the objects, upon which we in truth do not stand at all" (*Hua* 22, p. 317).

The idea that in relating to non-existent object, we are only acting as if we were relating to an object, even applies to logic, and mathematics. In logic and mathematics, we can make conditional claims about objects which may not be true. But then we are only talking as if there were such objects (*Hua* 22, pp. 321–328).

FROM INTENTIONAL OBJECT TO FUNCTIONAL ROLE

The idea that non-existent objects are ones to which we merely pretend to refer is not completely satisfying. There seems to be a difference between believing that centaurs exist and pretending to believe that centaurs exist. Fortunately, Husserl has a deeper suggestion for how we might understand reference to objects that do not exist. He suggests that the notion of an intentional object, in the

[20] Alexius Meinong, "The Theory of Objects," in R. Chisholm (ed.), *Realism and the Background of Phenomenology.*

sense of an object that must be represented if an act of consciousness is to have content, should simply drop out in favor of the distinctive inferential role played by the content expressed by a certain act of consciousness:

> It is worth considering ... whether talk of immanent objects of representation and judgment cannot be understood as an inauthentic one, such that in general there is nothing contained in the acts themselves, that there is nothing there in them in the authentic sense of which it could be said that this is the object which the act represents or rather recognizes or rejects; that therefore acts, if they need an existing stuff to be acted on in the way that activities do, cannot have the stuff they need in the objects "at which they are directed"; but that talk of containment and the whole difference between "true" and "intentional" reduces to certain individual features and distinctions in the logical function of representations, i.e. in the forms of possible valid connections, in which the representations can enter, regarded solely with respect to their objective content. ("Intentional Objects" section 4, *Hua* 22, p. 311)

For Husserl, the idea that the intentional object is nothing but a function of the distinctive functional role that a certain way of representing things can play in reasoning and the making of logical inferences is itself the expression of the distinction that he draws between the ideal and the real or psychological content of linguistic and other representations.

> The distinction between the ideal and the psychological content of representational acts pushes us from the outset to such a conception. The former points to certain connections of identification in which we grasp the identity of the intention (in some cases with evidence), while the individual representations do not have any psychologically identical constituent in common. We assigned the objective reference of representations from the outset to their ideal content, representations of identically the same meaning can display objective difference, representations of different meaning identity. Here talk of representations that represent the same object was based on nothing other than synthesis in judgment, or rather in cognition. Looking at the matter precisely, the posited connection here is based on the objective content of the referential representational acts, in their essence. ("Intentional Objects" section 4, *Hua* 22, pp. 311–312)

Here we must distinguish three things, (1) the real or psychological content, (2) that aspect of the ideal content that constitutes the meaning of an act, and (3) that aspect of the ideal content that constitutes its intended reference. Unfortunately, the opening section of "Intentional Objects" in which Husserl develops the idea that intentional directedness of representations is part of their ideal content is no longer fully extant.[21] However, the ideas that he articulates here are an anticipation of the more developed account to be found in the *Investigations*. The intended reference of a representation is determined by the object which it purports to represent. Husserl takes successful reference to involve cognition of the object to which one is intending to refer. The possibility of cognition of a certain object by means of a certain set of representations is, however, determined by the essence of the acts to which they belong, and this, in turn, is the basis for the distinctive functional roles that different acts play in inference:

> Thinking, we are always directed at objective connections. But the latter concern the mere function of representations, this does not mean that object and objective connection in representation and judgment lead an idiosyncratic "mental existence." ("Intentional Objects," *Hua* 22, p. 335)

INTENTIONAL AND INTENSIONAL OBJECT IN THE "INVESTIGATIONS"

The analysis of the intentional object that Husserl develops in the late 1890s, with its distinction between an authentic and an inauthentic, or merely significative, intentional object, prepares the way for the position that he articulates in the *Investigations* (1901). The authentic intentional object is an object that exists as we take it to be, while the inauthentic intentional object is an object that merely seems to exist because we can meaningfully (significatively) talk about it. Working with these distinctions Husserl argues in the *Investigations* that the intentional object of consciousness is really neither inside nor outside of consciousness. The context is purely intensional:

> I present the god Jupiter, that is, I have a certain presentational experience; in my consciousness there occurs a presenting-of-the-god-Jupiter. One may dissect this intentional experience by descriptive analysis in any way one pleases, but one will naturally not find anything like the god Jupiter; the "immanent," "mental" object does not belong therefore to the descriptive (real) constitution of the experience, thus it is not really immanent or mental. Of course, it is also not *extra mentem*, it does not exist at all. But that

---

[21] A more complete version of the German text of "Intentional Objects" than that to be found in *Husserliana* is now available in *Brentano-Studien* 3 (1990–1), 136–176.

does not affect the fact that the presenting-of-the-god-Jupiter is actual. (*LU* v, section 11).

While the claim that the intentional object is neither inside nor outside of consciousness is initially somewhat mysterious, it can be made sense of by thinking of the intentional object as an adverbial modification of intentional states.[22] Something appears to consciousness even in cases of non-veridical perception and fictional discourse. But in such cases there is no object internal to or external to consciousness and thought to which one is in fact existentially committed. Instead what appears to be an object is merely a way of perceiving, believing, imagining, or thinking. Thus while there is a logical or grammatical object that is intended, there is no actual object, and hence no genuine reference. By contrast, where perception and belief are veridical, they do involve existential commitments to objects (*LU* v, sections 34ff.). In this way, Husserl rejects both the immanentist and the externalist versions of the object account of intentionality.

The act of consciousness creates an intensional context in which the existential generalization from the thought that Pa to $(\exists)xFx$ is not in general licit.[23] However, failure of existential generalizability of the kind involved in intensional contexts is not a sufficient condition for intentionality. The statement "Klingons fight wars" is intensional, it fails to support existential generalization, since Klingons do not in fact exist. However it does not necessarily involve intentionality. There is also no reason to think that failure of existential generalizability is a necessary condition of intentionality. Knowledge involves intentionality, and yet on the traditional interpretation of knowledge as justified true belief knowledge supports existential generalization.

Especially in his later career, Husserl makes much of the kind of immunity to reference failure involved in I thoughts. He attributes the highest level of "Evidenz" (support for the truth of a claim) to such thoughts because we cannot even think them without their

---

[22] The intentional object in the *Logical Investigations* is also given an adverbial interpretation by David Woodruff Smith and Ronald McIntyre, *Husserl and Intentionality* (Dordrecht: Reidel, 1982), p. 142, and by Barry Smith, *Austrian Philosophy: The Legacy of Franz Brentano* (La Salle: Open Court, 1994).

[23] While Chisholm has attempted to spell out logical criteria that are necessary and sufficient conditions for intentionality, I think it is fair to say that he has not succeeded in doing so. A detailed criticism of his account may be found in L. Jonathan Cohen, "Criteria of Intentionality," *Aristotelian Society Supplementary Volume* 42 (1968), 123–142.

being true, and thus having an object that exists. Non-extensional occurrence, or intensionality, is also not a logical criterion of intentionality, since there are non-intentional sentences, particularly modal sentences, such that replacing a phrase, p, with a phrase, p₂, having the same truth value as p, in a sentence, s, will result in a sentence with different truth value than s. Referential opacity also fails to distinguish intentional from non-intentional sentences, since many non-intentional sentences with modal operators are referentially opaque. It is, however, reasonable to say that intentionality provides some of the most significant examples of intensionality, and referential opacity. In those circumstances, however, in which consciousness actually represents the object as it is, and hence existential generalization is possible, the intentional object of consciousness is simply the external object of consciousness. In those cases, however, in which what is represented by us does not in fact exist, the intentional object is merely an adverbial modification of the act of consciousness through which it is represented.

HUSSERL'S BRENTANO CRITIQUE

Working with an immanentist interpretation of Brentano's theory of perception, Husserl accuses Brentano of confusing the real contents of consciousness by means of which an object is presented to us in individual experience with the intended object of those experiences. From the immunity of such contents to error in the presentational immediacy of individual experience, Brentano then falsely infers that inner experiences are the only objects that one can truly perceive ("wahr-nehmen"), where he should have claimed that such contents are not perceived at all in our immediate experience of them (Addition to *LU* VI, section 6). In contrast to Brentano, who maintains that sensations are mental phenomena and are characterized as such by intentional inexistence, Husserl insists that sensations are not intentional, in the sense that they do not have referential or content intentionality, although he regards them as mental states or experiences ("Erlebnisse") with a certain content. As such, sensations have what contemporary philosophers of mind would call "phenomenal content." There is something that it is like to experience a sensation.

While Husserl makes Brentano's emphasis on the intentional inexistence of the mental his own, he rejects both the latter's thesis that all mental states are characterized by intentional existence, and his conception of intentional objects as objects that are always immanent to consciousness. Husserl introduces the notion of mental acts to characterize mental states that are directed at objects. Such object-directedness is what makes them inherently intentional. Mental acts are thus distinguishable from other mental states, such as sensations, that contribute to the way in which mental acts are directed at objects, but are themselves mere subjective states of the percipient. It is in virtue of such object-directedness that mental acts have meaning. For meaning is the way in which an object presents itself to consciousness. Mental states that are not object-directed have meaning only in virtue of the contribution they make to mental acts that do have intentionality.

Brentano emphasizes the fact that sensations are representations whose objects are internal to the mind, and hence have intentional inexistence. Thus the sensation of pain may be said to have an object. But this object is not independent of the experience of having the pain. Husserl maintains that sensations must be distinguished from perceptions precisely because sensations have objects that are not logically distinct from sensations themselves. Only the latter representations, that is, perceptions, which interpret the content provided by sensations are characterized by intentionality, or genuine directedness at an object. For it only makes sense to talk of a directedness at an object if the object is logically distinct from the representation of it. In discussing Brentano's views on inner perception, Husserl notes that in perceiving a painful tooth we are quite capable of error. For, in this case, "the perceived object is not the pain, as it is experienced, but the pain, as it is interpreted transcendently, that is, interpreted with respect to the tooth" (Addendum to *LU* vi, section 6). It is one thing to have an immediate experience of pain, it is another to perceive what one is experiencing as the pain belonging to one's tooth. For the tooth is something that is not in any sense an essential part of one's experience of pain.

Again in the case of emotional states, Husserl distinguished states such as hope or fear that seem to have an obvious object, and states such as joy that may not have an object that is logically distinguishable from the state itself (*LU* v, section 15). Sensations and emotional states provide the mind with an immanent content. A sensation of pain or a feeling of unease has a content that seems in some ways inseparable from our having the experience of pain or unease. To this extent, Brentano seems to be correct in thinking of sensations and some kinds of feelings as being characterized by intentional inexistence. However, Husserl also seems to be right in denying that such mental states are about anything. The immanent content of consciousness gives consciousness its *particular* directedness at an object even though such states are not themselves directed at objects prior to being conceptualized by us.

We may have an intentional relation to spatio-temporal objects, to mental states, to abstract objects such as numbers, and universals, and even to facts. It is often thought that we may have an intentional relation or attitude to a meaning or proposition. When we believe, or hope, or desire that something is the case, we seem to have an intentional relation to a proposition that is referred to by the clause in question. Husserl rejects the idea that we ever have an intentional attitude to a proposition. Instead he argues that so-called propositional attitudes involve an intention to refer to a fact by means of a thought that instantiates a proposition.[24] In this way, he can argue that propositional attitudes do not require the existence of the concrete object which is referred to in the proposition unless the proposition is true and thus states a fact.

Husserl allows for acts of consciousness endowed with intentionality and meaning that are not explicitly propositional in structure. A perception falls, for instance, into this category of what he comes to call monothetic acts. Indeed, unlike philosophers in the Kantian and Fregean traditions, Husserl does not think that the primary bearer of meaning is the proposition. However, he does maintain that singular and general terms have a meaning that expresses itself in the distinctive contribution that they make to the different propositions in which they can play a semantic role. Since propositions are abstract objects of a certain kind, Husserl concludes that meaning in general must be conceived of in terms of abstract

---

[24] The contrast between the popular idea of propositions as objects referred to by that clauses and Husserl's notion of a proposition as an abstract object instantiated in thought is emphasized by Dallas Willard, "The Paradox of Logical Psychologism: Husserl's Way Out," *American Philosophical Quarterly* 9 (1972), reprinted in J. N. Mohanty (ed.), *Readings on Edmund Husserl's Logical Investigations* (The Hague: Martinus Nijhoff, 1977), pp. 43–54.

objects, species, that are instantiated in the different thoughts or sentences in different persons and in different languages that have the same functional role. These meanings provide standards of conceptual roles that underwrite linguistic competence and the understanding of concepts. Although they are independent of any of the actual contents of our minds, these functional or conceptual roles govern the instantiation of repeatable representational contents in non-repeatable experiences. Here, Husserl succeeds in articulating some of the insight that lies behind Aristotle's idea that thought and perception are based on species that are instantiated in the mind, while freeing the idea of Brentano's tendency to think of intentional inexistence in terms of facts about individual and collective psychology.

Interpreting meaning in terms of functional role leads to a conception of intentionality in which the intention to refer to an object is ultimately itself something ideal, rather than a real feature of psychological states. The very intention to refer to an object cannot be understood independently of the proper use of the term that purports to refer. On the other hand, the account of intentionality in the *Investigations* is in an important respect less radical than it first appears to be. It is tempting to conclude that because there are no objects that we must take to exist either within or outside of the mind when we are directed at objects, there is also no state of consciousness that must be somehow before the mind if we are to experience things outside of or inside of the mind. Now it is unclear whether Husserl thinks that there must always be some occurrent state of consciousness whenever one has an experience or understanding of anything. Husserl thinks that at least some of our recognitional capacities are dispositional. This suggests that at least some of our beliefs might turn out to be purely dispositional in character. But, on the whole, he thinks that any directedness at an object, regardless of whether the object exists or not, depends on the existence of experiences ("Erlebnisse") in the mind. This pervasive assumption in Husserl's account of intentionality is one that becomes a central target of Heidegger's critical attack on the Husserlian conception of intentionality. Emphasizing the connection between Husserl's account of intentionality and the idea that intentionality is a property of a crucial class of experiences, while also advocating a realist interpretation of Brentano, has the effect of making the differences between their views less significant than they at first appear to be. However, Husserl's Platonist conception of the species in the mind that allow us to direct ourselves in thought and perception at objects has the effect of taking his thought in an entirely different direction from that of Brentano.

CHAPTER 2

Husserl's methodologically solipsistic perspective

In this chapter, I want to look at Husserl's first-person singular account of experience, as he develops it in writings after the *Investigations*. This account of experience is methodologically solipsistic. By this I mean that Husserl acknowledges the existence of an external world and other minds, but insists on suspending belief in the existence of the external world and other minds in order to explain how external objects and other minds are to be understood by each of us individually. I shall argue that Husserl is not completely successful in reconstructing the intersubjective and objective world from within the perspective of methodological solipsism.

THE PHENOMENOLOGICAL REDUCTION AND THE TRANSCENDENTAL EGO

The phenomenological reduction is the key theoretical tool that Husserl develops after the *Investigations* for engaging in a distinctively philosophical form of reflection on experience. In the first volume of his *Ideas on a Pure Phenomenology and Phenomenological Philosophy* (henceforth *Ideas* 1), Husserl talks of different phenomenological reductions but does not explicitly distinguish between the psychological, phenomenological, and eidetic reductions. In subsequent work, especially his lectures on *First Philosophy* (1923–4: *Hua* 8), Husserl distinguishes between three forms of reduction: (1) A psychological reduction is one in which one reflects on the contents of consciousness. We restrict our attention to what we are aware of in self-conscious reflection. But we do not abstract from the existential commitments of the mental stages upon which we reflect. (2) In the phenomenological or transcendental reduction, we understand the contents and objects of consciousness as objects of a purely theoretical investigation that takes no interest in the objects of reflection other than a theoretical one. The phenomenological reduction brackets existence claims about entities in the world, thus suspending questions about the ultimate referent of expressions and mental acts. (3) In an eidetic reduction, we inquire into the essence of what is meant. We do so by abstracting from the way what is intended by us actually exists for our consciousness and by representing what is meant in a way that is constant through different possible permutations of the way in which it is meant. If this is unclear, it is because Husserl fails to identify a non-circular way of picking out what is essential to what is indented.[1]

In the *Investigations*, Husserl rejects the very idea of a Kantian or neo-Kantian transcendental ego as the ultimate source of unity in our experiences in favor of the more commonsensical idea that the only unity that the self has is one that is available to us in experience, and grounded in identity of the physical bearer of experience. He continues to reject the idea of a "pure ego as point of reference, center, and the like" as a "fiction" in a letter to William Ernest Hocking (July 9, 1903).[2] But, between 1903 and 1905, Husserl begins to move away from the purely empirical conception of the self that he defends in the *Investigations*. The influence of Paul Natorp's neo-Kantianism and discussions with Dilthey seem to have been decisive.[3] He begins to insist, with the neo-Kantians whom he had hitherto criticized, that the unity of the ideal structures that are the distinctive topic of philosophical and logical investigation, can only

---

[1] There have been a number of criticisms of Husserl's method of eidetic reduction or eidetic variation. The basic problem of the theory is that Husserl never addresses the worry that eidetic variation must already presuppose a prior understanding of the natural kinds that it is supposed to make accessible to us in the first place. For we can only grasp something as the same through different possible permutations in imagination if we already have some antecedent grasp of what the identity of the object is that we are supposed to hold fixed through such permutations; see David Levin, "Introduction to Husserl's Theory of Eidetic Variation," *Philosophy and Phenomenological Research* 29 (1968), 1–15; Edward Casey, "Imagination and the Phenomenological Method," in Elliston and McCormick (eds.), *Husserl: Expositions and Appraisals*, pp. 70–82; Donald Kuspit, "Fiction and Phenomenology," *Philosophy and Phenomenological Research* 29 (1968), 16–33; Richard M. Zaner, "The Art of Free-Phantasy in Rigorous Phenomenological Science," in F. Kersten and R. Zaner (eds.), *Phenomenology: Continuation and Criticism* (The Hague: Nijhoff, 1972), pp. 192–219; Richard M. Zaner, "Examples and Possibles: A Criticism of Husserl's Theory of Free-Phantasy Variation," *Research in Phenomenology* 3 (1973), 29–43. The theory of free variation is developed in *Ideas*, section 70 and, more extensively, in sections 39–42 of *Experience and Judgement*.

[2] *Edmund Husserl Briefwechsel*, vol. 3, p. 148.

[3] Husserl suggests in a letter to Georg Misch dated Jan. 27, 1927 that talks with Dilthey trigger his move towards a transcendental phenomenology. See Georg Misch, *Lebensphilosophie und Phänomenologie* (Darmstadt: Wissenschaftliche Buchgesellschaft, 1967), pp. 327ff.

be understood by reference to a pure ego that is itself ideal in structure. Like the neo-Kantians, he refers to this pure ego as the transcendental ego. And, like neo-Kantians, such as Natorp, who emphasize Kant's notion of an impersonal "consciousness in general" as the basis for all objective experience, Husserl initially avoids the conclusion that there is a multiplicity of different pure or transcendental egos. Objects of reflection are to be understood by a consciousness that is impersonal in the sense that even the ego is something that transcends the impersonal perspective of theoretical consciousness: "The thought of which it speaks [the phenomenological reduction] is no one's thought [*niemandes Denken*]. We abstract not only from the ego, as if the ego were in fact to stand in it and just not be referred to, but we exclude the transcendent positing of the ego and hold to the absolute, to consciousness in the pure sense."[4]

In the same context of his lectures on "Things and Space," Husserl claims that the appeal to a pure consciousness that logically precedes all individual self-consciousness allows him to avoid solipsism. What is experienced in pure or absolute consciousness is experienced in a way that is prior to and independent of any individual consciousness and hence cannot be said in any interesting sense to be internal to such individual consciousness. However, by September 1907, Husserl begins to worry that the move to an impersonal consciousness that is pre-personal fails to deal with the problem of the unity of the individual consciousness that engages in phenomenological reflection: "This is indeed a big question that I have too much avoided, the Evidenz of the ego as an identical, that therefore cannot consist of a bundle."[5]

In *Ideas* I in 1913, Husserl gives up the neo-Kantian emphasis on a pure consciousness in general in favor of a less Kantian and a more Cartesian or Leibnizian interpretation of pure consciousness according to which pure consciousness consists of independent streams of consciousness belonging to different transcendental egos. From the point of view of Husserl's new philosophical method, the transcendental reduction, whatever it is that gives my particular experiences their unity seems initially to be a matter from which one can safely abstract. However, the consciousness of the investigating self, not merely the self whose experiences are being investigated, must have an inherent unity to it, if there is to be any analysis of the structures

---

[4] E. Husserl, *Ding und Raum. Vorlesungen 1907, Hua* 16, p. 41.   [5] *Hua* 24, p. 421.

that objects have as they present themselves to consciousness. This fact forces Husserl to concern himself with the source of the unity that even so-called pure consciousness has. Now Husserl regards even pure or absolute consciousness as a flux of time-consciousness, although one that does not flow relative to anything else. A question then arises as to why one should think of any particular set of states of consciousness as belonging together in a single stream. It would be circular to attempt to account for the unity of consciousness in terms of associations that themselves require co-occurrence of states of consciousness in one consciousness. This unity cannot be provided by an empirical ego, for the empirical ego is a kind of spatio-temporal unity from which one abstracts in reflection of the kind involved in the transcendental reduction. The need to find a source of unity for the subject that engages in the kind of reflection involved in the transcendental reduction requires Husserl to regard even the objects of pure consciousness as the objects of a particular pure ego. For each empirical ego we now need a particular transcendental ego to serve as the bearer of absolute consciousness.

While the need to account for the unity of time-consciousness seems to have provided the starting-point for Husserl's commitment to numerically distinct transcendental egos, in some respects time-consciousness and the transcendental ego make competing or at least mutually complementary claims to provide the unity of all experience. For time-consciousness is in some sense responsible for the constitutive unity of an individual ego, just as the unity of that ego is presupposed in the individuation of time-streams. As Husserl puts it in very late remarks: "The structural analysis of distinctive presence (the standing, living streaming) leads us to the ego-structure and to the continuous substratum of the ego-less flux that founds it; the flux in turn leads by consistent questioning to what makes the sedimented activity what it is, as well, to that which is radically prior to the ego" (*Hua* 15, p. 598).

In the *Ideas* and more later work, Husserl regards Descartes' *Meditations* as an important inspiration for the phenomenological method. The structure of his *Ideas* follows the general structure of Descartes' own investigations. In *Ideas* 1, Husserl attempts to isolate a sphere of experience belonging to the *cogito* (the I think). This domain of experience, the domain of pure consciousness, is supposed to be characterized by the kind of certainty that find in thoughts about our own present existence. The experiences that belong to pure consciousness are given absolutely. They cannot fail to exist insofar as they are given in consciousness at all. Husserl connects this absolute existence of experiences with their immanence in consciousness. In a paraphrase of Descartes's notion of a substance, experiences require nothing else in order to exist ("nulla re indiget ad existendum"). Absolute existence, immanence, and independent existence are thus constitutive of what it is to be an experience in contrast to an object that exists outside of consciousness (for instance, a physical object).

Like Descartes, Husserl insists that the first-person claims about one's own mind have a special status. It is here that we must begin if we are to know other things with any certainty at all. Like Descartes, Husserl thinks that one needs to start with the epistemically privileged domain of the mind (something that Husserl does in *Ideas* i) in order then to work through an account of material bodies to a full account of how the mind is connected to the body (the topic of *Ideas* ii). Husserl argues that the kind of immunity to reference failure that the expression "I" has when used to articulate one's thoughts establishes an epistemically privileged immanent domain. The dubitability of all claims with respect to external objects, such as tables and chairs, is supposed to contrast with the indubitability of all claims about experiences themselves. For instance, my belief that the table is round is dubitable, but my claim that I believe that the table is round, is supposed to be indubitable. Husserl summarizes this thesis in the following claim: "Any bodily given thing can also not be, no bodily given experience can also not be: that is the law of essence that defines the latter necessity and the former contingency" (*Ideas* i, p. 98). For Husserl, "bodily given" ("leibhaft gegeben"), refers to any immediate epistemic relation of the subject to an object or experience. Thus he wishes to argue that things can turn out not to exist, while experiences are in a certain sense self-verifying.

Husserl takes the view that Descartes had stopped at a psychological reduction of experience in the First Meditation and never really gone beyond such a psychological reduction. Descartes' investigations are insufficiently philosophical. But, despite such reservations about Descartes' account of what is revealed by philosophical reflection on one's states, Husserl is strongly attracted to the Cartesian conception of mind as a kind of inner theater in which mental events can be observed to come and go. The Cartesian interpretation of the reduction as a search for contents of

consciousness with respect to which we can have certain knowledge
leads to a conception of meaning or representational content that
can be understood in terms that are internal to the mind. The
investigation of intentionality occurs in a manner that does not
require one to go outside of consciousness itself. It involves an
"immanent perception" of an act of consciousness in which
consciousness reflects on itself. In such reflection, that act reflected
upon is literally ("really") contained in the act which reflects upon it.
Inner perception or philosophical reflection thus constitutes a sphere
of "pure immanence," as Husserl likes to describe it (*Ideas* i, section
38, p. 78). Although Husserl's discussion in *Ideas* i can easily suggest
that questions of existence play no role once we have bracketed the
existence of objects external to consciousness, in fact he wants to
argue that existence and being take on a new sense once we bracket
the assumptions of our natural attitude to objects.[6] In contrast to the
reality that characterizes objects experienced in the natural attitude,
phenomenologically reduced experience has to do with "absolute
being." The being of consciousness is absolute in the sense that
consciousness can be immediately given to a (reflective) consciousness that is itself the basis for all meaning and hence for all existence
claims. Consciousness is self-sufficient, it requires no other existent in
order to exist, while all other kinds of entities are supposed to have
being only relative to consciousness.

The claim that there is an immanent domain belonging to acts of
consciousness which is accessible to reflection is based on the
internalist assumption that acts of consciousness are available as
objects of reflection independently of the objects that they are about.[7]
However, it is important to note that the object that we investigate
within the sphere of pure immanence is itself immanent in a
distinctive way. It is not just what is immediately given to consciousness now, but rather a transcendence in immanence. There is always

---

[6] The distinction between phenomenologically reduced or bracketed being and being for the
natural attitude has been compared to the distinction between the substitutional
interpretation of quantifiers (for terms with non-trivial equivalence relations involving
infinitely many equivalence classes) and the objectual interpretation of quantifiers by
Charles Parsons, "A Plea for Substitutional Quantification," in *Mathematics in Philosophy*
(Ithaca: Cornell University Press, 1983), p. 66.

[7] "If experiences of consciousness were unthinkable without connection to nature in the way
that colors are not thinkable without extension, then we could not regard consciousness as
an absolute distinctive region for itself in the way that we must do ... It [the domain of
experience as absolute entities] is independent of all worldly, natural being, according to its
essence and does not require that being for its *existence*" (*Ideas* i, section 47).

something represented indirectly (appresented) that is involved in what we directly represent. What is indirectly represented, for instance a thing as such, as opposed to a particular aspect of the thing, transcends what we are immediately and immanently conscious of. But even the knife-edged immanent now of awareness is strictly speaking an abstraction from the lived present of actual experience. The lived present always includes a whole continuum of different abstractly distinguishable nows in it. The nows of the immediate past and future are appresented in the lived or specious present of actual experience. Thus all experience whatsoever is strictly speaking a transcendence in immanence, not just the experience of physical objects or the other minds that we experience through the way they manifest themselves in bodies endowed with life.

In works in the early twenties that may have been written under the influence of Heidegger's anti-Cartesian criticisms, Husserl notes that the kind of immanence of consciousness that plays such a role in *Ideas* I is inherently misleading. For it suggests that we simply forget the world in the phenomenological reduction in favor of inner experiences that are intelligible independently of their relation to the world, when in fact the world as it is intended by us becomes itself the proper topic of investigation in the phenomenological reduction. Husserl's worries about the misleading character of the Cartesian version of the reduction lead to the alternative path to a phenomenological reduction taken by a universal phenomenological psychology. In this case, the world is the starting-point and the topic of universal psychology: "By bracketing the world nothing is lost, but world knowledge is won as something ultimately justified" (*First Philosophy*, *Hua* 8 (1923), pp. 275, 279). Later, in the *Crisis*, Husserl articulates a still further way of entering into the phenomenological reduction. We can proceed directly from the everyday life-world of the natural attitude and disengage ourselves from its constitutive interests, while regarding that life-world merely in terms of how it is intended by us. Even here, Husserl continues to maintain that a process of deconstruction ("Abbau") should ultimately take us from the environmental social world of everyday life to a perceptual world in which we exist as independent individuals with independent spheres of perceptual consciousness from which we construct the intersubjective world.[8]

[8] An excellent critical exposition of the different approaches that are possible to the phenomenological reduction may be found in Iso Kern, "The Three Ways to the Transcendental Phenomenological Reduction in the Philosophy of Edmund Husserl," in

While Husserl attempts in such late works as *Experience and Judgment* (1936) to provide a genetic account of how intentionality and our understanding of meaning may be understood from within the context of everyday spatio-temporal experience, he continues to maintain that the objects available to the life-world depend on individual time-consciousness, while the inner experience of such time-consciousness is itself completely autonomous. By revealing a level of experience that is at least equi-basic with that of the unity of the ego itself, the theory of time-consciousness leaves open a route to the phenomenological reduction that is in principle independent of its Cartesian interpretation. However, Husserl never completely succeeds in freeing himself from his Cartesian presuppositions. Even in his last work in philosophy, the *Crisis* (1936), written with an eye to responding to Heidegger's critique of his internalism, Husserl is committed to the possibility of a narrow representational content that does not depend essentially on the particular broadly social environment that a person happens to occupy. Thus Husserl continues to distinguish a perceptual level of experience that is independent of one's cultural background and indeed from the existence of other persons from a culturally mediated "cloak of ideas" that is overlaid on such perceptual experience.

In the *Crisis*, Husserl maintains that the socially structured life-world of everyday life is what we encounter first in experience. The life-world consists in part of things that all human beings experience in common, and in part of the distinctive contributions of particular cultures. The life-world of the everyday experience is itself supposed to be intersubjectively constituted. Intersubjective experience is in turn constituted indirectly in terms of the way other persons present themselves to the first-person singular perspective. Transcendental intersubjectivity continues to be constituted in the "primordial ego" ("Ur-Ich") which can never lose its uniqueness.[9] One abstracts in this first-person singular perspective from everything beyond what is given to one here and now. Such first-person experience does not require the existence of other persons, or of other objects at all.

F. Elliston and P. McCormick (eds.), *Husserl: Expositions and Appraisals*, pp. 126–149, see also Rudolf Bernet, Iso Kern, Eduard Marbach, *Edmund Husserl: An Exposition of his Thought* (Bloomington: University of Indiana Press, 1994), chapter 2, section 1.

[9] *The Crisis of European Sciences and Phenomenology*, trans. David Carr (Evanston: Northwestern University Press, 1970); *Hua* 6, section 54b, p. 188.

FROM I TO WE EXPERIENCE

In developing an account of how the subject itself is constituted, Husserl distinguishes between a purely first-person singular level of subjectivity, and a first-person plural level of subjectivity. But he maintains that the we-intentionality through which persons as groups can be directed at objects is always ultimately based on a prior understanding of objects in the form of I-intentionality, that is, group understanding always builds on the kind of understanding that is had by an individual consciousness directed at an object. He interprets the external world as a construct of intersubjectivity and then argues that intersubjectivity is somehow accessible in my own private sphere of consciousness, just as the past and the future are included in the duration of the specious present my actual experience.[10]

Not only theory and its objects, but also practical and evaluative behavior can be built up ("aufgebaut") from prepredicative perceptions that belong to the successive synthesis of momentary perceptions in the time-consciousness of a (transcendental) subject. From here one can then construct an intersubjective, historically and culturally structured world. The intersubjective world then becomes the basis for an account of the objectivity as nature as the x that unifies the different ways in which things appear to different subjects with their different standpoints and different perceptual and sensory capabilities.

In *Ideas* II, Husserl follows Descartes in distinguishing and investigating the relations between two fundamentally different kinds of things that are accessible to us by the kind of certain reflection investigated in *Ideas* I. These two things are extended things (bodies) and thinking things (minds or spirits). Overall, Husserl displays a striking level of sympathy with Descartes. This sympathy will later allow Heidegger to use Descartes as substitute target for Husserl in *Being and Time*. In the context of his criticism of Descartes' putatively worldless subject, Heidegger notes on p. 98 in his personal "hut copy" of *Being and Time*: "Critique of Husserl's structure <*Aufbau*> of 'ontologies'! just as the whole Descartes critique was put here with this intention" (*GA* 3, p. 442).[11]

---

[10] Husserl's most succinct discussion of the levels of immediacy and mediation involved in consciousness is perhaps that to be found in his lectures on *First Philosophy, Erste Philosophie Hua* 8, pp. 175ff.

[11] Heidegger alludes to *Ideas* II in a footnote to *Being and Time* (*SuZ*, p. 47n), where he notes that the "second part [of the *Ideas*] brings the realized analyses of constitution and deals in

In *Ideas* II, Husserl distinguishes four different "regions of being" that are involved in an account of intersubjectivity: (1) matter and bodies ("Materiel, Körper"), (2) lived body ("Leib"), (3) psyche ("Seele"), and (4) spirit ("Geist"). Husserl maintains that, ontologically and epistemically, spirit is primary, since everything else depends for its existence on the possibility of being identified by spirits. The lower cognitive capacities that Husserl identifies with the psyche are also of great importance. Animals have psyches or souls ("Seelen"), but no spirit. These psyches constitute the sentience that characterizes a lived body.

Animals and human beings have two aspects to their psyche (in the case of human beings and other beings capable of reasoning, spirit draws on the immediate experience provided by the psyche) and, on the other hand, their bodies. Both bodily states and the states of the psyche are inherently dispositional. They can only be characterized in terms of how a creature would react to a certain constellation of environmental factors. Now the lived body is that aspect of a human being or other sentient creature that directly interacts with its environment, while psychic states are that aspect of the sentient creature that endow it with a distinctive point of view. Husserl regards the unifying point of view of the creature in question as its psyche or soul. This is why he wants to argue that the psyche is the dominant aspect of the two aspects of a sentient creature. The soul, unlike the spirit or person is directly dependent for its states on the body of the creature that has it.

Husserl construes matter with Descartes as extended substance: "The physical thing or material thing is res extensa" (*Ideas* II, p. 33). But he also argues that to be a substance is to be the sort of thing that can be involved in causal relations with its environment. The properties of a thing are dispositional. They are defined by what the thing would do in a certain causal situation (*Ideas* II, p. 45). Physical things are the proper topic of the physical sciences which are concerned with determining the causal connections between things that make them behave as they do.

three sections with: 1. The constitution of material nature. 2. The constitution of animal nature. 3. The constitution of the spiritual <*geistige*> world (the personalistic attitude in opposition to the naturalistic one)." This is the construction that Heidegger is indirectly attacking in his critique of Descartes. A helpful discussion of Heidegger's use of Descartes as a foil for criticizing Husserl may be found in Jean Luc Marion, "Heidegger and Descartes," trans. in Christopher Macann (ed.) *Critical Heidegger* (London: Routledge, 1996), pp. 67–96.

Our epistemic access to physical things is rather complicated, since Husserl thinks of it as mediated through different levels of sensory experience. A sound, color, or other sensation exists in time, but not in space. On the basis of these sensations, I am able to perceive an object that displays itself in my private perceptual space and time in a certain distinctive way. We then need to distinguish the way perceptual objects appear to standard observers under standard circumstances from the way that they appear to me here and now under what may well be quite non-standard perceptual circumstances. The perceptual object that I see here and now can turn out to be wholly delusive, in which case we have what Husserl calls a phantom object. The object that I perceive may, however, also present itself in a certain way to standard observers under standard circumstances. In this case, the perceptual object exists in public space and time. Finally, a physical object is whatever causes standard observers under standard circumstances to experience certain sensations and on the basis of these to perceive certain things.

Veridical perception of the kind that standard observers have under standard circumstances is supported by an appeal to causal relations that allow us to pick out what the standard circumstances for standard observers are. These causal relations allow us to define an object that causes standard observers to have certain perceptual experiences under standard causal circumstances. This notion of an object that is independent of the way that it is perceived by observers is what Husserl refers to as a physical object or thing:

> Thus in principle the thing is something intersubjectively identical and something that does not have any sensible intuitive content that *could be given* intersubjectively *identically*: rather it is instead only an empty identical something as correlate of the identifications that are possible and justified according to rules governing the logic of experience by subjects standing in an intersubjective connection of appearances. (*Ideas* II, p. 88)

While the primary properties of physical objects are not perceptible by any creature, they provide the basis for rules governing how those physical objects appear to different creatures under different circumstances according to the preceptual set of those creatures.

Material bodies have identity conditions that are fixed by their causal–functional relations to each other. Material bodies or physical objects have identity conditions that are tied up with causal–functional identifiability in space and time. As such, material objects are identifiable only to the extent that we can identify and re-identify the spaces and times that they occupy. From this connection of material to spatial and temporal location, Husserl infers that material objects are necessarily mind-dependent; in language that he borrows from Kant, they are transcendentally ideal. "Objective thinghood determines itself physically, but as a this it determines itself only in relation to consciousness and the subject of consciousness. All determination refers back to a here and now and with that to a some subject or context of subjects" (*Ideas* II, p. 301). We can think of material bodies as having a spatial and temporal identity only in virtue of our capacity to pick out spatio-temporal locations. But we do not have any means of picking out such locations that is independent of our capacity to use such demonstratives as "here" and "now" to assign some zero point to a spatio-temporal coordinate system. And, finally, such demonstratives refer back essentially to a subject of thought, a spirit. Demonstratives, and the spaces and times to which they refer, are, as it were, egocentric particulars, so they cannot be understood independently of egos or spirits. By contrast, spirits are supposed to have an identity that is identification-independent. I am who and what I am, and distinct from who and what you are regardless of whether anybody is in a position to recognize that distinctiveness about me: "All individuation of the former [physical appearances] depends on the absolute individuation of the latter [persons], all natural existence depends on the existence of absolute spirits" (*Ideas* II, p. 302). Even if successful, this argument supports only a form of epistemic rather than ontological idealism. As such it lends support to a modest reading of Husserl's transcendental idealism as an epistemic rather than as an ontological thesis.

If successful, the argument would show that our ability to identify physical objects is parasitic on our ability to grasp our identity as persons. This claim seems to be first personal. Each of us has an immediate awareness of his or her own experiences as his or her own; in this sense "the experiences in the flux of consciousness have their absolutely own essence, they bear their individuation in themselves" (*Ideas* II, p. 300). Husserl maintains that the ego and its experiences are constitutive of a distinctive non-repeatable history in which no distinction can be drawn between existence and the concrete essence of a certain life history because each ego has its own distinctive motivational structure that is not derived from its location in space and time.

However, it is also true that persons or spirits need to be linked up to lived bodies through their psyches. The psyche provides the mind or spirit with experiences corresponding to sensory states of the lived body. Such experiences are needed if minds or spirits are to be able to perceive objects and thus to be able to individuate physical objects. Moreover, Husserl does not deny that our ability to identify ourselves according to public criteria that also apply to other persons depends on our ability to identify bodies, so the priority of minds in identification depends on the problematic assumption that we have direct access to the identity of our own minds. But there does not seem to be any more reason to think that we have a grip on the identity of our own minds that is independent of space and time than there is for thinking that we have a grasp of the identity of material objects that is independent of space and time. Husserl concedes at least that we can only identify other minds relative to spatial and temporal situations.

Our experience of other persons is indirect, but in a slightly different sense than that in which we can have only abstract knowledge of physical objects as they are in themselves. We infer the existence of physical objects on the basis of the phemomenal objects that appear to us as colored, heavy, hot, cold, noisy, etc. Our access to other persons is non-inferential, although also indirect and mediated by our experience of bodies endowed with phenomenal properties. We have what Husserl calls a mediated apperception of another person and his or her representations of the world. Here apperception, or what is added to perception ("ad-perceptio"), refers to a representation in what we experience of something that goes beyond what is immediately present to us in perception. Mediated apperception is based on our own direct apprehension of the spatio-temporal identity of our own distinctive stream of consciousness as it expresses itself in the lived body ("Leib") that gives us our own distinctive spatial point of view. The here from which I perceive other spatial objects comes to be linked together associatively with my awareness of the physical and psychological identity of another stream of consciousness. The psycho-physical identity of the other presents itself from a position which is over there in my private spatial environment. Consciousness of another person is based on an associative pairing of one's consciousness of one's own sentient body with the consciousness of the other person's body. This associative pairing is in turn based on an awareness that the other body that I

am perceiving is like my own. The similarity is based on exhibiting
, regularities of behavior of the kind that require explanation in terms
of a lived body ("Leib") as opposed to a mere body ("Körper"). A
lived body is a body that experiences sensory stimulation of however
rudimentary a form.

Husserl's solution to transcendental solipsism raises some difficult
questions. The kind of associative pairing involved in appresentation
of the other is supposed to take place at the level of a pre-judgmental
passive synthesis. Tracing recognition of other minds to dispositions
based on pre-judgmental habits of association has the merit of
avoiding the quite implausible view that we are engaged in a
continuous process of inferring that others are persons from the
behavior of their bodies: "Such apperception of others is not an
inference, not an act of thought" (*CM*, p. 141). But treating the
recognition of a similarity relation between different lived bodies as
a matter that is antecedent to all judgments puts a rather heavy
strain on what one could reasonably recognize at a pre-judgmental
level. For in this case we are asked to recognize another body as like
ours. We must therefore have a grasp of the unity of the different
perceptual fields of our own body and an ability to recognize
another body as a distinctive body. The way my body is present to
me as percipient is different from the way other bodies are present to
me. To the extent that there is an analogy between the way my body
is present to me and the way other bodies are present to me, it is
insofar as my body is an object of perception rather than constitutive
of my point of view as percipient. Perhaps, even more significantly,
we must also recognize that body as a lived body, as the body of a
person, or at least of a sentient being. To recognize similarities of
behavior of this level of sophistication requires rather developed
powers of conceptualization.[12]

In order to account for the realm of public experience, Husserl
maintains that we can think of each subject with its own sphere of
ownness as also appresenting other subjects from their own distinctive spatio-temporal points of view. Thus each subject has a
direct consciousness of itself and its own proper sphere of experience and an indirect consciousness of other subjects with their own

---

[12] Alfred Schutz argues that the kind of similarity involved is much too complex to be handled
at the level appresentation in: "The Problem of Transcendental Intersubjectivity in
Husserl," in *Collected Paper: Studies in Phenomenological Philosophy* 3 (The Hague: Nijhoff, 1966),
pp. 51–91, esp. pp. 63ff.

distinctive spheres of experience. But in representing oneself as having a certain point of view on my body and the body of the other self, and the other self as having a different point of view on my body and his or her body, I am constrained to represent these selves as belonging to a common nature, that is an intersubjectively accessible space in which each of the bodies is determinately related to the others (*CM*, section 55). It is then on the basis of this common nature that I come to think of the temporal sequence of my experiences as related to the temporal sequence of the experiences of other subjects in a determinate way. In this way I have the notion of common, intersubjective, or world time.

Husserl argues that the objectivity of nature must be understood relative to intersubjective agreement. But there are real worries of circularity here. He constructs intersubjectivity by appeal to the recognition by each person of another person that occupies a different spatio-temporal standpoint, or a here relative to the first person's there. The other person's here is then there for me. But the other person's here is only a there for me if I already think of both of us as belonging to a public space that we have in common. Thus, far from constituting an objective space and hence an objective time, Husserl's account seems simply to presuppose such a space and time in interpreting the other as a person who has a distinct body with its own distinctive spatial standpoint relative to mine. Husserl sometimes explicitly concedes the point:

But the basic form of identification for intersubjective givens of sensible content is such that they all necessarily belong to the same *system of location*; and its objectivity displays itself in this that every "here" is identifiable with a relative "there" in respect to every new "here" that results from every "change of place" of the subject, and then also in respect to every here that belongs to another subject. (*Ideas* II, p. 83)

What seems most problematic about Husserl's account of other consciousness of other minds is that he wishes to argue that it is distinct from a self-consciousness of what is properly one's own sentient experience and the standpoint of one's own lived body. The idea that there is self-consciousness which does not involve some implicit consciousness of others leads Husserl to insist on the possibility of a reduction of experience to a "sphere of ownness." It does not seem to be possible to reduce our experience to a distinctive "sphere of ownness" relative to which we can then go on to bring in a "sphere of otherness." Any consciousness of myself as a distinctive

individual seems to involve some at least possible consciousness of
another person.

There is some difficulty in understanding what a reduction to a
sphere of ownness can mean from within the perspective of Husserl's
phenomenology. In the sphere of ownness we abstract from all cultural
contributions. This leaves us without writing and indeed without
language in general. We might have some minimal notion of thought,
but it is not at all clear that we have enough of a distinction between
correct and incorrect representations to be able to characterize what
our experiences are at all. It thus seems impossible for the sphere of
ownness to comprise the standpoint from which the phenomenological
observer investigates experience. It is just not rich enough to support
the level of abstraction required by the phenomenologist. The sphere
of ownness does not have the resources required for the theoretical
standpoint to which Husserl wishes to give ultimate primacy.

Probably under the influence of Heidegger's criticisms of his
theory of empathy, Husserl finally gives up the idea that a distinctive
sphere of ownness can be pried apart from the sphere of otherness in
a manuscript from 1931: "Being with others cannot be disconnected
from me in my living presencing-oneself and this presence with
others founds worldly presence, that in turn is the presupposition for
the sense of all world-temporality and world-coexistence (space) and
temporal sequence."[13] Perhaps a more appropriate way of thinking
of the sphere of ownness than as the standpoint for the phenomenological observer, is to think of the sphere of ownness as the most
basic level or original level of experience from which all experiences
are in some sense derived. In contrast to the claim that the sphere of
ownness is primary for the theoretical observer, we could say that it
is primary for the individual subject of experience (the individual
transcendental ego). In this case, we would be thinking of the sphere
of ownness as the most basic stratum of an individual experience.
This seems to fit Husserl's view that only presocial subjectivity with
its subjective world of appearances as environment is accessible
through original perception (presencing). The intersubjective world
is something that we have access to only through the mediation of
empathy through which one has access to other points of view. Thus,
whereas our immediate private world of present experience is

[13] Manuscript of March 1931, cited from Iso Kern's introductory remarks to, E. Husserl, *Zur
Phänomenologie der Intersubjektivität: Hua* 15, p. XLIX.

directly present to each of us, the intersubjective world is something that is only indirectly present to us through an appresentation based on the immediacy of our experience of our own distinctive existence.

THE PERSONALISTIC AND NATURALISTIC PERSPECTIVES

Husserl's account of intersubjectivity in general, and the social in particular, pulls in two different directions. This is most apparent in *Ideas* II, a manuscript that Husserl sent to Heidegger in the fall of 1924 as Heidegger was working out early drafts of *Being and Time* (1926).[14] The necessary role that Husserl assigns to perceptions of bodies in space in the recognition of other minds leads Husserl initially to construct human beings and their minds as appendages or "annexes" to their bodies. This is the way that human beings and their minds are to be understood from the vantage-point of natural science and the naturalistic attitude. But Husserl ultimately argues that human beings and in particular persons cannot be adequately understood by appeal to the naturalistic attitude for which persons are mere appendages to bodies. From the vantage-point of the personalistic attitude, persons are primary and bodies and other things exist only relative to the efforts of persons to integrate their spatial and temporal perceptions into a coherent whole of experience. One would expect Husserl to provide an account of how we recognize other minds both from the naturalistic standpoint in which bodies are what is primary and from the personalistic standpoint in which persons are primary. But, even from the personalistic standpoint, Husserl takes the body to be the primary object of perception and the mind to be presented only indirectly. Indeed his account of how we recognize persons builds on his account of how we come to recognize bodies as lived or animated.

In the personalistic attitude, what we experience are not bodies *per se* but persons or human beings. However, these persons are apperceived, that is, grasped indirectly through their bodies. The contrast with the naturalistic attitude is in the way that human beings are understood. They are directly experienced as human beings rather than as bodies or embodied minds. This also involves understanding individuals in terms of their motivations. Each person acts in the way that he or she does in virtue of his or her distinctive

[14] Heidegger makes it clear that he has received and studied the manuscript of *Ideas* II in his pre-*Being and Time* lectures on *Prolegomena to the Concept of Time* (1925), *GA* 20, p. 168.

motivational set. This motivational set constitutes the character of the person (*Ideas* II, p. 271). Such a character or motivational set is constituted by the person's beliefs together with their desires and other reasons for acting. While the most basic level of a person's personality is based on instincts and drives, there is also a more autonomous level of human action determined by reasons or what Husserl calls motivations of reason (*Ideas* II, p. 255). Among these other reasons for acting, one must put pride of place to the values that the person has. Although each person has a character that is absolutely individual, each person also exhibits regularities of behavior over longer periods of time, and shares certain regularities of behavior with other persons. We understand ourselves and other persons in terms of the relatively constant character or type that motivates us over a certain period of time. It is in terms of the character type that is distinctive of that individual, and the more general character type that the person has in common with others, that we are able to make sense or rationalize the person's behavior.

Husserl thinks that the matter of reconstructing the social is relatively straightforward once we have an account of how we are able to recognize the existence of others minds. We can then think of groups or institutions as collections of individuals that have common interests, and thus behave in ways that make it reasonable for us to ascribe to them a common typical character that is independent of the existence of any particular individual that participates in the common identity, but a function of the interactions between the members of the group or institution. It is in terms of such typical motivational features that we can then come to understand other cultures and the individuals who belong to those cultures which Husserl thinks of as constituting distinctive life-worlds within the general shared live-world that all human beings have in common.

While Husserl maintains that his account of intersubjectivity provides the basis for a notion of shared experience, in fact his reconstruction of intersubjectivity seems to be ineliminably first-person singular. The first-person plural, we, of experience is always constituted only through one's relations to a nature that one has the same kind of first-person singular perspective on as other subjects do. While Husserl's first-person singular perspective on the social brings in a certain limitation or bias in his account, he can make some sense of the social in terms of intersubjective agreement about the natural world. He maintains that there are some fundamental features of the natural world that individuals can agree on no matter what their beliefs and desires. These fundamental features of the natural world constitute the a priori of the life-world. There are difficulties for Husserl in stating precisely which features of the natural world must be shared by all human beings in their experience of the world. It is even more difficult to state which features would be shared by all rational or sentient beings. Even basic distinctions such as those between the mental and the physical are not clearly intelligible across cultures. It is not clear that "animists" have a clear distinction between the mind and the body. However, Husserl insists that such fundamental shared features are the key to one being able to understand what is distinctive about individual cultures and individual human experiences within those experiences. It is in terms of a shared nature that we have a handle on the language, culture, and behavior of others in such a way that we are able to appreciate what is shared by persons who belong to distinctive language groups and cultures and then understand the differences between them.

Beginning around 1920, Husserl begins to address the status of history in his philosophy for the first time. By 1921 he can already maintain that "history is the great fact of absolute being" (*First Philosophy*, Hua 8, p. 506).[15] By this he means that the kind of creatures that have a history are also the ones upon whose procedures of identification others depend for their existence as objects, while creatures with a history themselves have identification-independent existence. There is clearly something wrong about this view. There is no more reason to think that persons have an existence as objects of consciousness that is independent of our procedures of identification than there is to think that physical objects are identification-independent. And there is no real reason to think that material things *per se*, as opposed to material *objects*, are identification-dependent, at all.

Husserl's positive point amounts to the somewhat suspect claim that to have a history is to have a unique set of non-repeatable motivations that cannot recur at another place in space and time. It is tempting to argue that the reason such motivations may be regarded as inherently non-repeatable is that they can only be understood

---

[15] The significance of Husserl's claim that history is the great fact of absolute being is discussed extensively by his former coworker, Ludwig Landgrebe, *Faktizität und Individuation: Studien zur Grundlage der Phänomenologie* (Hamburg: Meiner Verlag, 1982), pp. 38ff.

against the entire background of the whole complex of reasons that motivate individuals in a social context. But this argument would be in some tension with Husserl's methodological solipsism.

To be sure, Husserl regards history as a constitutive feature of culture that itself presupposes intersubjective experience. On the other hand, the historicity of human beings cannot be a fundamental fact about them, if such historicity involves a necessary dependence of persons on the existence of other persons. The interdependence of history and culture also accounts in part for the striking fact that, in dealing with history, Husserl makes no effort to connect history to time-consciousness.[16] From a certain perspective at least, the lack of any attempt to connect his account of history to that of time-consciousness is not altogether surprising. For an adequate account of history would involve understanding the development of human cultural institutions which are only comprehensible from the standpoint of the shared form of experience provided by the co-constitution of the self and other persons. As such, history belongs to the level of time-consciousness at which the objective temporal world is constituted, rather than to sensory or even perceptual time-consciousness.

The historical relativity of cultural institutions has implications for the very enterprise of philosophical inquiry. For philosophical inquiry itself has a form that cannot easily be detached from the cultural and historical situation in which it has arisen. Indeed, by the time of the *Crisis*, Husserl is willing to concede that the very idea of objectivity that governs his life-work is a prejudice that has its historical origin (*Hua* 6, p. 730). The conclusion that the very search for objectivity is something that may have an explanation in a certain historical and cultural context does not in itself nullify the goal of attaining objectivity, but it does have far reaching ramifications for any attempt to articulate a priori constraints on experience. For at the very least one must then allow for the possibility that these constraints are not in fact grounded in a truth that is radically independent of us. Such truth may turn out instead to be a reflection of the distinctive prejudice of our culture. And even if there is a culture independent truth, we may have no way of identifying it.

[16] Husserl's failure to connect his philosophy of history to his theory of time-consciousness is emphasized by Elizabeth Ströker, "Zeit und Geschichte in Husserls Phänomenologie. Zur Frage ihres Zusammenhangs," *Zeit und Zeitlichkeit bei Husserl und Heidegger*, pp. 111–137.

CHAPTER 3

Husserl's theory of time-consciousness

Consciousness of time is the most fundamental level of all experience. For Husserl, this includes both human experience and the experience of any other actual creature. Thus, any searching analysis of the make-up of experience must begin with the structure of time-consciousness. In this chapter I look at Husserl's development of the structure of time-consciousness that is inherent in any experience, and point out the way in which he tries to resolve the tensions inherent in his conception of successively present episodes of experience.

THE TEMPORALITY OF EXPERIENCE AND THE PHENOMENOLOGICAL REDUCTION

Husserl's theory of time-consciousness emerges out of an effort to understand how acts of consciousness are themselves constituted as experiences ("Erlebnisse"). To make sense of acts of consciousness, he thinks that we must trace experiences back to their origins in the most immediate form of experience. Husserl assumes that the most immediate form of experience consists of sensations. Such sensations do not represent an object that is logically distinct from the having of a certain sensory experience. Sensations are, however, self-intimating. To be an impression involves an immediate consciousness of a qualitative experience. As experiences ("Erlebnisse") they are conscious to the person who has them and as such involve a form of self-consciousness.

Sensations are not themselves the objects of perception, but they are experiencings that make a constitutive contribution to any perception. Unlike perceptions of objects, sensations do not seem to have intentionality. They represent objects, they are about objects, only in virtue of acts of consciousness in which the content of sensation is conceived of as or interpreted as belonging to objects. To make sense of such acts of consciousness endowed with referential intentionality, Husserl traces experiences back to their origins in immediate sensations. He realizes he must come to terms with the way in which sensations are retained and anticipated in a perceptual consciousness that is capable of sustaining a consciousness of short-term persistence or change. The way in which episodes of consciousness retain and anticipate each other should throw light on the very unity that any particular consciousness has, and thus on the unity of particular egos. It should also throw light on the nature of all states of consciousness.

And, as Husserl works on his theory of intentionality, he comes to think of sensations as experiences that have a kind of intentionality even though they do not involve referential intentionality. He comes to identify a form of intentionality in our very short-term experience of the past and the future in the specious present of sensation that does not involve a directedness at an object at all and does not, even initially, seem to involve any content intentionality. In the specious present we are supposed to be conscious of sensations as experiencings that involve connections to past and future experiencings without being conscious of an object of which they are the experience. This peculiar kind of intentionality is a feature of the self-intimating character of all experiences. It is not simply identical with the contemporary notion of a phenomenal or qualitative state of consciousness. However, this kind of horizonal intentionality, as Husserl comes to call it, in contrast to object or referential intentionality, is supposed to make phenomenal consciousness intelligible. For he comes increasingly to see that individual experiences are what they are only in virtue of their relation to other actual and possible spatial and temporal experiences. These other experiences constitute the horizon that determines the meaning of those individual experiences.

For Husserl, sense impressions are the most basic level of all consciousness and hence of all time-consciousness. This is an important motivation for him to concentrate on the kind of time-consciousness involved in sensation. However, he has an even more compelling reason to concentrate on the temporal relations between sensations. In the four to five years separating his initial lectures on time-consciousness from the *Investigations*, Husserl comes to develop a philosophical tool that will become central to the rest of his life-work. This is the so-called "phenomenological reduction." The purpose of the phenomenological reduction is to abstract from whatever presuppositions or interests that we may have in the objects of our experiences and reflect on the contents of our experience purely insofar as they present themselves to ourselves in consciousness.

To understand time in the sense required by the phenomenological reduction, Husserl proposes the "complete exclusion of every assumption, stipulation or conviction concerning objective time" (*Hua* 10, section 1, p. 4). The key here is to establish evident facts that Husserl takes to be indubitable: "We have evidence <*Evidenz*> which makes any doubt and any denial appear meaningless that the consciousness of a process of sound, of a melody, that I am just hearing displays a succession" (section 1, p. 5). Husserl thinks that certain facts about our experience of time are indubitable. While it might be doubted that things change, it cannot be doubted that they appear to us to undergo change. It is less clear whether Husserl takes all facts to be immune to revision that concern the way in which time presents itself to our consciousness. Husserl's own constant revision of his claims concerning phenomenological time would suggest that, at best, the most basic facts about temporal experience are immune to revision in the face of further reflection and further evidence.

Husserl describes the question that he is concerned with in the phenomenological reduction of time in Kantian terms. It is the epistemological question of the possibility of experience, where this is understood as the essence of experience. But Husserl also gives this epistemological investigation what initially seems to be a rather unKantian twist. He insists that the question of the essence or of the possibility of temporal experience is tied up with the origin of time. Despite prima facie appearances, Husserl's question concerning the non-psychological origin of our putatively a priori concept of time actually has a precise analogue in the transcendental deduction of time that Kant attempts in the Transcendental Aesthetic; this is a demonstration that time does not have its origin in experience, but independently of experience.

Still, there is something rather psychological and empirical in the particular way that Husserl proposes to link the origin of time with the essence of time. Anticipating Heidegger's later investigation into the origin of time, Husserl proposes to look for the origin of time in "the phenomenology of 'authentic' experience" (*Hua* 10, section 2, p. 9). In authentic experience, temporal objects, and hence time itself, are presented to consciousness just as they are themselves, that is, as they truly are. This is what privileges authentic experience in the process of justifying our beliefs about the nature of temporal experience. Husserl also thinks, rather fatefully and problematically, but completely in accordance with what we should expect from the *Investigations*, that the best procedure for identifying true, evident, or authentic experiences is to trace the experience of objects back to primitive experiences, that is, to experiences of objects that are as simple as possible. This leads him to claim that "the *question of origin* is directed at the *primitive* formations of time-consciousness in which the primitive differences of the temporal are intuitively and authentically constituted as original sources of all evidences concerning time" (*Hua* 10, p. 9). The kind of genetic investigation involved in Husserl's theory of time-consciousness appears to be psychological because it attempts to trace back higher-order structures to their origin in less complex mental states. However, there are two reasons for Husserl to reject the view that the kind of investigation in question is a psychological one. First, what is ultimately at issue is the epistemic warrant for our beliefs about time. That is, we are concerned here with an investigation of how our beliefs about time may ultimately be justified. Second, the investigation is concerned with the *essence of time*, where such essence is thought by Husserl to involve a kind of necessity and strict generality that eludes any purely empirical investigation of the kind undertaken by psychology.

Due to his preference for primitive experiences as the basis for understanding complex experiences of time, Husserl's analysis of time-consciousness is carried through using the example of a sound or series of sounds ("Töne"), as Heidegger will later note with obvious derision: "The whole investigation is instigated by the fact that he perceives the primary and original consciousness of time in the knowledge of a mere datum of sensation."[1] Heidegger's implicit objection is that we do not ever actually experience sensations or sense data. This worry needs to be taken quite seriously. In fairness

[1] M. Heidegger, *Metaphysical Foundations of Logic Starting from Leibniz* (1928), *GA* 26, p. 264. References to Kant's *Critique of Pure Reason* are to the first (A) and second (B) editions of the *Critique*. The pagination of the first (A) and second (B) editions is reproduced in Immanuel Kant, *The Critique of Pure Reason*, ed. and trans. by Paul Guyer and Allen Wood (Cambridge University Press, 1988) and the other German editions and translations of the *Critique*.

to Husserl, the earliest parts of the compilation of lectures that are published as *Lectures on Inner Time-Consciousness* represent a very early stage in his conception of the method of phenomenological reduction in which he was prone to restrict what is described to private experiences. Husserl soon moves away from this implausibly restrictive account of experience. However, he unfortunately never gets around to modifying his account of time-consciousness to do justice to his skepticism about the fundamental status he initially assigns to sensations in experience.

DURATION VERSUS PUNCTUAL MOMENT

In the tradition of the classical philosophical approach to time canonically articulated by Aristotle, Husserl combines a punctual or punctiform conception of the content of time-consciousness with a conception of time itself in which intervals are ontologically prior to punctual moments. Like Leibniz in his Sixth Letter to Clarke, and Kant in the Transcendental Aesthetic, Husserl maintains that time is essentially unitary. Moments of time are not parts of time, but abstract limits of intervals. But, like Kant in the Transcendental Deduction (A 99) and the Anticipations of Perception (A 168/B 210), and Leibniz in his Sixth Letter to Clarke, Husserl insists that sensations give empirical reality to time by picking out moments of zero temporal extension. This view goes back to Aristotle who distinguishes the continuity of time from the punctual now that is the basis for our capacity to enumerate different times.

Husserl's theory of time-consciousness is not so much a compromise between Bergson's conception of time as undivided duration, the saddlebacked specious-present conception of William James and the traditional knife-edged conception of the present advocated by theorists from Aristotle to Brentano, as an effort to take over those features of these rival theories that are requisite for a successful theory of time-consciousness. With James and other advocates of the specious-present conception, Husserl thinks that there is a difference between the short-term memory and anticipation involved in perceptual experience and the kind of recall or expectation involved in attending to the more distant past and future. But, unlike advocates of the specious-present conception of time, Husserl is not interested in identifying temporal building blocks or minima of temporal awareness. With Aristotle, Augustine, and Brentano, Husserl thinks that experience somehow how has its basis in successively existing momentary impressions. However, unlike such philosophers of time, who agree with him in regarding moments as abstractions from durations, Husserl does not look in punctual moments for the connection between past, present, and future. Even though he thinks that momentary impressions are in some sense the origin of all experience, he also regards the past and the future as equally real and subject to direct experience. Husserl's theory of time-consciousness not only attempts to mediate between the alternatives of thinking of temporal experience as consisting of intervals or of moments. It also combines an account of temporal experience, and indeed of time itself, as a temporal becoming of successively real past, present, and future experiences with an account of time that bases the structure of time in tenseless relations between events.

Husserl's starting-point for an understanding of time-consciousness is sensory awareness. Much of his project involves the attempt to trace our consciousness of past, present, and future back to original sensations that have no temporal extension. This project gives rise to difficulties in Husserl's account of how we are directly aware of short temporal duration. These difficulties have given rise to interpretations of his theory that treat it as very much of a piece with the knife-edge or punctual conception of the now favored by Brentano. On the other hand, other interpretations have tried to take the idea seriously that it is an account of time-consciousness in which we have bona fide direct awareness of short intervals of time in present experience. Husserl begins with a theory that is closer to the knife-edge view than he really wants, and is only able to find a way to avoid the problems besetting Brentano's theory in remarks dating from the teens of this century when he finally realizes that sensations are themselves mere idealizations from perceptions of changes.

Husserl regards temporality as the basic level of consciousness that is constitutive of intentionality. Temporality is fundamentally a process through which the past and the future are integrated into the present of experience, a present that he eventually comes to refer to in the 30s as "the living present." Husserl's analysis of time-consciousness thus follows a tradition going back from Brentano to Aristotle at least in giving primacy to present experience in understanding time, regardless of whether it also breaks with that tradition in regarding the knife-edged moment as an abstraction from actual present experience. He also insists that even the kind of non-object-directed experience to be found in sensations has its own distinctive form of time-consciousness. With time-consciousness comes a form of representation of the past and the future that is intentional, but that need not be object-directed at all. The intentionality of time-consciousness reaches below the object-directed level of perception down to the fundamental level of consciousness. Indeed, Husserl insists that the sequence of impressions that constitute the basic level of individual experience is past, present, and future only in virtue of the way in which those impressions present themselves to the mind. They have a tenseless ordering that becomes tensed only through the temporal intentionality that they have in virtue of being experiences. It is in terms of the way that episodes of consciousness constitute an awareness of themselves that Husserl proposes then to reconstruct both time-consciousness at its fundamental level and the very nature of the self as the subject of self-consciousness. This project is however itself only intelligible against the background of his new interest in the nature of the self and its constitutive role in experience.

Some commentators argue that Husserl endorses the principle at work in the early Brentano's view that an awareness of succession must involve simultaneous awareness of the different sensations involved in the succession and thus denies a specious present theory of time.[2] By contrast other interpreters have argued that Husserl is a defender of a sophisticated specious present conception of time.[3] While still other interpreters have argued that Husserl's theory of time-consciousness vacillates between a theoretical commitment to original punctual impressions from which all our knowledge is supposed ultimately to derive its legitimation and the idea that such original sources of knowledge are, strictly speaking, chimerical, because they are only abstractions from more complicated episodes occurring across temporal intervals.[4] It might be argued that the

[2] Izchak Miller, *Husserl's Theory of Perception* (Cambridge, Mass.: MIT Press, 1988), esp. pp. 109, 120ff., and 174.
[3] John Brough, "Husserl's Phenomenology of Time-Consciousness," in J. N. Mohanty and W. R. McKenna (eds.), *Husserl's Phenomenology: A Textbook* (Washington, D.C.: University Press of America, 1989), p. 279.
[4] Jacques Derrida, *Speech and Phenomena*, D. Allison trans. (Evanston: Northwestern University Press, 1973), pp. 49 ff., has emphasized the difficulties Husserl faces in saving his idea of an immediate source of experience in sensation given also his desire to bring out the mediated character of our experience of time. There seem to be some grounds for Jacques Derrida's charge that Husserl is actually committed both to a punctual moment conception of time-

argument could be resolved by noting that those who regard Husserl as a defender of a knife-edged theory of time, or as someone who vacillates between a specious present and a knife-edged theory have focused on the much more plentiful published material from his early theory, while the later more coherent approach to time-consciousness supports a specious-present interpretation. However, some interpreters have taken Husserl to move from a duration-based conception of temporal experience to one in which our experience of duration can be bracketed and effectively replaced with an experience of moments without temporal extension.[5]

Husserl takes Brentano's philosophical development of Aristotle's analysis of perception, memory, fantasy and time, as the starting-point for his investigations into the nature of time-consciousness. His first extensive treatment of the philosophy of time, and the lecture course from which his *Phenomenology of Inner Time-Consciousness* is largely derived, is a 1904–1905 lecture course entitled "The Major Parts of a Phenomenology and Theory of Knowledge" and consisting of four parts: (1) "On Perception," (2) "On Attention, Specific Opinion, etc.," (3) "Fantasy and Image Consciousness," (4) "On the Phenomenology of Time." At the beginning of that course Husserl notes that his inspiration for dealing with these issues comes from a lecture course given by Brentano in the mid 1880s entitled "Selected Psychological and Aesthetic Topics" (*Hua* 10, pp. 15–16). Most of Brentano's lecture course is a critical reconstruction of Aristotle's theory of sense and imagination. Husserl is particularly interested in developing a more adequate account of how we are able to experience the short durations of time within individual states of consciousness that are widely referred to as the specious present.

While Aristotle argues in *Physics*, Book IV that we directly perceive

consciousness and to an interval conception of time-conception and vacillates back and forth between them. Husserl is defended against this critique by J. Claude Evans, *Strategies of Deconstruction: Derrida and the Myth of the Voice* (Minneapolis: University of Minnesota Press, 1991), but only by ascribing to Husserl a straightforward defense of the specious-present conception of time that is difficult to defend as an interpretation of Husserl. Rudolf Bernet, "Is the Present Ever Present? Phenomenology and the Metaphysics of Presence," *Research in Phenomenology* 12 (1982), 85–112, is much more sensitive to the complications in Husserl's view and much more sympathetic to Derrida's critique; see also Rudolf Bernet, *La vie du sujet: Recherches sur l'interprétation de Husserl dans la phénoménologie* (Paris: Presses Universitaires de France, 1994), esp. pp. 282ff.

[5] Gerd Brand argues that Husserl changes from a phenomenological conception of time based on an extended present to one in the thirties that allows one to reduce the temporal present to punctual moments, see G. Brand, *Welt, Ich und Zeit nach unveröffentlichten Manuskripten Edmund Husserls* (The Hague: Martinus Nijhoff, 1955), p. 75.

change, Brentano, working with Aristotle's assumption of a knife-edge present, finds such perception of change incomprehensible, except as a present representation of the immediate past. In this context, Brentano notes: "But Aristotle seems to have been of the opinion that time can be perceived, and that is, by means of the 'now,' which as a limit is the end of the past and the beginning of the future ... The true solution is to be found in not assuming any perceptual representation of time and motion, and the like. For us, it is important that everything that is past or future is only accessible in its tendency in fantasy."[6] Brentano argues that we only directly experience the present. The past and the future are available to us only through our fantasy or imagination. To account for the memory that we have of the immediate past, Brentano invokes the idea of an original association. According to Brentano, there is a psychological law that induces each representation to give rise to a series of imaginings of past episodes. We then come to have a representation of the future through an expectation that there will continue to be new representations in our experience. This expectation is, in turn, generated by our habit of associating ever new present episodes with ever new past episodes. Since Brentano thinks that only the present is real, he is forced to think of the series of temporal episodes as one in which future episodes are continually popping into existence as they become present, and popping out of existence as they become past.

Brentano's theory cannot distinguish between the experience that we have of the immediate past that is part of the extended present of any experience and bonafide memory of past occurrences. Husserl regards this failure to distinguish the immediate past of the species present from bona fide memories of the past as a fundamental difficulty of Brentano's theory, as is its limitation of existence to present existence. The limitation of existence to present existence seems to make time-consciousness itself incomprehensible. For how can one be conscious of the past and the future on the basis of present episodes? The items that we originally associate with the present must themselves be present if they are to exist. But, if they are themselves present, how are they to account for our conscious-

[6] Franz Brentano and F. Mayer-Hillerbrand (ed.), *Grundzüge der Ästhetik* (Bern: Francke, 1959), p. 47. This book contains a substantial part of the lecture course: "Selected Topics from Psychology and Aesthetics" which Husserl heard and upon which he based his critique of Brentano's theory of time. The quote is from that lecture course.

ness of the past and the future? It might seem that we can solve the problem in question by thinking of the associated items as representations of the past and the future. But then we have left precisely the nature of our consciousness of time unexplicated.

Husserl insists against Brentano's early view that protention and especially, retention are involved in all perception, except completely original perception, that is perception of the present conceived most narrowly. Thus, in some sense we directly perceive the past and the future.[7] By responding to and modifying Brentano's theory of time, Husserl indirectly takes over important Aristotelian assumptions. He agrees with Aristotle against Brentano that we directly perceive the past and such things as change. Indeed, his whole manner of arguing against the thesis that we have no direct perception of the past involves an acceptance of the Aristotelian idea that the present in the strict sense of the term is a punctual now that exists only as a limit of a continuous manifold of temporal states. Any experience of a content lasting through some temporal interval requires anticipations and, especially, reproductions of the immediate past in an immediate present that is ultimately punctual in nature. Husserl refers to anticipations as protentions, and reproductions as retentions. It is through protentions that we experience the future, through retentions that we experience the past, and impressions that we experience the present.

Husserl is quite clear that he wants to reject the popular view, defended, for instance, by Brentano and Meinong, that one must somehow be able to compare past and future experiences with present experiences in present consciousness in order to be aware of present experiences as present, past experiences as past, or future experiences as future. But he nevertheless seems to get himself into

[7] Brentano gave up the doctrine that we only directly experience the present by 1911, in favor of the idea that past, present, and future are available to us through different modes of perceptual consciousness. There is, however, no evidence that Husserl took cognizance of the later Brentano's idea that we have a direct perception of the past, an idea that Brentano referred to as proteraesthesis. This theory of proteraesthesis has striking similarities with the conception of time-consciousness that Husserl defends until about 1908. According to both theories, we account for our immediate experience of past, present, and future by means of present impressions of past, present, and future episodes that are interpreted by consciousness as past, present, and future. Fortunately, Husserl came to see the inadequacy of this theory by 1908. There is a useful account of the later Brentano's account of our perception of time in Oskar Kraus, "Toward a Phenomenognosy of Time Consciousness," originally published in German in *Archiv für die gesammte Psychologie* 75 (1930), 1–30, and now available in English translation in L. McAlister (ed.), *The Philosophy of Franz Brentano* (London: Duckworth, 1976), pp. 224–239.

difficulties because he wants to say that we retain the past, and expect the future in the immediate present (*Hua* 10, section 13, p. 34).[8] The claim that the past and the future is retained in a punctual present, and not only in an interval of some duration, is most apparent in Husserl's response to Meinong's effort to do justice to our experience of duration. According to Meinong's account of our perception of duration and change, there must be some present act of perception that grasps the whole of a temporally extended object, since the perception of a temporally extended object cannot consist of momentary perceptions.[9] In responding to Meinong's view, Husserl concedes that consciousness must reach beyond the now in every momentary act, while denying that there is any distinct act that must grasp the whole of the perceived event. But he also notes that the momentary act is not itself the perception of a temporal object, but is a mere abstraction which serves as a necessary condition for perception (*Hua* 10, p. 227).

Izchak Miller appeals to Husserl's claim that "it belongs to the essence of temporal intuition that it is consciousness of *what has just been* in every point of its duration (which we can make an object reflectively) and not mere consciousness of the now-point of the objective thing appearing as having a duration" to support his ascription of the Principle of Simultaneous Awareness to Husserl. This is the principle that awareness of succession can only derive from simultaneous features of the structure of awareness, not from any succession of awarenesses.[10] The claim that Husserl accepts the Principle of Simultaneous Awareness conflicts with Husserl's negative answer to the question that he addresses at the view: "Can a series of *coexistent* primary contents ever bring a *succession* to intuition?" (*Hua* 10, pp. 322–323).

---

8 Husserl is often construed as arguing that the immediate past is present in the immediate present as a retention: "Presenting is dimensioned in itself, that is, moved-stretched out, in a way that with the consciousness of completely unmediated original givenness in the momentary now of the 'original impression,' a continuous connection of implication goes together with precisely this momentary now, consisting of 'retentions,' that is, of near term nested memories in which consciousness allows the given to glide out of the original impression unthematically while also holding on to it," Klaus Held, "Phänomenologie der Zeit nach Husserl," *Perspektiven der Philosophie* 7 (1981), 196.
9 Alexius Meinong, "Beiträge zur Theorie der psychischen Analyse," *Zeitschrift für Psychologie und Physiologie der Sinnesorgane* 6 (1893), 447ff., and "Über Gegenstände höherer Ordnung und deren Verhältnis zur inneren Wahrnehmung," *Zeitschrift für Psychologie und Physiologie der Sinnesorgane* 21 (1899), 248ff.
10 Miller, *Husserl's Theory of Perception*, p. 109.

Husserl insists that

> I see with self-evidence that *the endstate is only possible as endstate* and that *a time intuiting state in general* is only possible as an *extended state* [I also see with self-evidence] that a [*state*] *intuiting a time point* is only possible in *connection* [with other states], and that the consciousness of time itself time, the consciousness of duration, [requires] duration, the consciousness of succession, [requires] succession. (*Hua* 10, p. 192)

It might seem that Husserl accepts part of Miller's Principle of Simultaneous Awareness; it might seem that he accepts the idea that the momentary present must contain the past and the future in it if we are to be able to make sense of the experience of time. But then again his conception of temporal experience would differ from that of Brentano in detail only. Husserl obviously does not accept the further claim that our experience of the past and the future derives exclusively from what is contained in the momentary present, and involves no appeal to the succession of what is perceived.

Ascription of a modified version of the Principle of Simultaneous Awareness seems to derive support from Husserl's view that the immediate past and the immediate future are perceived by us by means of retentions and protentions that attach to the punctual present that is constituted by an original impression. Husserl does construe retentions or protentions as states of consciousness contained in the immediate present: "Every actual now of consciousness is subject to the law of modification. It changes in retention of retention and that continuously. A continuous continuum of retention is the result such that every later point is a retention for every earlier" (section 11).

For Husserl then, every moment in time retains its immediate past, and less directly its mediate past; it is a consciousness of what has been and what was before whatever it is conscious of as having been. The same point applies to our protention of the future.

Miller runs together Husserl's principle that one must be aware of the past as past and hence as a state that is no longer now with the principle that all awareness of the past must be a present punctual awareness of the past. Similar remarks apply to our awareness of the future. From Husserl's point of view, the Principle of Simultaneous Awareness fails to accomplish precisely what Brentano and Miller would like it to accomplish; it fails to account for why we think of the past as past, and the future as future. To account for the pastness of the immediate past, the presence of the immediate present, and the futurity of the immediate future, we need episodes that are past, present, and future in relation to each other, and hence not all present at the same moment, but we also need a perception of those episodes as belonging to distinct nows of which we are conscious (that is, that we perceive) not at a moment, but across an interval of time.

Although Husserl talks of momentary impressions as the origins of all experience, his actual view is that the punctual present is really an "ideal limit," "an abstraction that cannot exist independently" of the continuum of retentions and protentions that make up our experience of duration (*Hua* 10, section 16, p. 40). In Husserl's theory, time-consciousness is based on the perception of objects by means of sensations that have zero duration. But these sensations are themselves ultimately abstractions from the continuum of time. Each temporal interval can always be divided and subdivided into further retentions and protentions. Despite the emphasis that Husserl places on the idea of original momentary sensations or impressions as the source of time, he ultimately regards these impressions themselves as abstractions. In what seems to be a later addition to a manuscript written between 1908–1909: "Original sensation is something *abstract*" and, in a note on the margins of the same page that is clearly of later origin, Husserl notes: "I say original sensation, that refers to the non-self-sufficient phase of originality; sensation *tout court* refers to the whole time-constituting consciousness, in which an imminent content is constituted" (*Hua* 10, p. 326). Thus Husserl ultimately seems effectively to follow Findlay's good advice: "Perhaps Husserl should have dropped the whole notion of retention as in some sense a derived or modified state of awareness harking back to one that was more 'originary.'"[11] Original sensations are abstractions from the continuous flow of experience.

The Third Part of the *Lectures on Inner Time-Consciousness* is later in origin than the first two parts, since it derives from notes written in the early teens of the century. In the Third Part, Husserl argues that "the tone c is first a concrete individual as temporally extended. The concrete is in each case what is alone given, and obviously it is intellective processes of analysis which allow such distinctions" (*Hua* 10, section 41, p. 86). The knife-edged present seems really to be a

---

[11] J. N. Findlay, "Husserl's Analysis of the Inner Time-Consciousness," *Monist* 59 (1975), 10.

theoretical postulate that we introduce from our efforts to apply mathematics to temporal experience. We could thus take Husserl to be engaged in the use of "idealized fictions cum fundamento in re" that he describes as the procedure of theoretical physicists in the Prolegomena to the *Investigations* (*LU* section 23).

The key to Husserl's attempt to formulate a viable alternative to the specious present and the knife-edged views of time is his idea that even the kind of time-consciousness involved in the sensation of a pain has a certain intentionality to it. At first, the idea that even non-intentional states such as pains are somehow intentional after all is puzzling to say the least. These states do not have referential intentionality. They are not about objects that are distinguishable from those states of consciousness themselves. In what sense do they have intentionality at all?

The past or future content that is presented by retention and protention is not itself present in the retention or protention as a real content or impression. The sensation theoretically exists at a moment, and is presented as past in a retention, and presented as future in a protention, at which times the original sensation has already ceased to exist. But, nevertheless, the past sensation is retained as past in a retention that comes immediately after it, and a future sensation is anticipated as future in a protention that comes immediately before it. Each retention is a retention of something immediately past as something that has been, and of everything in the past of that immediate past as something that has been before. This leads to a whole series of retentions of retentions, and, by force of parallel, protentions of protentions.

Husserl ascribes a combination of what he calls horizontal and vertical intentionality to all impressions. In virtue of its horizontal intentionality, each impression is a consciousness of the immediate past and of the immediate future. It retains the impression in consciousness that immediately preceded it, and anticipates the impression which immediately succeeds it, although the retained or anticipated sensation is not itself a real constituent of the retention of protention. At the same time, each retention of a past sensation is also a retention of the retentions of sensations that are retained in the original sensation. Each protention is again not only an anticipation of an individual future sensation, but also an anticipation of the sensations that are anticipated in that future sensation. In virtue of its horizontal intentionality, each impression is a retentive consciousness of all past retentions, and a protentive consciousness of all future protentions.

Following William James, Husserl draws a sharp distinction between primary memory and secondary memory. Like James, Husserl regards retention as the primary kind of memory, and thinks of recall or recollection as a secondary kind of memory that is only possible because we have retained information. Unlike James, there is no tendency for Husserl to identify retention with some neurophysiological phenomenon of information storage, although Husserl could readily acknowledge that there might be some neurophysiological basis for retention of the past in experience.[12]

Secondary memory represents the past. Unlike primary memory, it does not directly present us with the past. Perhaps the easiest way to see the point in question is by appeal to perceptual experience. We are able to listen to music rather than to individual notes, because we are able to directly perceive a series of different notes that belong to the specious present. These notes present themselves to us in a temporal sequence. They are not all perceived simultaneously, or we would again have no experience of them as a succession of notes. But the way in which we perceive different notes in the specious present is quite different from the kind of recall of past notes involved in a memory of a concert that happened several months ago. For, when we remember notes in the second sense, we do not hear them, but represent them to ourselves as we heard them or as if we were hearing them.

Secondary memory is also unlike primary memory in that it is to some extent up to us. We can choose to recall or represent situations in the past to ourselves. And we can also alter the contents of what we remember in our imagination. All this is not true of our immediate experience of the most immediate past. In the case of the

---

[12] William James, *Principles of Psychology* (New York: Henry Holt, 1890), I, p. 654: "The retention of e, it will be observed, is no mysterious storing up of an 'idea' in an unconscious state. It is not a fact of the mental order at all. It is a purely physical phenomenon, a morphological feature, the presence of these 'paths,' namely, in the finest recesses of the brain's tissue. The recall or recollection, on the other hand, is a *psycho-physical* phenomenon, with both a bodily and a mental side."

experience of the very immediate past, error seems to make no sense. Without reliable experience of the very immediate past, we would have no determinate experiences at all. For experiences take at least some amount of time.

In developing his own account of secondary memory or recall, Husserl criticizes the image or representative theory of memory that has a lineage going back to Aristotle, and defends a realist theory of memory instead.[13] According to the representative theory, to remember is to experience some representative, in general a memory image, of some past experience. According to the realist theory of memory by contrast, to remember is directly to experience some past experience as past. Husserl argues that the representative theory has a number of crucial defects. These defects lead him to reject mental images as the basis for memory, although it is important to note that he does not deny that memory can be accompanied by mental images.

The image theory cannot account for the fact that memory is direct knowledge of the past. Since, according to the image theory, we never directly represent the past, but only an image of what is past, we find ourselves in conflict with our intuition that we remember past objects rather than images of past objects. Husserl makes the point with the example of a memory of a "lighted theater." What I remember when I remember the lighted theater is often only the lighted theater, not my having perceived the theater (*Hua* 10, section 27, p. 58). The representative theory also provides us with no way of accounting for our experience of the past in memory. The image that we have of the past in memory is a present image, so it is unclear why we think of it as remembered, that is, of the past at all.

Thus Aristotle already asked himself "how it is possible that, although we perceive only the impression, we remember the absent thing which we do not perceive."[14] His response is not, however, one which Husserl finds satisfactory. According to Aristotle, we are aware of the past through a present experience in the same way that we can perceive Koriscus when we look at a portrait of him. But

---

[13] A helpful discussion of Husserl's theory of memory may be found in John Brough, "Husserl on Memory," *Monist* 59 (1975), 40–62. Brough pays particular attention to Husserl's critique of theories of memory according to which memory is based on imagery.

[14] Aristotle, "De Memoria et Reminiscentia," trans. in Richard Sorabji, *Aristotle on Memory* (London: Duckworth, 1972), pp. 50–51 (Greek: 450 b15ff.).

then it seems that the present memory image has a resemblance or similarity relation to the original experience that itself needs explanation. The fact that we are presented with an image of something might seem to be enough to indicate to us that what we are experiencing is remembered. The problem with this suggestion is that there are clearly images that are not memories. So, even if being an image were a necessary condition for being a memory, it is not a sufficient condition. Husserl notes that we can imagine things without remembering them (*Hua* 10, section 23, p. 51).

Husserl's own account of memory treats memory as a direct experience of the past. This direct experience of the past is then the basis for our immediate, non-inferential knowledge of the past, but it is not strictly speaking identical with immediate knowledge of the past. Unlike primary memory (retention), secondary memory, that is, memory properly so-called, is fallible. While memory is a success term, so that in a sense one can say that, if one remembers something, then it actually did occur, there is also a sense in which it is clearly possible to misremember the fact. In this case, one believes oneself to have a memory of the past, but does not in fact. Such delusive memories are not phenomenologically directly distinguishable from bona fide memories.

While Husserl criticizes the Brentanian view of time-consciousness and the representative view of memory for failing to account for our ability to be conscious of the past, in a sense this might seem to leave him open to an *ad hominem* attack. For Husserl himself has nothing more to say about the nature of our ability to be aware of the past than the fact that we do, in fact, represent the past. The same remark holds for his account of how we represent the future. In unpublished writings, Husserl does, however, point out how the distinction between past, present, and future has to do with different ways in which repeatable objects present themselves to us, while maintaining their qualitative identity or, in the case of objects that undergo change, while undergoing changes in their qualitative features.

Husserl takes recall to be the key to attributing reidentifiable features to objects and thus to the whole notion of repeatable objects. It is significant that Husserl notes that

to have a representation of something, that is in itself in contrast to possible observations that it make it conscious: in other words, an object [Kant's empirical notion of a thing in itself as something within experience, not his transcendental notion of a thing in itself as something completely independent of experience] ... one needs reproduction and recognition, as Kant already saw in the transcendental deduction (although restricted to spatial objectivity). What makes perception originally conscious as an existing, becoming unity in the flux of original impressions and retentions and protentions, must be something that I can recall in repeated recollections and know as the same something that I perceived previously.[15]

Husserl seems to identify all recall with what has come to be called personal memory, that is memory based on personal experience. For, despite the fact that he denies that all secondary memory involves an explicit awareness by the person who remembers of the fact that he or she had a certain experience, he does insist that secondary memory always involves some implicit consciousness of the fact that one has oneself perceived something: "it belongs primarily to the nature of memory of memory that it is consciousness of having-been-perceived" (*Hua* 10, p. 57). By this locution, Husserl might mean having been perceived by someone, which would be consistent with it not having been perceived by me. However, Husserl actually insists that it is I who must have perceived things: I am aware in the "present representation of the past consciousness that I had the perception" (p. 195).

Now there are obviously instances of memory in which I remember something that I have never perceived. This seems to be true of a good deal of so-called factual memory. I remember that the Greeks defeated the Persians at Marathon without having perceived them to do so. However, it might be argued that I have this knowledge based on some kind of perception – I read a book at some point or I was told this fact by someone – and even if I do not consciously remember this fact it might in some sense be regarded as an implicit fact about my memory. The problem with the suggestion that an awareness of the fact that I have myself experienced something in the past that provides me with evidence for anything that I remember when I remember it, is that it is a claim that I have no way of verifying or falsifying.

ABSOLUTE TIME-CONSCIOUSNESS

It is customary to think of time as consisting either of the mutually exclusive properties of being present, past, or future or to think of

---

[15] Edmund Husserl, "Bewußtsein und Sinn – Sinn und Noema," (1920) in *Analysen zur passiven Synthesis (1918–1926)*, *Hua* 11, p. 327.

time in terms of relations such as x being earlier, later than, or simultaneous with y. J. Ellis McTaggart has given the popular epithets of the A- and B-series to these two aspects of time.[16] The A-series consists of events ordered in a sequence according to which each event is past, present, and future in relation to other events. The B-series consists of events ordered according to which event is earlier, later and simultaneous with other events. One may also distinguish between A- and B-series *theories* of time, according to which temporal series one regards as fundamental.

The only sense one can give to change in the B-series taken in isolation is that of differences between events which exist at different temporal co-ordinates. According to the A-series theory of time, states of things come to be and pass away in temporal sequence. The A-series theory of time conceives of time and reality essentially on the model of successive presence. The past may be defined as what was already present, but is no longer, and the future may be defined as what is not yet present, but will be present. Things and properties that were once future, become present and then become past. What is present is continually being replaced as one now succeeds another. This theory of time is thus associated with the thesis that reality is essentially becoming. Only what is present now exists, the past is no longer, and the future is not yet. Reality is relativized to what is present, but this present is constantly being replaced by a new and different one. Since the present is demarcated by synchronized clocks, time is again understood as sequence measurable by clocks. Unlike the B-series theory of time, the sequences of states tracked by clocks do not coexist, since actual existence has an essentially temporal meaning restricted to what is now. But, by conceiving of past, present, and future episodes as a sequence, the A-series view regiments time in a manner measurable by clocks.

A-theorists argue that time must involve some form of becoming. McTaggart argues, for instance, that the A-series is fundamental to time, because time involves change. He denies that events and their properties can come to be and pass away in an absolute sense. For each event has fixed properties and a fixed location in the B-series. This is crucial to the very identity of events. How does one account for change? Events become past, present, and future as they take on

[16] J. M. E. McTaggart, *The Nature of Existence*, vol. 2 (Cambridge University Press, 1927), Book v, ch. 33.

different de. rminations of the A-series. Without such changes in tense, there would be no changes at all. It would be difficult to determine that time had elapsed if there were no changes as changes are normally understood, namely as changes in the states of things. McTaggart does not deny that there are differences between events that correspond to our normal conception of changes in the state of things. But he does argue that such differences amount to genuine changes only if those differences are tied to changes in the determinations of the A-series. Without changes in the determinations of the A-series, the B-series would not be a time-series at all. It would be what McTaggart refers to as an atemporal C-series. For time is supposed to require change, and the B-series taken in isolation from the A-series involves only differences between events.

On the A-series theory of time, events or states of things seem to be required to satisfy two mutually exclusive conditions. They must be absolutely past, present, or future, where past, present, and future are mutually exclusive determinations. And they must also be past, present and future at different times in order for there to be temporal becoming. Thus each of the temporal modalities must involve the other in a specific way. If time involves the existence of states of things or events (as McTaggart would have it) with the absolute and mutually incompatible properties of pastness, present-ness, and futureness, then it is contradictory for any state of a thing or event to have more than one of these three properties. But the very successiveness that is constitutive of the distinction between past, present, and future seems to require that properties of things or of events be each past, present, and future and thus to have all three of these mutually incompatible properties. McTaggart concludes that the notion of time is contradictory and that time is therefore unreal.[17] He urges that the contradictory notion of time as some-thing successively real be replaced with an atemporal C-series.

The most popular way of responding to McTaggart is to argue that the B-series is not in fact parasitic on the A-series as he claims. Once one gives up the idea that time must involve past, present, and future, change without becoming is intelligible in terms of differ-ences between events ordered tenselessly according to earlier and

---

[17] A helpful articulation of the contradiction which McTaggart finds in the notion of temporal change is provided by Michael Dummett, "A Defense of McTaggart's Proof of the Unreality of Time," *Truth and Other Enigmas* (Cambridge: Harvard University Press, 1978), pp. 351–357.

later. Past, present, and future have generally been defined in the B-series theory in terms of being earlier, later, or simultaneous with some event which is distinguished as present by the use of the demonstrative "this." More recently, defenders of the B-series theory have backed away from the possibility of translating tensed discourse without remainder into tenseless discourse, and have tended to argue only that tensed discourse can be explicated in terms of a metalanguage that uses only tenseless discourse. They have even been prepared to concede that the different kinds of demonstrative expressions are exhaustively definable neither in terms of each other nor in terms of non-tensed discourse.[18] But even the interpretation of tensed discourse in terms of a metalanguage that does not involve tense raises the question posed by McTaggart of whether the relations of earlier, later, and simultaneous that remain are still genuinely temporal once they have been stripped of their connections to tensed discourse (their A-determinations).

In the Third Part of the *Lectures on Internal Time-Consciousness*, Husserl provides an account of the most fundamental level of subjectivity. Here he opts for a position that has striking similarities to McTaggart's view that we must account for the passage of time in terms of a C-series. While Husserl does not argue that the notions of past, present, and future are contradictory, he does, somewhat surprisingly, attempt to ground the distinction between past, present, and future experiences in a tenseless notion of sequence that he does not think can any longer be properly called time at all. The tenseless notion of sequence in question is supposed to be the flux of experiences that constitute time itself. Since the flux of experiences in consciousness is not in time, but is itself supposed to be responsible for the distinction between past, present, and future, it makes no sense to say that it could proceed at a faster or slower rate (*Hua* 10, section 35, p. 74). Husserl wants to deny that the flux in question is in "objective time" (section 36, p. 75). Thus he does not think of it as what McTaggart and contemporary philosophers would call the B-series, although he does think, like McTaggart, that the atemporal C-series, taken together with the A-series, provides the ultimate source of the B-series, and its temporal relations of earlier, later, and simultaneous.

---

[18] A valuable survey of the current state of the discussion may be found in L. Oaklander and Quentin Smith (eds.), *The New Theory of Time* (New Haven: Yale University Press, 1994).

It might be asked why we cannot regard the series of episodes in question as the B-series. For that we would already have to think of these episodes in distinctively temporal relations. But Husserl wants to argue that the kind of temporal relations involved in objective time, and, more specifically, in physical time, must themselves be regarded as constituted by the experiences belonging to this flux. For objects are taken by us to be in time only in virtue of their relation to the sequence of our experiences. Here Husserl's new transcendental idealism begins to intrude. We cannot presuppose objective time in an analysis of the fundamental structure of absolute time-consciousness because such time-consciousness is supposed to be the very basis upon which we can articulate an objective conception of time. To this it might be responded that what is claimed is an epistemological dependence and not necessarily a metaphysical dependence. It is a hallmark of Husserl's transcendental idealism to argue that relations of identification dependence must be ones that we can make sense of. To this extent they depend on the conditions under which we can make sense of the relations in question. In this case, the claim is that the only notion of time that we have is one that depends in some sense on our experience.

What is striking about absolute consciousness is that it is not itself in time, although its experiences are ordered according to what Husserl takes to be a linear parameter defined by the horizontal intentionality of a continuum of different mutually retending and protending experiences. Now, even though absolute consciousness is not in time, it is able to represent itself as being in time, and thus temporally "appear to itself" (*Hua* 10, section 39). For experiences, including sensations, are, for Husserl, as they are for Brentano, self-intimating episodes. Each of them is not only a state of consciousness, but also a state of self-reflexive awareness. The sequence of these different self-reflexive states of awareness distinguishes different presents, and hence pasts, and futures. It is the different sequentially ordered represented sensations, each in turn with its retentions and protentions, that then account for our experience of the flow of time, or of the shifting of the present, past, and future through different episodes.

Now there are different streams of consciousness corresponding to different persons. But these different streams of consciousness all belong together in a single encompassing stream of consciousness that includes all experiences. The single encompassing stream of consciousness is obviously not in the private experience of different individuals, but rather in the shared experience that makes a distinction between private and public experience possible in the first place. It is, in Husserl's new terms, time as it presents itself to consciousness in general, and hence to an ego that is not yet distinguished as any particular individual.

Husserl accepts the traditional view of time as passage, and explains our experience of passage in terms of the manner in which the states of consciousness belonging to absolute subjectivity represent themselves. Each immediate momentary representation represents itself, and also represents the past and the future, through its retention of sensations in its immediate past, and protentions of possible sensations in its future, together with its retention and protention of the retentions and protentions of those sensations. The experience of passage derives from our experience of the difference between retented, presented, and protended episodes of experience.

The most fundamental level of absolute time-consciousness allows for a tenseless description of experiences that is independent of a temporal standpoint. However, each claim that we make from a certain temporal standpoint within the sequence of representations of the absolute flux is, in fact, temporally relative. The contradiction induced in bringing together different tenses may be circumvented by relativizing the truth of statements about present, past, or future states to a certain time.[19] The claim "S is future" is true of a certain state S at time t_1, at time t_2 the claim that "S is present" is true of S, and at t_3 the claim that "S is past" is true of S. But then claims about past, present, and future states have no meaning in abstraction from a particular temporal perspective. Futurity, pastness, and presence apply to any thing or event, but they never apply to that thing or event from the same temporal perspective. It may still be said of the same event E that it is past at present, and it was in the future in the past, but once we relativize the truth of claims about the occurrence of events to different times we have eliminated the passage that McTaggart took to be constitutive of A-determinations. We have not, however, eliminated tenses entirely. They exist relative to a certain representation of absolute subjectivity which is an inevitable

---

[19] C. D. Broad defends the A-series theory of time by relativizing the meaning of past, present, and future, to different times in response to McTaggart in *An Examination of McTaggart's Philosophy* (Cambridge University Press, 1938), esp. Part I, pp. 277ff.

expression of the series of experiences belonging to absolute sub-jectivity itself.

Husserl's idea that we have an immediate non-inferential conscious-ness of a moment with zero duration seems quite implausible. For to be conscious of a moment as such we would have to have discrimina-tory powers capable of distinguishing the infinite number of different possible moments in any given duration from one another. By treating each retention as a retention of the retentions of past sensations, Husserl is able to connect all of the past punctual phases together in a temporal continuum. This gives a plausible account of how the past and future are involved in the present. However, there is a certain phenomenological cost to this construction. For not only are we forced to assume that individual punctual sensations that are phases in a temporal continuum represent both the past and the future, but we must also assume that they represent all of the other past and future phases. It is difficult to see how such a fine-grained consciousness of past and future can be reconciled with our rather finite capacities for temporal discrimination. To this, it may be responded that we do not have consciousness of such phases as objects. But there is some question of whether we can have consciousness of them individually and as a continuum at all.

Husserl denies that our knowledge of the knife-edged present is inferential. He thinks that such a view would force us to regard immediate impressions as unconscious representations, a view that would deprive us of any immediate access to completely original experience and also undermine a key assumption about conscious-ness that Husserl takes over from Brentano, namely any state of consciousness is always conscious to the person who is in that state (Addition ix, *Hua* 10, p. 119). The kind of consciousness of conscious-ness involved in original sensations is, to be sure, not a consciousness of any object, in Husserl's terminology it is not an interpretative act, but it is, nevertheless, a consciousness of a content belonging to consciousness.

Husserl denies that time-consciousness has a metric that can be measured by clocks. So we cannot even think of distinct moments as limits of intervals that, in principle, might be measured by clocks. Since we cannot appeal to time as perceived in changes in perceptual objects, and we cannot appeal to time as measured in changes in physical objects to understand original time-consciousness on pain of circularity, the claim that we immediately experience a knife-edged present through each original impression that we experience must bear the weight of the view that the punctual moment is something more than a mere abstraction. The obvious objection to assuming that we are immediately conscious of impressions that exist at, or rather define what it is to be, punctual moments, is that our threshold of conscious discrimination is not sufficiently fine-grained to distinguish one such momentary impression from another. Ricoeur has noted that there is a real threat of circularity in Husserl's account of how objective time is constituted by inner time-consciousness. The problem is that Husserl must draw on the structure of objective time, for instance the idea of a linear temporal parameter in order to explicate inner time-consciousness.[20] Husserl avoids the circularity in question by the extremely problematic idea that we have an immediate experience of punctual moments that exists as boundaries of intervals, which, in turn, are constituted by a continuum of retentions and protentions involved in any momentary awareness. Once Husserl gives up the distinction between content of interpretation ("Auffassungsinhalt") and interpretative acts ("Auffassung") in perception, and with it the "universally dominant data-sensualism" (*Hua* 10, p. xl), there is no longer any reason to postulate momentary knife-edge awarenesses at all. But there is no evidence that Husserl ever clearly drew the conclusion in question.[21] For, even though he sees that one cannot think of sensations as independent entities, but rather as parts of the flux, he never seems to quite free himself of the implausible idea that we could have direct consciousness of a continuum of sensations.

[20] Paul Ricoeur, *Time and Narrative*, K. Blarney and D. Pellauer trans. (University of Chicago Press, 1988), vol. 3, p. 44.

[21] A helpful discussion of the implications of Husserl's rejection of the content-interpretation schema may be found in John Brough, "The Emergence of Absolute Consciousness in Husserl's Early Writings on Time-Consciousness," F. Elliston and P. McCormick (eds.), *Husserl: Expositions and Appraisals* (University of Notre Dame Press, 1998), pp. 83–100.

CHAPTER 4

Between Husserl, Kierkegaard, and Aristotle

In this chapter I first introduce Heidegger's conception of human experience against the background of his critique of Husserl's consciousness-based conception of experience. I then discuss the manner in which Heidegger comes to understand human experience as a process of disclosure. I argue that this conception of human experience as disclosure is based on a critical interpretation of Husserl's notion of *Evidenz* against the background of a new interpretation of Aristotle. I then look at the way Heidegger appropriates and transforms Husserl's theory of categorial intuition so that it forms the basis for his own conception of truth as disclosure. Then I look at the manner in which Heidegger uses the notion of truth as spatial and temporal disclosure to undermine the subjective implications of the notion of consciousness and intentionality. I conclude with some of the skeptical implications of Heidegger's own conception of truth.

INTENTIONALITY, THE CONCEPT OF A PERSON, AND HUMAN
EXISTENCE

Heidegger claims that it is a reading of Brentano's discussion of the different senses of being in Aristotle that initially sets him on his philosophical path.[1] In fact, Heidegger initially comes to study Husserl through his interest in the way that Husserl has developed Brentano's philosophical reinterpretation of the scholastic notion of intentionality. This interest in Brentano is, in turn, motivated by

---

[1] Heidegger claims that Brentano's first work: *On the Several Senses of Being in Aristotle*, trans. Rolf George (Berkeley: University of California Press, 1975), is the key text that starts him on his way to thinking about philosophy in general and his own concern with being in particular, cf. Heidegger's preface to William Richardson, *Heidegger from Phenomenology to Thought* (The Hague: Martinus Nijhoff, 1963), pp. xiff.

Brentano's philosophical reconstruction of key scholastic doctrines using the resources of Aristotle's thought.

After writing a dissertation on the problem of psychologism in the theory of judgment that is already strongly influenced by Husserl's *Investigations*, as well as by *Ideas* I, Heidegger goes on to discuss the scholastic theory of intentionality, meaning, and categories in his habilitation (1915). His habilitation concerns the theory of meaning and categories articulated in a work that he attributes to Duns Scotus, the *Grammaticae Speculativae*, now generally thought to have been written by Thomas of Erfurt. It draws heavily on the philosophical tools provided by Husserl and Brentano to reconstruct a classical text of scholasticism.[2] But, by the late teens, in the course of collaboration with Husserl, Heidegger begins to move away from his initial neo-scholastic approach to philosophy and becomes correspondingly critical of Brentano's neo-scholastic interpretation of Aristotle.

In his lecture course on *The History of the Concept of Time* (1925), in which he works up many of the positions developed and defended in his early *magnum opus*, *Being and Time* (1927), Heidegger writes of Brentano:

> He sought to interpret Aristotle against the horizon of medieval philosophy, above all that of Thomas Aquinas. Such an interpretation is the distinguishing mark of his work, which is not to say that this is really the way to understand Aristotle. On the contrary, through this kind of interpretation Aristotle essentially undergoes a drastic reinterpretation.[3]

The general emotional, political, and cultural upheaval brought on by the First World War makes Heidegger increasingly hostile to the neo-scholastic appropriation of Aristotle that first attracts him to Husserl's writings via a reading of Brentano. Heidegger now thinks that a "distorted" interpretation of Aristotle has prevented the scholastic tradition from coming up with an adequate understanding of human existence and of the very notion of intentionality that it ultimately owes to Aristotle.

In the early twenties, Heidegger begins to use the term "life," in place of the Husserlian notion of consciousness to describe what is distinctive about human experience. "Life" is a term he takes over from Wilhelm Dilthey, a philosopher who, like Brentano and

---

[2] Martin Heidegger, *Die Kategorien- und Bedeutungslehre des Duns Scotus, GA* I, esp. pp. 273ff.

[3] Martin Heidegger, *History of the Concept of Time*, Theodore Kisiel trans. (Bloomington: Indiana University Press, 1985), *GA* 20, p. 23.

Kierkegaard, had himself once been a student in Berlin of Adolf Trendelenburg, the great nineteenth-century critic of Hegelianism and renewer of the Aristotelian tradition.[4] Like Husserl, Dilthey tends to describe his project of understanding life in the potentially misleading Brentanian terms of a "descriptive psychology." As Dilthey understands descriptive psychology, it is concerned with the individual experiences ("Erlebnisse") that make up an individual life as well as with the distinctive way in which human beings experience their lives in different societies and historical epochs.

In commenting on Brentano's psychology in an unpublished paper written immediately before *Being and Time*, Heidegger notes that, for Brentano,

> the historical tradition through which he came into contact with theology remained alive (Middle Ages and *Aristotle*). Greek psychology was something different from experimental psychology. Psychology was a doctrine of life, of human existence itself. Not only *Dilthey*, but also *Husserl* is determined by *Brentano's* psychology, that does not want to explain psychological processes, but basic constitutions.[5]

Heidegger invests the term "life" with the less subjectivist perspective of Aristotle's conception of psyche (which is more appropriately translated as "life" than as "soul"). Soon, however, under the influence of Karl Jaspers' interpretation of Kierkegaard in his *Psychology of Worldviews*, Heidegger begins to place the process of existing, or living a life, at the center of his work. He now gradually replaces the term "life" with the Kierkegaardian term "existence." This reflects his view that the notion of life upon which the philosophy of life is premised involves a metaphorical use of an expression from biology that is not even clearly understood in biology itself. Now the notion of self is to be understood in terms of the notion of existence:

> Existence is a determination of something; insofar as one wants to characterize it regionally, although this characterization ultimately and actually <*eigentlich*> turns out to be a misinterpretive digression relative to the sense of existence, it can be grasped as a determinate way of being, as a

---

[4] The systematic use of the term "life" goes back to Hegel's early work, cf. H. Marcuse, *Hegel's Ontology and the Theory of Historicity* (Cambridge: MIT Press, 1987), pp. 201ff. Dilthey appropriates it from Hegel. A detailed look at the development in Heidegger's position from the notion of life to that of *Dasein* may be found in T. Kisiel, *The Genesis of Heidegger's Being and Time* (Berkeley and Los Angeles: University of California Press, 1993), pp. 201ff., pp. 161ff.

[5] Martin Heidegger, "Wilhelm Diltheys Forschungsarbeit und die historische Weltanschauung," *Dilthey Jahrbuch für Philosophie und Geschichte der Geisteswissenschaften* 8 (1993), 155.

determinate sense of "is" that essentially "is" (I) "am" – sense, that is not genuinely had in theoretical intending, but rather had in the enactment <*Vollzug*> of "am," a mode of being of "I." The being of the self thus understood, means, formally indicated, existence.[6]

Heidegger's emphasis on the idea of life or human existence as "enactment" ("Vollzug") reflects the influence of personalistic psychology on his conception of human existence (*SuZ*, pp. 47–48). Scheler's conception of a person is easily recognizable in Heidegger's account of the self. His claim in 1919–1920 that existence is a particular mode of being "which is not genuinely had in theoretical intending, but rather had in the performance (*Vollzug*) of 'am,' a mode of being of the being of the 'I,'" betrays the obvious influence of Scheler's view of the person as a performer of acts that are not primarily cognitive:

Person is the unknown and never "cognitively" given individually experienced (*erlebte*) unitary substance of all acts which a being performs; therefore no "object," certainly no "thing." What can therefore be given to me objectively is always only 1, another body, 2, the unity of the body, 3, the ego and the vital "soul" which belongs to it. This applies to each individual in relation to himself. A person can only be given to me in "mutually carrying out" his acts – cognitively in "understanding" and "reliving," ethically in "following."[7]

According to the notion of a person developed by Husserl in "Philosophy as a Strict Science" (1910), more extensively in *Ideas* II, and by Scheler, a person is a "performer of acts" who exists only by "living through," enacting, or performing those acts. This conception of a person as, above all, a bearer of responsibility for actions may be regarded, in turn, as a development of the Kantian idea that persons are ends in themselves, that is, beings whose existence involves pursuing the goals of agency. Scheler's personalist psychology takes up the Kantian idea of a person as a project of self-realization, but avoids Kant's view that the self to be realized, the authentic self, is the rational self, that is a self that is motivated by impersonal reasons.

---

[6] *Critical Comments on Karl Jaspers "The Psychology of Worldviews," GA* 9, p. 29. Hermann Schmitz sees these remarks as an indication that Heidegger was really disinterested in questions of ontology at this stage in his career and not continuously driven from the start of his career by the question of being as he himself retrospectively claims, cf. *Husserl and Heidegger* (Bonn: Bouvier, 1996), pp. 189ff.

[7] Max Scheler, *Wesen und Formen der Sympathie* (Bern: Francke, 1973, original 1913), *Gesammelte Werke* 7, p. 168.

Heidegger's emphasis on human beings as individuals who are what they are through the way they determine themselves to be may be regarded as a development of the Kantian conception that underlies Scheler's concept of a person. However, Heidegger finds personalist psychology to be too dependent on a theory of process based on successive states of consciousness (experiences in the sense of "Erlebnisse"). As I have already indicated, it is customary in late nineteenth- and early twentieth-century philosophy to think of persons as streams of experiences. These experiences are understood to be states of consciousness broadly conceived, i.e., "Erlebnisse."[8] This emphasis on states of consciousness is also apparent in the description of persons as performers of *acts*. The connection that is drawn between these states of consciousness and the notion of life compensates for the preoccupation with states of consciousness by linking consciousness to non-cognitive aspects of human existence. But this enrichment in the concept of a person still fails to make any headway in getting away from the framework provided by the notion of episodes of experience. As Heidegger sees it, personalist psychology, like its predecessors, does not assign fundamental importance to the ontological issue of what it is to be a person. It simply assumes a problematic theory of experience based on states of consciousness.[9]

CATEGORIAL INTUITION AND ONTOLOGY

As Heidegger makes clear on a number of occasions, Husserl's theory of categorial intuition in the *Investigations* is the point of departure for his own account of truth with its account of being.[10] It

---

[8] There is an interesting critical discussion of the concept of "Erlebnis" in Konrad Cramer, "Erlebnis: Thesen zu Hegels Theorie des Selbstbewußtseins mit Rücksicht auf die Aporien eines Grundbegriffs nachhegelscher Philosophie," *Hegel-Studien*, Beiheft 11 (1974), 537–603. However, Cramer's claim that Husserl's notion of experience fails to do justice to the reflexively self-referential character of self-consciousness seems rather implausible. For one of the advantages of the self-intimating character that Husserl ascribes to experiences is that problems of how to account for self-consciousness are relatively easily avoided.

[9] Heidegger provides a concise version of this criticism at the beginning of division I of *Being and Time* (*SuZ*, pp. 46ff.). There is a more extensive critique of this notion of a person in *History of the Concept of Time* (*GA* 20, pp. 161ff.).

[10] Ibid., *GA* 20 (1925), pp. 63ff., cf. also *Seminare*, *GA* 15, pp. 376–377; "My Way to Phenomenology," in *Time and Being* (New York: Harper and Row, 1972), pp. 74–82; and Heidegger's letter to W. J. Richardson of April 1962 published as the preface to Richardson, *Heidegger from Phenomenology to Thought*, pp. vii–xxiii. Very clear and instructive discussions of these texts may be found in Françoise Dastur, "Heidegger und die Logischen Untersu-

provides the background for Heidegger's break with Husserl's general conception of ontology, as well as his break with Husserl's more specific ontology of persons. According to the theory of categorial intuition, categories are themselves just as given to us as are objects of perception, even though their being given to us depends on our perceptions of concrete objects. Thus, the category of substance, or, even more generally, of being, is something that we have an intuition of, although it is clearly not something of which we could have an empirical perception. The categories that we intuit in categorial intuition, such as being, have their basis in the syncategor-amical terms that are needed in order for us to be able to make sense of what we perceive. These categories are implicit in the ways in which we process ("synthesize") objects of perception. They may then be objectified in acts of reflection that are directed at the structures of objects displayed by the procedures through which we construct the objects of perception. The perceptual intuition of objects is thus the indirect basis for all knowledge.

From Heidegger's perspective, categorial intuition provides a way of seeing how a general ontology could be developed that, unlike neo-Kantianism, does not depend on a subjectivization of the subject-matter of ontology. It is much easier to see the contrast that Heidegger has in mind by looking at Husserl's *Philosophy of Arithmetic*, than it is by studying the *Investigations*, despite the more subjectivist approach in the former work. While the *Philosophy of Arithmetic* is concerned with what Husserl calls a psychological investigation of the origin of number, he thinks of his account largely as an alternative to the Kantian accounts of how we grasp number. Where Kant and such neo-Kantians as Friedrich Ernst Lange base our grasp of number on an experience of temporal, or spatial, or better spatio-temperal sequence, and thus give primacy to ordinal numbers, Husserl thinks that the key to understanding number is in terms of a concept derived from our activity of collecting items together in consciousness. This leads him to give primacy to the cardinal, as opposed to the ordinal numbers.[11]

chungen," *Heidegger Studies* 7 (1991), 37–52, and *Heidegger et la question du temps* (Paris: Presses universitaires de France, 1990), pp. 22ff., and Rudolf Bernet, "Transcendence et intentionalité: Heidegger et Husserl sur les prolégomènes d'une ontologie phénoménolo-gique," in F. Volpi et al. (ed.), *Heidegger et l'idée de la phénoménologie* (Dordrecht: Kluwer, 1988), pp. 195–216.

[11] It is instructive that Husserl discusses Kant's thesis in the Schematism that number can be understood as that through which time itself is generated (*Hua* 12, pp. 32–33). For this gives

Heidegger also thought that Husserl's approach had the further merit that it did not involve an attempt to derive categories from basic logical notions (as, for instance, in Kant's use of the purported completeness of his table of judgment to derive a complete table of categories as forms of objects corresponding to the basic forms of judgment): "There are acts in which ideal constituents show themselves in themselves, which are not constructs of these acts, functions of thinking or of the subject" (*GA* 20, p. 97). The claim that such acts are not functions of thought is somewhat more problematic, since categories are objectifications for Husserl of the connections established in and between objects by logical constants functioning in propositions as syncategoramical expressions. But it has some justification in Husserl's insistence in the *Investigations* that categorial intuition is based on connections between aspects of perceived objects rather than on a reflection on the character of the mental acts involved in perception: "Not in reflection upon judgments, nor even upon the fulfillments of judgments, but in the fulfillments of judgments themselves lies the true source of the concepts states of affairs and being (in the copulative sense). Not in these *acts as objects*, but in *the objects of these acts*, do we have the abstractive basis which enables us to realize the conceptions in question" (*LU* VI, section 44).[12] The somewhat psychologistic account of mathematical knowledge in the *Philosophy of Arithmetic* claims, by contrast, that our grasp of numbers is based on reflection on our mental acts of collecting. So, even if Heidegger's interpretation that Husserl does not want to think of categorial intuition as based on the structure of thought seems problematic, he is at least right that Husserl wants to avoid any derivation of categorial structures from psychological states.

As Heidegger sees it, the Husserlian approach to non-sensible objects in the *Investigations* effectively frees the notions of being and truth from the way they had come to be linked to judgment in the

---

Heidegger's claim some justification that Husserl's analysis of categorial synthesis is a form of alternative to Kant's theory of how categories come to have temporal instantiations through a process that the latter refers to as Schematism, and which Heidegger would later argue is the central doctrine of the whole *Critique of Pure Reason* in his *Kant and the Problem of Metaphysics* (*GA* 6), cf. also his *Phenomenological Interpretation of Kant's Critique of Pure Reason* (*GA* 25) (1927–28), P. Emad and K. Maly trans. (Bloomington: Indiana University Press, 1997).

[12] It has been noted by Jacques Taminiaux, "Remarques sur Heidegger et les *Recherches Logiques* de Husserl," in *Le regard et l'excédent* (The Hague: Martinus Nijhoff, 1977), pp. 178ff., that Heidegger was able to see the idea that we have an understanding of being that transcends entities, but is the basis of our understanding of entities, in Husserl's idea that perceptual intuition and higher-order intuition involves an implicit intuition of being.

post-Kantian tradition. The theory of categorial intuition also paves the way for a conception of the a priori that is free of the close connection that the a priori has with subjectivity in the Kantian tradition. However, Husserl's theory of categorial intuition does have the problem that it invokes a notion of intuiting abstract objects that is modelled on the analogy of perception, but is unable to explain exactly why the difference between (empirical) perception and intuition of abstract objects still allows enough theoretical space for an account of how it is possible for us to have a non-empirical intuition of abstract objects. For, even though Husserl thinks that we have an intuition of being, categories, and abstract objects, he rejects the idea that they are perceptible in the strict sense of the word. They involve an excess of meaning that goes beyond anything that is perceptible in the normal sense of the word. The idea that being and categories of being could be directly given to us in perception as something that is necessary to the interpretation of perceptual information gives Heidegger a way of making sense of being as something that is given, and not just as an abstraction from entities, as he points out in a seminar given in Zähringen late in his life (*GA* 15, p. 376).

What emerges from Heidegger's discussion is that he rejects the main aim of the theory of categorial intuition which is to provide an account of how we can have knowledge of abstract objects. Heidegger has no sympathy with Husserl's Platonism. However, Heidegger thinks that something crucial remains standing in Husserl's theory of categorial intuition even once one has rejected the idea that we can intuit abstract objects. Heidegger takes Husserl to have shown that there is a way in which we can directly apprehend not only categories, but also being and truth, without thinking of them as projections of the mind. The categories, and even being and truth, have their source in the process of the activities through which we make sense of the world.

READING HUSSERL THROUGH THE EYES OF ARISTOTLE

Now working with Husserl, and studying Aristotle, Heidegger becomes convinced in the late teens that the key to understanding Husserl's conception of intentionality and the distinctive process of human existence is the notion of truth. He also comes to think that, in interpreting the notion of truth in terms of his conception of

Evidenz, Husserl has, in effect, rediscovered the Greek, and, more particularly, the Aristotelian notion of truth as *aletheia*. Heidegger refers to this notion of truth as disclosure.

In a retrospective account of the importance of Husserl's *Investigations* for his thought, Heidegger emphasizes the connection he comes to see between intentionality and the Greek notion of unconcealment through rereading the *Investigations* with older students in the period prior to the articulation of *Being and Time*:

> In this way I experienced – at first more directed by premonition than from justified insight – this one thing: What takes place for the phenomenology of acts of consciousness as the-self-announcement of phenomena is thought more originally by Aristotle and in the whole of Greek thought and existence as *Aletheia*, as the unhiddenness of what is present, its disclosure, its self-display. What the phenomenological investigations have found to be the supportive attitude of thought proves to be the basic tendency of Greek thought, if not of all philosophy.[13]

What Heidegger refers to here as the self-announcement of phenomena, is Husserl's notion of *Evidenz* in which objects present themselves as they truly are. The passage thus makes clear that Heidegger comes to see Husserl's notion of *Evidenz* as the basis of what he took to be Aristotle's notion of truth as the disclosure of entities as they are. *Evidenz* is itself based on a process of recognition. Heidegger argues that we must understand this process of recognition as the process of human life itself. This establishes an intimate link between Heidegger's concern with human existence and his interest in Aristotle's conception of truth. The process of human life turns out itself to be the process of having an understanding of what is true. And this process in turn underwrites our understanding of the different kinds of being.

Heidegger emphasizes the manner in which intentionality is rooted in the Aristotelian conception of motion or process as well as in the Aristotelian notion of truth. This notion of process has an immediate antecedent in Husserl's idea that *Evidenz* is something that is grasped in the process ("Vollzug") of engaging in acts of consciousness. The importance of process to Heidegger is most apparent in the early accounts that he provides of Aristotle's

---

[13] "Mein Weg in die Phänomenologie," in *Zur Sache des Denkens* (Tübingen: Max Niemeyer, 1969), p. 87, trans. "My Way into Phenomenology," in *On Time and Being* (New York: Harper and Row, 1972), p. 79.

philosophy in a long lost Introduction to Aristotle written in 1922.[14] The Introduction, intended to provide a research survey for coming years, supported his application for an associate (extraordinary) professorship at Marburg. Heidegger argues that intentionality emerges in Aristotle as a "how of the movement of life, life which is somehow 'noetically' illumined in its dealings. Entities in the aspect of being moved – in the basic aspect of 'being directed at something' – are the project, i.e. the condition for the ability to emphasize intentionality as it becomes explicit in Aristotle and as it, for the most part, makes the basic character of logos visible" (*PIA*, p. 49). In the terms of Husserl's account of intentionality, intentionality is to be understood in terms of the enactment ("Vollzug") of acts of consciousness. Such enactment is in turn for Husserl something to be understood in terms of the constitutive intentionality of time-consciousness. Heidegger is able to reinterpret this temporal process of enactment by way of Kierkegaard's appropriation of Aristotle's conception of the process of life (the kinesis of the psyche). For, in insisting on the recalcitrance of human existence to any Hegelian conception of pure consciousness, Kierkegaard notes that Trendelenburg's critique of Hegel brings out the importance of movement or process as something that cannot be grasped in purely abstract terms, that is, in terms of the notion of pure consciousness. This leads Kierkegaard to claim that Trendelenburg's "merit consists among other things in having apprehended movement as the inexplicable presupposition and common factor of thinking and being, and as their continued reciprocal relation."[15] Heidegger draws on this Kierkegaardian attack against Hegel's conception of absolute consciousness, and redirects that attack against absolute consciousness as Husserl's notion of such consciousness.

Heidegger takes the noetic illumination that accompanies life in all its dealings with other entities to be truth, or rather uncovered-ness. In this way, he takes up the Husserlian idea that an understanding of the content of acts of consciousness must be based on an understanding of the kinds of *Evidenz* situations in which those acts

---

[14] Martin Heidegger, "Phänomenologische Interpretation zu Aristoteles (Anzeige der hermeneutischen Situation)," *Dilthey Jahrbuch für Philosophie und Geschichte der Geisteswissenschaften* 6 (1989), 228–274, trans. Michael Bauer, *Man and World* 25 (1992), 358–393. I will refer to the manuscript henceforth as *PIA* and cite it according to the pagination of the original typescript which has been reproduced in both the German publication and the English translation.

[15] Søren Kierkegaard, *Concluding Unscientific Postscript*, p. 100.

of consciousness would grasp things as they really are. This *Evidenz* or rather uncoveredness that constitutes truth is supposed to be prior to all judgment and possible correspondence between a judgment and its object (*PIA*, p. 30). In fact, Heidegger rejects the standard interpretation of the Aristotelian notion of truth according to which Aristotle is committed both to a version of the correspondence theory of truth and to the thesis that the locus of truth is primarily in judgment. He does, however, acknowledge that there is a sense in which truth is in the understanding: "The *on hos alethes* [being insofar as it is true] is not authentic being, nor is it the authentic field of being, or the domain within which true judgments are valid, but it is rather being itself in the manner (*hos*) of its uncovered being intended. It is *en dianoia* [in the understanding] as *noeton* [as intelligible object], in the 'understanding,' as that with respect to which understanding grasps" (*PIA*, p. 32).

The connection that is suggested here between Aristotle's notion of the object of the understanding and Husserl's notion of a *noema* (the intended object as such) is even more obvious when Heidegger introduces the notion of truth as uncoveredness: "Aletheuein does not mean: 'to seize hold of the truth'; it means rather to seize the being that is intended, and which is intended as such, as uncovered in truthful safe-keeping" (*PIA*, p. 31).

Following Aristotle, Heidegger distinguishes between acts of intentionality in which one immediately grasps an object without interpreting the object as such and such, and acts of intentionality involving interpretation. The former acts divide into sensible acts of perception, and intelligible or noetic acts of immediate insight (*PIA*, pp. 31–32). *Noûs* or intellectual insight itself divides into practical insight ("phronesis") and theoretical insight ("sophia"). Heidegger identifies practical insight with the kind of understanding that one needs in order to come to terms with one's life (*PIA*, p. 35). But he argues that Aristotle assigns primacy to theoretical insight ("sophia") because in theoretical insight the object of insight is given simultaneously with the insight itself (*PIA*, p.39). The primacy that Aristotle assigns to theoretical insight is based on his ontology of motion or process, which, in turn, takes the idea of production as a paradigm (*PIA*, p. 38). Theoretical insight is the highest form of life for Aristotle not because it is shown by him to be constitutive of human life, but because in theoretical insight life achieves the kind of closure demanded by the process product model of being suggested by taking production as the model of all being. In theoretical insight, the product of the process is internal to the process itself. Theory is thus completely actual ("energes"), and not merely potentially complete, as ordinary motion is which has a goal external to itself. Here, Heidegger already indicates a certain level of skepticism about the Aristotelian project. The value of the theoretical form of life does not seem to him to derive from its value for human existence, but rather from its completeness relative to a model of being based on production. In this way, Heidegger plays Kierkegaard out against Aristotle. For Kierkegaard already emphasizes the (subjectivist) notion of truth that is linked to understanding how to live one's life against the objective notion of truth that consists in grasping objective states of affairs.

Heidegger's interpretation of Husserl's conception of intentionality in the light of his own interpretation of Aristotle's notion of truth does not exhaust the Aristotelian twist he gives to intentionality. Heidegger also interprets Aristotle's doctrine of the species involved in perception and thought in terms of Husserl's notion of an intentional object intended by me in thought as such. This is what it is to be an object of perception or thought (a *noema* in the language of both Aristotle and Husserl). Such an object is not numerically distinct from objects taken independently of being perceived or thought, but rather our way of understanding just those objects that exist independently of us. However, in reflection, we are able to focus on the object of thought as thought by us rather than merely directly perceiving or thinking a mind-independent object (*PIA*, p. 31). Heidegger goes on to argue that we are able to perceive or think things only because, as human beings, the process of our lives (which Aristotle refers to as kinesis) is such that we are always already directed at entities in the world in the sense that we always already have some insight into what they are. The process of human existence becomes the crucial factor in understanding the intentionality of our behavior. We already have some basic understanding of what it is to be an entity of a particular kind, because disclosure of the way entities are (which Aristotle refers to as truth) is constitutive of the distinctive way in which we exist as human beings.

By developing the link in Aristotle between our ability to understand things as they are in truth ("hos alethes on") and the project of human existence (i.e. the kinesis or motion through which the soul sustains itself and its body), Heidegger seeks to move back behind the conception of intentionality and time-consciousness developed by Brentano and Husserl to a conception of the temporal and disclosive character of human existence that no longer needs to think of human understanding in terms of a quasi-relation between consciousness and its objects. Indeed, the whole notion of the different ways consciousness relates to its objects is to be reinterpreted as different ways in which we comport ourselves toward, or behave in respect to, different entities. The problem set for Husserl by Brentano – how can we relate to objects that do not exist? – becomes transformed into the question: how can we fail to disclose or understand the world as it is?

DISCLOSURE AND CORRESPONDENCE

In *Being and Time*, Heidegger introduces his notion of truth as disclosure as a presupposition of Husserl's account of the corroboration involved for Husserl in truth as correspondence (*SuZ*, p. 218). In the *Investigations*, Husserl bases his notion of corroboration on the identification of a statement or a propositional act of consciousness with the fact corresponding to it. Thus, for Husserl, corroboration is a matter of determining whether a statement or thought is true or not. He maintains that when the object of an intentional act is actually present to that intentional act then that object displays itself in the act as it truly is. Heidegger agrees with Husserl that in a corroboration the entity in question shows itself to be the same in the statement or thought as it is in itself. From the fact that in corroboration the entity displays itself to thought as it is in itself, Heidegger concludes that corroboration presupposes that the entity in question display itself as it truly is. And this is only possible insofar as the cognition in question is a way of discovering the entity in question as that entity is in itself (*SuZ*, p. 218). He suggests that an individual perception of an object, such as a picture on a wall, could itself corroborate the statement "the picture on the wall is hanging crooked." I can in some sense know that the picture on the wall is hanging crooked by seeing it to be hanging crooked. Here I am treating seeing or perceiving as a success word.

Thus far, Heidegger's analysis follows Husserl's own understanding of corroboration. But, where Husserl maintains that the justification of the truth claim of an act of consciousness always requires a further judgment to determine that the intended object corresponds to the actual object, Heidegger argues that one does not need to justify the belief that one is perceiving by appeal to some further belief, because this would lead to an infinite regress of justification (*GA* 21, p. 108). This leads Heidegger to reject the whole project of justifying a correspondence relation between a certain putative cognition and its object. However, it is one thing to maintain that justifications must end somewhere; it is quite another to give up on justification altogether.

Heidegger rejects the idea of comparing "contents of consciousness" and thus our ability to individuate beliefs or propositions that can then be compared and contrasted with one another (*SuZ*, p. 218). Our understanding does not, on his view, allow of any but a relatively arbitrary regimentation into individual beliefs, since such beliefs have their meaning only in relation to the whole general context of one's understanding. Heidegger's skepticism about propositional truth revenges itself in his failure to explain how truth may be distinguished from falsity. This does not mean that the normative force that is constitutive of the meaning of truth cannot, in principle, be expressed by the idea of disclosure or unconcealment. Unconcealment does not provide a criterion of truth, but it does not preclude one from identifying some other criterion of truth, such as coherence. Heidegger's tendency in *Being and Time* to argue for the truths of claims by their ability to express the totality ("Ganzheit") of existence suggests that he tacitly appeals to some form of coherence criterion of truth.

Heidegger's lack of interest in justification and the determination of criteria for truth encourages him, however, to regard rightness and wrongness as extraneous to the notion of truth. There is clearly a problem here. But Ernst Tugendhat somewhat overstates the problem by arguing that this leads Heidegger "in making the word truth a basic concept to pass over precisely the problem of truth."[16] To be plausible, Tugendhat's critique must be understood as taking the problem of truth to be the problem of how to distinguish truth from falsity rather than the problem of what truth means. Unfortunately, like Heidegger, Tugendhat does not clearly distinguish the problem of what truth means from the problem of what the criteria for truth are.

---

[16] Ernst Tugendhat, "Heidegger's Idee von Wahrheit," in Otto Pöggeler (ed.), *Heidegger: Perspektiven zur Deutung seines Werkes* (Köln: Neue Wissenschaftliche Bibliothek, 1969), p. 296, trans. "Heidegger's idea of truth" in *Critical Heidegger*, pp. 238ff.

To be sure, even if one denies that the problem of what truth is should be resolved by answer to the question how a claim to truth should be justified, there should still be some way of distinguishing truth from falsity. Heidegger's obsession with playing off disclosure and unconcealment as the meaning of truth against the idea of correctness leads him to a very ambivalent stance to the normativity of truth. This interest in playing out disclosure or unconcealment against correctness stems from his concern with the kind of truth that must obtain if one is to be able to have a distinction between the truth and falsity or correctness and incorrectness of specific claims. In fact, Heidegger is much more interested in the nature of intentionality or, rather, of transcendence, as he calls it, and tends to run together the condition for the possibility of transcendence with truth. This leads to a tendency for him to shift between construing disclosure as making something accessible either delusively (as mere appearance) or non-delusively, the higher-order truth that makes specific true or false beliefs possible, and construing disclosure as the making accessible of things as what they (truly) are.

Heidegger does distinguish between disclosure in the mode of mere appearance ("Schein") and disclosure of things as they really are, even though he does not make enough of this distinction (*SuZ*, p. 224). Also, in the *Basic Problems of Phenomenology* (1928), *GA* 24, p. 308, he notes that "only because it [human existence] exists *essentially* in the truth, can it err as such and can there be hiddenness, displacement, and closedness of entities." Thus Heidegger distinguishes between truth as the condition under which there is a distinction between truth and error, and truth in a sense that contrasts with error.[17]

The tendency to run together truth with justification is already latent in Husserl's notion of *Evidenz* as the experience of a correspondence relation between a belief and some fact. Husserl himself never really addresses the question of how we can determine whether we have a bona fide instance of *Evidenz*.[18] It is an obvious danger inherent in the tendency that both Husserl and Heidegger have to

---

[17] On Heidegger's implicit distinction between truth and falsity, see the helpful discussion by Barbara Merker, *Selbsttäuschung und Selbsterkenntnis zu Heideggers Transformation der Phänomenologie Husserls* (Frankfurt: Suhrkamp, 1988), p. 55.

[18] For a good development of Husserl's failure adequately to deal with criteria for *Evidenz*, the reader is referred to David Levin, *Reason and Evidence in Husserl's Phenomenology* (Evanston: Northwestern University Press, 1970), pp. 51ff.

favor intuition over less immediate forms of discursive thought in thinking about our access to truth. And this idea of a direct access to things is just what attracts Heidegger in Husserl's account of intentionality. For Husserl, acts of intentionality, including statements expressing propositions, but also singular terms and perceptions (monothetic acts in Husserl's technical terminology), are true of their objects just when those objects themselves are indeed present to the person who is directed at those objects through those acts. This notion of truth provides the basis for a reconstruction of the cognitive content or meaning of an intentional act. We understand the meaning of an act just when we understand what would "fulfill" that act, that is, when we understand what would make that act true of its object. This suggests to Heidegger that the ultimate source of meaning and truth is in the objects of intuition themselves. For we only succeed in referring to an object or stating a true proposition when the object itself displays itself to us as it really is (*GA* 20, p. 73).

In his extensive discussion of Husserl's contributions to the understanding of intentionality in lectures on *The Concept of the History of Time*, Heidegger notes, even before the publication of *Being and Time*, that by thinking of even pre-predicative acts of perception (monothetic acts in Husserl's terminology) as acts that can be true of their objects, Husserl already frees himself of the widespread prejudice that truth is only a property of propositions and the judgments that express propositions. He claims that Husserl has, in effect, worked his way back to the Greek notion of truth, although Husserl demonstrates no awareness of the connection between his own views about truth and the conception of truth articulated in Greek thought.

"DA-SEIN" AND DISCLOSURE

Heidegger's rejection of the traditional conception of states of consciousness as the basis for understanding human existence expresses itself in his choice of terminology. In contrast to Jaspers, who prefers the Latinate expression "Existenz," Heidegger uses the more Germanic term "Dasein." This term has connotations that are absent from the expression "existence." *Dasein* literally means "to be here," but also "to be now," and "to be there." All three of these demonstrative aspects of the spatio-temporal adverb "da" express the contextual nature of our existence. Heidegger insists that demonstratives like "here" and "there," "now" and "then" can only be understood by a being whose very existence is constituted by the disclosure of spatial and temporal relations: "The entity that is essentially constituted by being-in-the-world *is* itself in each case its 'there.' According to the familiar meaning of the word, 'there' points to 'here' and 'there' ... 'Here' and 'there' are only possible in a 'there,' that means if there is an entity that as the being 'there' has disclosed spatiality" (*SuZ*, p. 132). The spatial and temporal circumstances in which a human being is situated are not something that a human being can opt out of, since they make each of us who we are and are the basis for anything that has any truth for us as human beings. Heidegger maintains in *Being and Time* that the most fundamental notion of truth is that of disclosure (*SuZ*, p. 223).

For Heidegger, to be a human being ("Dasein") is literally to be the truth in which one understands what is here from what is there, and what is now from what is then (*SuZ*, pp. 132–133). To be human is then to have at least sufficient understanding of what is true to be mistaken about something. This is why, on Heidegger's view, some understanding of truth in general and also of the truth about oneself is necessary to being a human being. For in understanding what is here from what is there and what is now from what is then one already has some understanding of the context in which one exists.

Heidegger's identification of the original form of truth with disclosure or even with discovering at first suggests the idea that truth is radically subjective. It is, however, in fact a denial of the possibility of radically immanent truth, that is, truth about purely subjective states, as Husserl understands it. Intentionality is now understood in a radically externalist way as the transcendence of the self to things in the world. This makes it impossible to bracket the existence of external objects. In order to ascribe any cognitive attitudes to ourselves we must already have some grasp of truth. This truth cannot be purely immanent, because the very notion of spatiality and temporality that is constitutive of human existence requires a there for the here of human existence ("Da-sein"). To this it seems natural to respond that the heres, theres, nows, and thens in question might actually be subjective. This objection assumes that we have an interesting distinction between the subjective and the objective available to us. Heidegger rejects this assumption. The spatial and the temporal are neither subjective nor objective on this view. Spatial and temporal entities can display themselves as they are, or they may appear to be differently than they are, but this distinction itself depends on spatial and temporal entities being in some way disclosed to us.

Heidegger's prepropositional understanding of truth finds its most drastic expression in the view that traditional refutations of skepticism, such as that to be found in Kant's Refutation of Idealism, are based on a mistaken assumption that skepticism can or needs to be refuted. Part of Heidegger's disagreement with such arguments stems from the fact that they are expressed in the form of propositions. Such arguments require the assertion of something, at which point the skeptic can suggest suspense of judgment as a way of avoiding the objection that he or she is committed to a self-refuting claim. By leaving this opening for the skeptic, they fail to get at the basic problem for the skeptic.

Once one takes an understanding of some truth about one's spatial and temporal situation as an enabling condition for human existence, then one cannot genuinely deny the existence of truth or suspend belief about everything without denying oneself the very conditions under which one can exist at all. One does not even have to have any propositional beliefs at all for this objection to hold. Heidegger puts the point somewhat drastically, for effect. A skeptic who exists in the negation of truth, and presumably even in suspension of belief, would have to commit suicide (*SuZ*, p. 229).

This response to skepticism is convincing given an acceptance of Heidegger's ontological notion of truth which requires spatial and temporal engagement with the world as a condition for human existence. It is open for the traditional epistemologist (for instance, a Kantian) as well as the skeptic to point out that the Heideggerian response to skepticism itself has a premise that must also find expression in the form of a propositional truth. Heidegger is not unaware of this difficulty. This is why he winds up walking away from the problem of skepticism instead of offering an argument against it. As soon as one formulates arguments against skepticism, one has already moved to a theoretical position that, in principle, is always assailable.

What is perhaps most revolutionary about Heidegger's conception of truth is that it is not supposed to be a relation between our beliefs and the world. Instead, to be true is to have genuine as opposed to merely apparent being, to be real ("Wirklich-Sein," *GA* 20, p. 71). That which appears to us must have some reality in order to appear to be thus and such. Something can only dissemble, to the extent to which it displays enough of a resemblance to what it is supposed to be to allow error to occur in the first place.[19] Thus, the standard for truth is to be taken from the things themselves rather than from the subject or its practices.

There is something to this account of correctness and incorrect-ness, but it is also incomplete. We cannot simply help ourselves to the way things themselves are, for we may take something to be true of them which is in fact not true of them. Heidegger's conception of truth is complicated considerably by the way in which he makes use of the success grammar of the terms "disclosure" and "discovery." When we have discovered something, when something is disclosed to us, we have succeeded in understanding something about it. It is certainly appropriate to think of truth as a normative notion that determines the adequacy of our understanding of something. This need not be understood purely instrumentally, since in many cases understanding the way something "truly" is may actually impede one from attaining the goals that one has set oneself. The problem with Heidegger's exploitation of the success grammar of his terms for truth is that he also wishes to assign to truth a role in misunderstanding as well as in understanding.[20] On his view, some-thing can be both true and untrue. Indeed, he regards truth and untruth to be equally constitutive features of human existence (*SuZ*, p. 222). This does not involve a contradiction, since the respect in which something is true would be different from the respect in which it is untrue. In fact, he gives priority to truth. If there is some untruth then there must be something about which one is mistaken. But for one to be mistaken one must have some understanding of truth. Falsity is traced back to dissemblance ("Schein"). It is disclosure in the mode of dissemblance (*SuZ*, p. 222). That is, something is disclosed to us, but the way it discloses itself to us deceives us about what it really is. Heidegger's paradigmatic example of disclosure in the mode of dissemblance is what he refers to as inauthenticity. We are inauthentic to the extent that we fail to understand the truth

---

[19] Heidegger's most sophisticated development of this point about falsity is to be found in *GA* 21, pp. 185–190.

[20] This distinction between a very wide notion of truth as disclosure and a more narrow normative notion of disclosure is emphasized by Ernst Tugendhat, *Der Wahrheitsbegriff bei Husserl und Heidegger* (Berlin: de Gruyter, 1967). Tugendhat argues that Heidegger fails to do justice to the normative notion of truth because he also extends the notion of truth to include any understanding of anything at all.

about ourselves. We are authentic by contrast when we understand the truth about ourselves. But he seems to think that truth and untruth apply to anything that displays itself either as it is or as it is not.

Heidegger's use of the notion of truth or rather disclosure to characterize the conditions under which it is possible to exist as a human being pushes Husserl's theory of experience in a radically non-subjective direction. This is particularly true of the spatial dimension of disclosure. However, as Heidegger begins to exploit the temporal dimension of disclosure and intentionality, his thought seems to take a rather different course.

In his lectures on inner time-consciousness, Husserl emphasizes the importance of the construction of temporal experience in the constitution of absolute consciousness. He interprets intentionality in terms of the normative goal of making an object present itself to us in perception. The presence of the object to consciousness that is intended by consciousness is what makes for the truth of the act in question. In this way, truth comes to be identified first with the evidence that would make a certain statement or act true of its object, and then with the presence to consciousness of the actual object to which one intends to refer. Being present to, and hence simultaneous with, a state of consciousness is a natural way of expressing the immediacy of intuition.

Through the link between truth and the circumstances under which an act would be true of its object, truth itself seems to take on a certain temporal meaning, since knowledge is justified true belief and the objects that serve to justify belief are objects that are present: "The thesis that all knowledge is directed as means at 'intuition' has the temporal sense: all knowledge is presencing ... *Husserl* uses the expression 'presencing' to characterize sensible perception ... The *intentional* analysis of perception and intuition in general would have had to suggest this 'temporal' description of the phenomenon" (*SuZ*, p. 363n). From this perspective, it seems to be reasonable to interpret truth as the intuitive presence of things themselves to our understanding. Due to the connection between being true and being, this leads to the idea that the truth of being is to be understood as presence ("Anwesenheit"). Husserl suggests

Heidegger's reconstruction of intentionality as temporality by interpreting intentionality as presencing.

Heidegger argues that in order to understand the way in which
intentionality is constituted one must look to the distinctive temporality of human existence: "Since my being is continually such that I
am ahead of myself, I must come back to what I encounter from my
being ahead of it in order to grasp it. Here an immanent structure of
simply grasping, of *as* behavior displays itself that proves on closer
analysis to be *time*" (*GA* 21, p. 147). Time itself turns out to be the
basis for the context of interpretation that is constitutive of meaning.

For Husserl, truth is always understood in terms of what is
objective in the sense that it can be an evident experience for any
rational being. Evident experience is experience in which the object
of consciousness is immediately present to consciousness. The object
is then said to be self-given or bodily there. To find oneself in this
situation of *Evidenz* is to have an authentic experience and hence to
"live in truth." However, Husserl initially insists on the independence of truth and being from any actual presence to consciousness
and hence from temporality.[21] For Heidegger, by contrast, to live
authentically, to "live in truth" means something quite different. It
means to relate to one's own unique life-situation in the unique way
that adequately expresses that life situation. He tends then to carry
this idea of expressing or disclosing one's distinctive situation over to
truth in general, which becomes relativized to a particular historical
situation. Thus for Heidegger, "objectivity as general validity,
universal bindingness ... has nothing to do with truth."[22]

Partly as a consequence of his identification of truth with disclosure or unconcealment, and partly as a consequence of his temporal
interpretation of disclosure, Heidegger wants to restrict the existence
of truths to the time in which they have been "discovered." His
favorite example of truth existing only so long as there are dis-
coverers is the truth of Newton's laws (*SuZ*, p. 226). The example of
the subject and temporally relative truth of Newton's laws is derived
from Husserl's critique of Sigwart's relativization of truth to knowers
at certain times in the *Investigations*. Heidegger endorses one of the
very conclusions that Husserl urges as a reductio of anthropologism
in the Prolegomena: "The judgment that expresses the equation for

---

[21] "But the truth itself is beyond all temporality, i.e. it makes no sense to ascribe to it a
temporal being, becoming, passing away" (Prolegomena, *LU*, section 24, *Hua* 18, p. 87).
[22] *Platon: Sophistes*, *GA* 19 (1924–1925), p. 24.

gravitation would not be true before Newton" (Prol., section 38). Where Husserl defends an atemporal notion of truth against Sigwart's temporalized and subject-dependent notion of truth, Heidegger effectively takes over Sigwart's position.

Husserl argues that "one cannot relativize truth and hold on to the objectivity of being. To be sure, the relativization of truth presupposes an objective being as reference point and therein lies the relativistic contradiction" (Prol., section 38). Heidegger avoids the contradiction in *Being in Time* by accepting the consequence that not only truth, but also being itself are given only so long as there are human beings ("Dasein"): "Being – not entities – 'is given' only insofar as there is truth. And it [truth] *is* only insofar and so long as there is *Dasein*" (*SuZ*, p. 230). Thus the existence of the absolute reference point is precisely what Heidegger denies. He argues that the assertion of "eternal truths" is really based on theological assumptions that philosophers should no longer accept (*SuZ*, p. 229). The idea seems to be that we can only meaningfully assert that there are eternal truths if we can make sense of a standpoint from which such truths might be grasped, and this can only be a God's-eye point of view.

If truth is not independent of us in the way that Husserl maintains that it is, then the relativistic contradiction that Husserl diagnoses disappears. However, Heidegger's relativization of truth is quite problematic. For it leads him to maintain that there is no more difference in truth between Aristotle's notion of the natural place of bodies and Newton's first law than there is between the plays of Sophocles and Shakespeare.[23] It is undeniable that the meaning of terms changes as the world conception to which they belong changes, but this is not itself enough to establish the incommensurability of the terms involved in different world conceptions. This claim of incommensurability ignores, for instance, the greater explanatory power of the Newtonian notion of inertia.

Heidegger's relativization of truth to particular historical epochs so eviscerates the notion of independence that the notion of truth can provide that he then asserts the transcendence of nature relative to truth in order to maintain the independence of nature. This leads him to distinguish the way things are in themselves from the way

---

[23] M. Heidegger, "The Age of the World Picture," *The Question Concerning Technology and other Essays* (New York: Harper and Row, 1960), p. 117, *GA* 5, p. 77.

they are in relation to us in a way that is independent of what is intelligible to us. This has to do with his view that nature is what is only contingently intelligible. In lectures both before and after the publication of *Being and Time*, Heidegger asserts that nature's being is independent of its truth.[24] Such assertions border on incoherence, since they assert something to be true that is supposedly independent of being true. It might seem that there is no way to avoid contradiction here, since Heidegger also wants to link being, but not entities, to truth and disclosure. Since being is supposed to presuppose the existence of truth, there is being, or rather being is given only *so long* as *Dasein* exists. It seems that there cannot be being independent of *Dasein*.

Husserl responds to Heidegger's criticism of atemporal truths directly in *Experience and Judgment* without however mentioning Heidegger by name:

> Objects of the understanding as irreal occur in the world (a state of affairs is "discovered" <*ein Sachverhalt wird "entdeckt"*>); they can be thought again and arbitrarily often, be experienced in their way after they have been discovered. But afterwards it is said: even before they were discovered, they had "validity," or they are in all of time – insofar as there are subjects in it [time] and conceivable in it that are capable of generating <*erzeugen*> them – they are to be taken as generatable and have this mode of omnitemporal existence: in all possible generations they would be the same. (*Experience and Judgment*, section 64c)

Husserl's notion of genetic phenomenology, the idea that we must understand how all objects can be constituted leads him to agree with Heidegger that even putatively atemporal truths are in a certain sense temporal. We have to be able to understand how abstract objects can be generated from objects of experience by means of processes that confer on them epistemic warrant, that is, that show that our use of them is legitimate because it can be justified by some kind of recourse to our immediate experience. In this sense, Husserl is perfectly happy to link truth to the process by means of which we discover truth. However, he plausibly argues that we need to link truth to the actual existence of someone who has

---

[24] "Unhiddenness is a determination of entities insofar as they are encountered. Alétheia does not belong in that sense to being, as if it could not be without unhiddenness. For nature is present at hand (*vorhanden*) even before (*bevor*) it is discovered," *Platon: Sophistes* (1924–1925), *GA* 19, p. 17. "Nature does not depend in its being (*Sein*), that or whether it is an entity (*Seiendes*) or not, on whether it is true, i.e. unveiled and as something unveiled is encountered by Dasein, or not" (*GA* 24 (1928), p. 313).

discovered the truth in question. It is enough for us to regard a truth as one that could be justified by some possible knower.

Against Heidegger's rather radical contextualism, Husserl insists that Heidegger cannot develop the general claims he makes about human existence; he cannot articulate the existentials or conditions of the possibility of any human existence except by considering the idea of what it is to exist as a human being in a manner that purports to be context-independent. Heidegger's concern with the contextuality and historicity of human existence and truth is in some tension with his project of identifying conditions for the possibility of human existence that apply to human existence ("Dasein") in general, rather than in a specific culture or historical epoch.

It seems extremely likely that Husserl's relatively late insight that the philosopher must regard "all the things he takes to be obvious as *prejudices*, and that all prejudices are unclarities out of a traditional sedimentation" (*Crisis*, section 15), is a result of coming to terms with Heidegger's critical emphasis on tradition and historicity.[25] Husserl now recognizes the need for a deconstruction ("Abbau") of the assumptions derived from tradition. But there is a crucial difference between Husserl's (later) acknowledgment of the historical relativity of all our background knowledge and Heidegger's own conception of an essentially historical ontology. Husserl's theory of a basic a priori structure of the life-world that informs the more specific life-worlds constituted by different cultures and historical traditions (*Crisis*, section 36) allows him to do justice to the contextualist claims that Heidegger wishes to defend without undercutting the more general project of articulating completely general conditions for the possibility of intelligibility. Thus, Husserl eventually comes to argue that the relative and absolute notions of truth are interdependent: "What if the relativity of truth and of evidence of truth on the one hand, and on the other hand, the infinitely distant, ideal, absolute truth beyond all relativity – what if each of these has its legitimacy and each demands the other?"[26]

The problems faced by Heidegger's contextualism make Husserl's

[25] Heidegger claimed in response to Gadamer's interpretation of the relation between him and Husserl that he influenced Husserl to include a richer account of history and the social in the constitution of human experience, cf. Otto Pöggeler, *Martin Heidegger's Path of Thinking* (The Hague: Martinus Nijhoff, 1987), p. 286). This seems to be quite plausible.
[26] E. Husserl, *Formal and Transcendental Logic* (1929), trans. D. Cairns (The Hague: Martinus Nijhoff, 1969), *Hua* 17, section 105.

notion of omnitemporal truth look much more attractive. For
Husserl, there is always a distinction to be drawn between the
description of how our concepts and beliefs arise and what gives
them their normative force. He can account for the relation between
the descriptive and the normative precisely because, for him, the
real objects that conform to normative principles and the ideal
structures that underwrite normativity constitute different domains
of objects.

From Husserl's perspective, Heidegger's attempt to formulate
universal conditions for the possibility of human existence (Heidegger's existentials) must fail, because it must be either an empirical or
a non-empirical investigation. As an empirical investigation, it could
claim to have only relative generality. It would at any rate require
support from empirical disciplines such as anthropology that provide
us with our knowledge of human beings. Heidegger does not wish to
make substantive use of such empirical evidence. But, as a non-
empirical investigation, Heidegger's enterprise cannot depend on
evidence that is itself standpoint-dependent. What seems to be
needed is some form of non-empirical knowledge of the empirical
(conditions of human existence).

Husserl worries that, by focusing on the conditions of human
existence rather than of subjectivity in general, Heidegger anthro-
pomorphizes philosophy: "Heidegger transposes or twists the constitutive phenomenological clarification of all regions of entities and
universals, the total region of the world, into the anthropological.
The whole problematic of this transfer, *Dasein* corresponds to the
ego, etc. In this way everything becomes unclear in a deep way and
it loses its philosophical value" (κ x Heidegger 1 to p. 13 line 8 of
SuZ).[27] In some ways even more trenchant is Husserl's question on
the title page of his copy of *Being and Time*: "Isn't this anthropology?"

From Husserl's point of view, Heidegger's conception of existential conditions is a subtle version of psychologism, a "transcendental
psychologism" to which he thinks Kant also falls victim in his
relativization of the a priori to human sensible conditions. The
alternative is to think of "transcendental psychology" as concerned
with the conditions under which any rational being would have to
understand things. The charge of anthropologism is not unwar-

---

[27] Husserl's critical remarks about Heidegger's anthropological approach to philosophy in his
copy of *Being and Time* are reproduced by Alwin Diemer, *Edmund Husserl* (Maisenheim: Hain,
1965), pp. 19–21n.

ranted. We need only look at Husserl's account of anthropologism in his critique of psychologism in the Prolegomena to the *Investigations* to see why he would find Heidegger guilty of this form of psychologism. According to anthropologism, as Husserl understands it in the Prolegomena section 36, all truth is species-relative. But to give truth this species-relative meaning is to make it dependent on the fact that a certain species is constituted in a certain way. This is to make truth depend on something individual and temporal, whereas Husserl maintains that it is eternal.

Heidegger responds to the objection that his fundamental ontology is really a kind of anthropology immediately after publication of *Being and Time* by distinguishing between human beings and the existence ("Dascin") in them: "If the human being is only a human being *on the ground of the Dasein in him*, then the question concerning what is more original than a human being cannot be an anthropological one. All anthropology, even a philosophical one, has already posited human beings as human beings."[28] By distinguishing *Dasein* from human beings Heidegger's thought moves in the direction of Husserl's later idea that "every human being 'bears a transcendental ego in himself'" (*Crisis*, section 54). Indeed, Heidegger's claim that all anthropology has already "posited" human beings as human beings might be taken as another way of saying that to be a human being is to be a "self-objectification of the relevant transcendental ego" (*Crisis*, section 54). For, in Husserlian vocabulary, to be posited and to be an object of experience are one and the same thing.

Heidegger insists, to be sure, that "the rejection of a 'consciousness in general' does not mean the negation of the a priori, any more than the supposition of an idealized subject guarantees that the a priori character of *Dasein* is factually grounded" (*SuZ*, p. 229). Heidegger is right that the existence of a priori knowledge does not seem to require the existence of a "consciousness in general," that is, an abstract Kantian ego. However, Heidegger is committed to the stronger claim that there is no absolute truth. It is not at all clear how one can sustain a claim to contextualized a priori structures of human existence without falling into anthropology or shifting to something like the assumption of transcendental consciousness.

In one sense, Heidegger's response to Husserl is subtle, for what

---

[28] *Kant and the Problem of Metaphysics* (1929), section 41.

Heidegger is arguing is that he is not really basing truth on facts about human beings, but rather on the conditions under which anything could be intelligible to us. However, this does not really resolve the issue, since Heidegger also wants to say that we cannot get behind the way we as human beings must understand the world to raise the question of whether this way of understanding might be false. Husserl would argue that this relativizes the notion of truth in a way that is inconsistent with the absolute character of truth claims. There is a good deal of force to this remark as a claim about how we understand the truth. Our understanding of truth does not seem to have an implicit relativization to a species perspective in it, however it might be argued that this relativization is not part of our notion of truth because we do not in general ask the question of whether we can say that what we as a species take to be true might in fact turn out to be false.

There is some merit in the claim that our ordinary notion of truth is not sufficiently well defined to support the claim that truth must be radically independent of us. A more interesting position is, however, open to Heidegger. He can make the stronger case that in making truth dependent on *Dasein*, he is not suggesting that we could take ourselves to take fundamental truths, such as those of logic, to be true that creatures who are not *Dasein* could take to be false. For we can only think of other creatures as the kind of beings that can take things to be true to the extent that we think of them as being the kind of beings that have *Dasein*. The relativistic contradiction cannot arise, since the only access that we have to the truth is from our own point of view. Such a position is not, however, wholesale relativism, since Heidegger is deeply interested in what we must together take to be true.

CHAPTER 5

Heidegger's critique of Husserl's methodological solipsism

In this chapter, I look at Heidegger's critical response to Husserl's Cartesianism and his effort to articulate a conception of human existence that undercuts the methodological solipsism that provides the general epistemological and metaphysical framework for Husserl's analysis of experience. Heidegger's conception of human existence is intended to undermine the Husserlian assumption that sense and meaning are things that are intelligible in the terms set by methodological solipsism.

The contemporary philosophy of mind has been considerably interested in the merits and demerits of internalist and externalist conceptions of the mental. According to internalists, it is possible to understand at least some contents of the mind in the narrow terms provided by introspection and first-person awareness that does not appeal to any knowledge of other persons or objects outside of the person in question. It is thus possible to investigate such contents of consciousness in a manner that is methodologically solipsistic. Externalists, by contrast, argue that there is no interesting notion of mental content left over once one abstracts from the relations of persons to the public institutions that constitute our linguistic conventions. The externalist argues that these conventions are themselves underwritten by the objects belonging to a shared environment. It is the natural kinds into which objects fall in our environment that give determinate structure to the concepts that persons have.[1]

---

[1] Hilary Putnam presents the externalist view in terms of the slogan: "Cut the pie any way you like, meanings just ain't in the head!" Hilary Putnam, "The Meaning of Meaning," *Mind, Language, and Reality: Philosophical Papers* 2 (New York: Cambridge University Press, 1981), p. 227. While Putnam ultimately bases the meanings of words, especially natural kind terms, on the natural environment, our access to this environment is mediated for him by our knowledge of the environment. We depend for our knowledge of natural kinds on experts in particular fields. Putnam refers to this social aspect of meaning as "the linguistic

Heidegger has a wide reputation for his efforts in breaking down the inner–outer distinction of post-Cartesian epistemology and philosophy of mind. Instead of thinking of understanding on the model of a subject that confronts an object, he suggests that we understand human existence as being-in-the-world. Here, what it is to be a human being involves an essential relation to other entities and in particular to the world in which such entities are to be found. The primacy of being-in-the-world expresses what might be called Heidegger's externalist conception of what it is to understand things and to be a human being. But it is not quite correct to describe his position as externalism. Externalism presupposes the traditional inner–outer distinction, and argues for the dependence of the inner on the outer, whereas Heidegger thinks that the traditional inner–outer distinction is based on a mistaken ontology of human existence.

From Husserls point of view, the narrow representational content that we are presented with in our individual private experiences ("Erlebnisse") is the ultimate basis for the philosophical investigation of the conditions under which both narrow and wide content are possible. Husserl does not, to be sure, deny the existence of wide representational content. He thinks that a wide representational content based on our interactions with our environment and with other persons is of paramount significance in most inquiry. The nature of the disagreement between Husserl and Heidegger concerns the status of narrow representational content.

Heidegger maintains that there cannot be any distinctively narrow representational content and thus no contrastive notion of wide representational content. This leads him to give up on the notion of representation, in general, and propositional attitudes, in particular, in favor of different ways in which the world is disclosed to us. But Heidegger shares a basic assumption with Husserl in his account of how experience is to be investigated philosophically. Like

division of labor." While internalist philosophers such as John Searle do not deny that there is a natural and a social dimension to meaning, they do wonder where else meanings could ultimately be situated if they are not in the head, see J. R. Searle, *Intentionality: an Essay in the Philosophy of Mind* (New York: Cambridge University Press, 1983), chapter 8. According to Searle, "each of our beliefs must be possible for a being who is a brain in a vat because each of us is precisely a brain in the vat; the vat is a skull and the 'messages' coming in are coming in by way of impacts on the nervous system," p. 230. This strange claim is a consequence of Searle's dual commitment to an internalist conception of the mental and a form of naturalism according to which mental states are both features of the brain and caused by physical states of brain and nerve system.

Husserl, Heidegger thinks that philosophy is concerned with the manner in which human beings make sense of what they experience rather than with a nature that might ultimately prove to be inaccessible to our understanding. This shared emphasis on the meaning of what we experience is a consequence of their shared conception of the importance of how we experience the entities that we do experience. The key to understanding how we experience entities is to be sought in the notion of intentionality.

HEIDEGGER'S CRITIQUE OF HUSSERL'S PLATONISM

Heidegger's theory of meaning emerges from a critical appropriation of Husserl's account of meaning. Heidegger finds the Platonist idea that meanings are essentially non-temporal and non-spatial to be very problematic. He attempts to find an alternative to Husserl's Platonism and the psychologism that seems to be the obvious alternative to Husserl's insistence on the atemporal ideality of truth and sense (*LU* I, section 39). Heidegger's notion of a sense or meaning to being is best understood in the light of his rejection both of a psychologistic and of a Platonist theory of sense and meaning. From the very beginning of his career, Heidegger rejects both a psychologistic reconstruction of sense and meaning in terms of the contents of actual psychological states and the "hypostasization of the logical to a metaphysical entity."[2] This leads him to the view that the status of sense is the crucial problem of philosophy: "We must give up accommodating sense (*Sinn*) in the sphere of entities (*Seiendes*). Wherein should we place it? We stand with that in the face of a final principle problem with which the basic character of logic (of theoretical philosophy) and of philosophy in general should be decided."[3]

---

[2] "Neuere Forschungen in der Logik (1912)," *GA* I, p. 24. Heidegger was one of the first philosophers to pay any attention to Frege's work in the philosophy of logic, despite his reservations about Platonism, see *GA* I, pp. 17–43, esp. p. 20: "*G. Frege's* logical-mathematical investigations have not in my opinion been appreciated in their true significance, let alone exhausted. What he has written down in his works on 'Sense and Reference,' on 'Concept and Object' cannot be overlooked by any philosophy of mathematics; it is equally valuable for a general theory of concepts." He later argues that mathematical logic is limited by its use of formalisms which "hide the meanings and shifts in meaning of judgments," p. 42. This leads him to the somewhat vague, but by no means implausible conclusion that "mathematics and the mathematical treatment of logical problems reach limits where their concepts and methods fail, that is precisely where the conditions of their possibility lie" p. 43.

[3] Martin Heidegger, *Zur Bestimmung der Philosophie*, *GA* 56/57 (1919), p. 199.

While Heidegger agrees with Husserl that meaning is to be understood in terms of the way that things are given to us, he rejects Husserl's thesis that we can analyze those meanings in abstraction from the actual "real" environment and social context in which we understand them the way we do. Husserl's view that one can understand meaning in abstraction from the actual environment in which a person finds him- or herself, does not mean, to be sure, that Husserl interprets meaning in terms of a molecular model of propositions. According to the molecular model, the meaning expressed by acts of thought and statements articulating those thoughts would be comprehensible independently of one's understanding of the meaning of other thoughts and their corresponding linguistic statements. For Husserl, meaning is holistic and environmental. However, the environment in question is the notional environment that is internal to a given person's individual beliefs.

Thus, Husserl realizes that intentionality always has a horizon, or background, which is also constitutive of the meaning of expressions that are based on our intentional directedness at objects. Heidegger is aware of the importance of the horizonal dimension of Husserl's conception of intentionality. He emphasizes that particularly Husserl's theory of perceptual experience involves a totality of meaning: "the perceived thing is always presumed in its *thing-totality* ... The thing *adumbrates*, shades off in its aspects," (*GA* 20, pp. 57–58). But Heidegger also sees that Husserl's notion of horizonal intentionality is primarily first personal. It is consistent with the non-existence of things in the world and even other persons.

Heidegger appropriates Husserl's idea of "horizonal intentionality," with its holistic implication. But Heidegger insists that his meaning holism notwithstanding, Husserl's first-person singular Cartesian account of what is experienced through our intentional directedness at objects leads to a fundamental misunderstanding of intentionality. Instead of basing all intentionality on the transcendence of understanding in the direction of what is understood, Husserl falls back to Brentano's Cartesian emphasis on the immanence of mental states to consciousness. Heidegger objects to the immanence that Husserl ascribes to the mental in particular because he is skeptical of the very idea that whenever we have a belief or are in a certain mood we are therefore in some occurrent mental state. To understand human behavior on the model of consciousness is itself deeply misguided for Heidegger. Once one takes the notion of consciousness as basic to understanding, one inevitably finds oneself thinking of individuals as being either internal to or external to consciousness. The object of consciousness may be independent of consciousness, but our access to that object through consciousness involves some object that is internal to or immanent to consciousness.

The existence of such dispositions as moods, like anxiety and boredom, that do not have any obvious object, make Heidegger suspicious not only of the identification of the mental with acts of intentionality, but of the whole category of "mental states." Such moods as anxiety, sadness, happiness, and boredom track the individual's relation to his or her environment in a cognitively significant manner, but they do not easily fit into the usual dichotomy between the "mental" and the "physical." Although they may be object-directed, one can be sad, bored, or happy about x, they do not require any directedness of a subject at an object: "with the existence of a *Dasein* insofar and as soon as *Dasein* exists, something happens, history has begun – namely the unheard of event that an entity is and can be encountered by another, and without the subject directing itself at it in its own right" (*GA* 26, pp. 161–162).

Heidegger is also skeptical about the idea of a privileged access to such occurrent mental states. Doubts are certainly justified as to whether Husserl succeeds in identifying a bona fide distinction between the corrigibility of claims about objects that are external to consciousness and the incorrigibility of claims about experiences that are internal to consciousness.[4] The idea that the mental is somehow self-contained, reinterprets intentionality in a way that jettisons its essential relatedness to objects that are outside of the self. This is encouraged by thinking of intentionality in terms of states of consciousness that have abstract semantic structure that one can investigate through philosophical reflection which is immune to doubt about its objects.

Heidegger advocates a holistic conception of meaning based on the significance ("Bedeutsamkeit") of the patterned responses that

---

[4] According to Dagfinn Føllesdal, "Husserl on Evidence and Justification," in R. Sokolowski (ed.), *Husserl and the Phenomenological Tradition* (Washington, DC: Catholic University of America Press, 1988), Husserl is a fallibilist and rejects foundationalism. But the evidence that he cites for this interpretation comes from work of Husserl's beginning in the early twenties when Husserl came to be more critical of the Cartesian way into the phenomenological reduction.

human beings display as they engage with their world as a whole (*SuZ*, pp. 83ff.). This holistic conception of meaning is anticipated by Husserl's notion of the way things are given to us in everyday experience. However, in Husserl's theory, meaning holism does not come fully into its own because of Husserl's ideal of contents that are completely self-presenting to self-conscious reflection and his advocacy of methodological solipsism.[5] Heidegger thinks of human beings as beings whose very nature consists in their existence ("Dasein"); he thus rejects the endeavor to elicit the structures of intentionality in abstraction from the environment or world in which human beings exist.

The nature of intentionality cannot be understood by abstracting from the existence of the very objects to which consciousness is directed in intentionality. This is why Heidegger comes to argue that intentionality is based on transcendence. By using the notion of transcendence that Husserl uses to describe reference to objects that are external to consciousness, Heidegger rejects Husserl's internalist interpretation of intentionality.

HUMAN EXISTENCE AND THE ESSENCE OF THE INTENTIONAL

At least initially, Husserl maintains that it is possible to understand the nature of existence as an idea, that is, one can attempt to understand what it is that all things that exist have in common in pure consciousness. This leads Heidegger to argue that Husserl's phenomenology focuses solely on the content of experience without investigating the manner in which acts of consciousness exist: "Thus in the consideration and development of pure consciousness only the *what content* is extracted without asking about the being of acts in the sense of their existence" (*GA* 20, p. 151).

The way Husserl develops the distinction between existence internal to and external to consciousness raises the problem of what it is to be. But Heidegger maintains, somewhat tendentiously to be sure, that the distinction between entities inside and outside of consciousness is itself ultimately based on a univocal treatment of the

---

[5] The importance of the notion of horizon in Husserl's theory of meaning has been emphasized by David Carr, *Interpreting Husserl* (Dordrecht: Martinus Nijhoff, 1987), p. 240. The non-actional and horizonal dimension of Husserl's conception of intentionality becomes the basis for the general attack on Heidegger's Husserl critique to be found in Burt Hopkins, *Intentionality in Husserl and Heidegger* (Dordrecht: Kluwer, 1993).

kind of being that characterizes intentionality and consciousness and the kind of reality that things have which are outside of consciousness. Husserl does think that both minds and bodies are real in *Ideas* II. However, he also distinguishes such reality from the pure being that is characteristic of pure consciousness. Husserl's position in the *Ideas* clarifies the distinction between our everyday understanding of things and entities as they present themselves to philosophical reflection by sharpening the distinction between mental states and the meanings in virtue of which those mental states have intentionality. The former are real states while the latter have a distinctive form of being, pure or ideal being.

Husserl's developing position convinces Heidegger, however, that Husserl has, paradoxically, failed to explore what it is for something to be intentional, and indeed what it is for an entity to be capable of relating to other entities intentionally. The problem derived from Husserl's purported failure to see that there is not really a univocal meaning to what it is to be for different kinds of entities. This criticism has little force, given the distinctions that are characteristic of Husserl's worked out position. However, Heidegger does connect this criticism with another somewhat more plausible objection to Husserl.

The abstract consideration of representational content leads to a misunderstanding of the nature of intentionality. It prevents Husserl from understanding the distinctive nature of human beings who have intentionality: "If there were an entity, *whose what precisely it is, to be and nothing but to be*, then this ideational consideration in respect of such an entity would be the most fundamental misunderstanding" (*GA* 20, p. 152). As Heidegger sees it, Husserl misses out on the distinctive connection between existence and essence that characterizes what it is to be a human being and to have the kind of intentionality that characterizes human beings. The problem is that Husserl thinks of an idea or essence as an ideal structure that determines what an act of intentionality must be like. This notion of essence is juxtaposed to the existence or actuality of the act or thing of which it is the essence. While he agrees with Husserl that to be human is to have an intentional relation to something, Heidegger maintains against Husserl that the kind of essence that a human being has, and hence that intentionality has, is not something that can be distinguished from its essence. Husserl cannot do justice to intentionality precisely because he must think of the essence of an intentional act as something that is intelligible independently of its existence.

Heidegger's objection to interpreting intentionality in terms of the Husserlian notion of pure consciousness and its essences precisely parallels Kierkegaard's objection to Hegel's notion of pure consciousness.[6] In both cases, the aim is to establish the legitimacy of a notion of existence that is not thought of simply as an instance of an essence against the idea that all individual existence is simply an instance of essences that are independent of individual existence. Following Kierkegaard, Heidegger contrasts the how of the way that one lives a human existence with the what that characterizes the essence of other things.

From Heidegger's point of view, Husserl's emphasis on essences or ideal objects that are available in abstraction from the existence of the world in which they are instanced leads to a misunderstanding of the nature of intentionality. Husserl needs to be able to abstract from the real basis of intentionality in order to be able to get at the essence of different acts of consciousness and their objects, but he cannot do so completely without abstracting from intentionality itself. Thus, Heidegger's objection to Husserl's account of intentionality, that it presupposes an account of the real basis of intentionality that it must exclude from phenomenologically reduced experience, is initially quite plausible. The claim that Husserl does wish to abstract from real existence in the phenomenological reduction may seem contentious, but it has a solid basis in the text. Thus, in a famous paper from 1910 to 1911, "Philosophy as Rigorous Science," Husserl claims that:

pure phenomenology as science, so long as it is pure and makes no use of the existential positing of nature, can only be essence investigation, and not at all an investigation of existence <*Dasein*> ... To fix this essence as an individual, however, to give it a position in a "world" of individual existence, is something that such a mere subsumption under essential concepts can never accomplish. For phenomenology, the singular is eternally the *apeiron*.[7]

---

[6] Kierkegaard maintains, in his *Concluding Unscientific Postscript: to the Philosophical Fragments*, V. Hong and E. Hong trans. (Princeton University Press, 1992), pp. 196ff., that Hegel abstracts from human existence in interpreting the world from the vantage-point of a system constituted by a pure ego, thus failing to do justice to the nature of subjectivity. Given Heidegger's strong interest in Kierkegaard in the period after the First World War, it is altogether likely that this is an important source for his critique of Husserl.

[7] Edmund Husserl, "Philosophy as Rigorous Science," in Q. Lauer trans. *Phenomenology and the*

It thus often seems that, for Husserl, a full-fledged transcendental–phenomenological reduction will also involve an eidetic reduction. For he notes that "phenomenology allows *only individuation* to drop, but it raises the whole essential content in the fullness of its concreteness into eidetic consciousness and takes it as ideal identical essence" (*Ideas* I, section 75, p. 157).

However, despite Husserl's repeated insistence on the importance of the eidetic reduction, it is not clear that he excludes all investigation of the individual. With some justification, he can claim in a letter to the Plato scholar, Julius Stenzel, that the view that he cannot do justice to individuality has its roots in a conflation of the phenomenological with the eidetic reduction:

> I see that you also, following the suggestions of Scheler and Heidegger, as is now common, regard me as a kind of Platonist, or what is the same thing, confuse the phenomenological reduction with the eidetic reduction. No one seems to think it necessary to read and take seriously what *I* have to say about the reduction. In truth, I am further from Platonism and any a priori ontologism as any philosopher of the past and our time – much further than Dilthey. (Letter of March 28, 1934)

Husserl's own tendency to identify phenomenology with the investigation of species explains the confusion here. Thus, in a remark connected with the writing of *Ideas* I, he claims that "the *specifically phenomenological* consists in the consideration of essences which places us in the intentionally all encompassing consciousness which thus *relates everything that arises from eidetic consideration to the eidetic essence of consciousness* in which all being . . . is constituted" (*Hua* 5, p. 133)

Despite Husserl's tendency to shift quickly from the phenomenological reduction to the further step of eidetically reducing the contents of a phenomenological reduction, the two forms of reduction are logically independent of each other. There is thus, in principle, no reason why an investigation of facticity is not possible within the phenomenological reduction. To deny such a possibility is to confuse the two different senses in which consciousness can be pure, namely, consciousness can be pure in the sense of an object of

---

Crisis of Philosophy (New York: Harper, 1969), p. 116. Husserl also seems to regard the topic of phenomenology as restricted to the analysis of essences in the much later (1930) appendix to *Ideas* I, section 1, p. 141–142: "The facts that present themselves in each case serve only as examples – in the most general way similar to the way empirical examples serve the mathematician . . . In this volume it is a matter of an 'a priori' (an eidetic) science (directed at the originally-intuitive universal) which takes up the factual experiences merely as pure possibility."

disinterested investigation, and pure in the sense of being devoid of particular empirical content.

With considerable justification, Heidegger regards both senses of purity as problematic. However, an argument against treating human existence in the pure or rather abstract terms characteristic of the eidetic reduction would not have much force against Husserl's conception of a human being unless Husserl had no way of characterizing what it is to be a concrete human being. There is, however, evidence that the purely exemplary role that Husserl assigns to the individual relative to abstract essences actually breaks down in the case of an investigation of human beings. Heidegger is familiar with Husserl's claim that "experiences in the flux of consciousness have their absolutely own essence, they bear their individuation in themselves ... The only thing that is originally individual is concrete consciousness with its ego" (*Ideas* II, section 64, p. 301). Heidegger dismisses such claims as mere reproductions of the claim of the priority of pure consciousness (*GA* 20, p. 170). While Husserl does wish to argue that pure consciousness is ontologically independent, it is important to note that this is a claim he makes for individual experiencers, rather than for the abstract natures of such experiencers, as Heidegger would have it. Indeed, Husserl maintains that the distinction between essence and existence breaks down in the case of persons, since persons can only be understood adequately in terms of experiences that are repeatables in the sense that they fall into certain types, but are never actually repeated in their precise specificity. Husserl closes *Ideas* II with the remark that one can treat a human being as "a mere exemplar of a universal," but only insofar as one thinks of that human being in the limited terms of its existence as a natural object. One then misses out on the "specific individuality" that belongs to a human being as spirit" (*Ideas* II: *Hua* 4, p. 302). Thus if we substitute "person" for "Dasein," Husserl anticipates Heidegger's claim that "Dasein is thus never to be ontologically grasped as case or exemplar of a kind of entity as something occurrent <*Vorhandenes*>" (*SuZ*, p. 42). For both philosophers, it would be a fundamental naturalistic mistake to treat human existence as something that belongs to natural reality in the same way that a stone does.

In late reflections dating from the early thirties, Husserl notes that the standpoint from which all consciousness and its objects are constituted involves a collapse of the distinction between possibility and actuality, between essence and existence:

The being of an eidos, the being of eidetic possibilities, and the universe of these possibilities, is free of the being or non-being of any actualization of such possibilities, it is independent in being from all actuality, namely of corresponding [objects]. But the eidos, transcendental ego, is unthinkable without the transcendental ego as something factual [*faktisches*] ... Here we have the curious and unique case of a relation between fact and eidos.[8]

There is thus for Husserl, as for Heidegger, an ineliminable facticity to experience. But this is, for Husserl, the facticity of the transcendental ego. The connection between facticity and essence that Husserl allows is at any rate of a fundamentally different nature from the one that Heidegger wishes to emphasize. For, according to Heidegger, the very essence of being human is to exist in such a way that who one is can never be determined by a set of abstract possibilities of the kind provided by a Husserlian essence.[9] Husserl acknowledges the fact that our existence is indeterminate, but thinks that it is still legitimate to think of ourselves in terms of an idealization in which we do have a fixed essence: "Consciousness has its own essence, a flowing one and one that is not exactly determinable; but as idea it is to be assigned an exact essence, and within being posited it acquires a determinate this" (*Ideas* II, p. 301).

Heidegger rejects the whole idea that a human being has an essence, in the Husserlian sense of a whatness that Heidegger associates with the traditional philosophical notion of essence or *essentia*. To have an essence in this sense of whatness, even if it is an individual essence, is to be an "occurrent entity" ("ein Vorhandenes"):

The "essence" of *Dasein* lies in its existence. Thus the characters that can be displayed in this entity are not thus and such "looking" ["aussehenden"] occurrent entities with their occurrent "properties," but only possible ways for it in each case [i.e. it alone] to be and only that. All being-such of this entity is primarily being (*Sein*). For this reason the title "Dasein," with which we refer to this being does not refer to a what, like table, chair, house, tree, but to being. (*SuZ*, p. 42)

---

[8] E III, p. 73 (1931). Cited in Klaus Held, *Lebendige Gegenwart* (The Hague: Martinus Nijhoff, 1966), p. 147.

[9] There is an interesting discussion of this point about the nature of Heidegger's disagreement with Husserl's notion of pure consciousness in Michael Friedman, "Overcoming Metaphysics: Carnap and Heidegger," *Minnesota Studies in the Philosophy of Science* 26 (1996), esp. p. 63.

Heidegger's denial that the characters of *Dasein* are ones that "look" thus and such is a play on the connection of the Greek word "eidos" with the way something looks. *"Eidos"* is used by Plato to refer to the form of a thing and by Aristotle also to refer to its essence. Heidegger is thus denying that there is an essence to *Dasein* that could be understood in terms of some underlying form that it exemplifies. *Dasein* is not a thing in the sense of something that exemplifies properties that can be understood independently of the specific manner in which a life is lived. Human beings do not have properties in the same sense in which things have properties. The "properties" of a human being are adverbial modifications of the process through which it exists and has being; all "properties" that a human being may have are, in fact, modifications of the way in which it exists spatially and temporally, "ways which are possible for it to be in each case and only that" (*SuZ*, p. 42). Human existence is thus unlike the way things are what they are. Human existence *is* a possibility that can never become an actuality. This is a development of the Kantian idea that persons exist as ends to be realized.

Heidegger appropriates the idea from personalistic psychology that one must be able as a human being ("Dasein") in some sense to determine how one is to exist. This is what it is for human beings "to be." The idea that a human being is the kind of creature that is able to determine what it is for he or she to exist leads Heidegger then to define what it is to be human ("Dasein") as "to be" ("Zu-sein", *SuZ*, p. 42).[10] He later comes to characterize what it is to be more helpfully as to be oneself: "This to-be-oneself ("Zu-sich-selbst-sein") constitutes the being of "Dasein" and is not a faculty superadded to it, to be observed in addition to existence ... Rather to-be-oneself as being-a-self is the presupposition for the different possibilities of ontic behavior" (*GA* 26, p. 244).

A human being's properties are through and through disposi-

---

[10] There is a useful discussion of the notion of "to be" in Tugendhat, *Der Wahrheitsbegriff bei Husserl und Heidegger*, p. 299, and particularly in his *Selbstbewußtsein und Selbstbestimmung* (Frankfurt am Main: Suhrkamp, 1979), pp. 152ff. It is the merit of the later discussion that it also brings out the connection between Aristotle's notion of the human good as that for the sake of which we do all the things that we do and Heidegger's notion of resolute choice. One should also note that this conception of the human flourishing is sunk into Aristotle's philosophical psychology and its account of human existence as functional organization. The account of the soul as a functional unity is, in turn, part of his general account of the explanation of natural motion.

tional, and even the way that these dispositions will manifest themselves under appropriate circumstances is subject to change. For, as a human being's experience changes, his or her dispositions also change. These dispositions, or rather capacities for doing things and relating to things and other human beings, are not to be understood as not yet actualized possibilities as they are according to the Kantian and personalist conception of self (*SuZ*, pp. 143ff.). Unlike the personalist conception of self, a human being so conceived is not something that exists through a successive replacement of acts of consciousness. Thinking of the possibilities of the self as unactualized possibilities would mean that, once a behavior pattern were actually chosen, it would no longer be a possibility. By contrast, Heidegger insists that human beings can always make changes in the way that they appropriate their own history, so that their history is never fixed: "Whenever *Dasein* behaves according to a certain mode of behavior, this mode remains a possible one, that is it can in principle be given up, *Dasein* can in principle place itself in another, so that therefore the determination of possibility belongs in principle to modes of behavior, and the possibility cannot disappear when a certain behavior is factually chosen, lived" (*GA* 26 1925–1926, p. 228). The capacity that human beings have to alter the import of what they have done even after the fact does not mean that, if one has had a car accident, one can somehow make it the case that the accident never happened. But one can substantially alter the significance of an event by the different ways in which one comes to terms with it.

This potentiality or possibility must be understood as expressing something one can do, or, even more perspicuously, something one can be (see *SuZ*, p. 143). Understanding oneself in this freedom to do this or that is what Heidegger takes to be the sense in which one is one's own possibilities. Such possibilities are to be understood as genuine potentialities of behavior for a certain individual as opposed to some weaker notion of possibility (such as logical possibility, *GA* 24, p. 392). We can never be said to be who we are in the way in which a thing has occurrent properties, because our histories are essential to who we are, and the way we relate to where we come from is a constitutive factor in what that background turns out to be in our own lives.

Heidegger argues that the problem with Husserl's account of intentionality is that its emphasis on abstract essences or ideal objects forces Husserl to make intentionality a feature annexed to the natural existence of human beings, rather than an expression of their very nature as selves. The notion of a nature or essence, as Husserl understands it, precludes him from thinking of being in an actual intentional relation as constitutive of what it is to be a particular self. Here Heidegger seems clearly to miss the mark.

Heidegger maintains that to do justice to intentionality one must get back to the original experience of intentionality in the natural attitude. He intimates that the being of the intentional, and by this he seems to mean the existence of the intentional, is something that one must look for in the natural attitude of everyday life rather than in phenomenologically reduced experience. This is a claim that Husserl would reject. However, even for Husserl, the very identity of each particular ego depends in a certain sense on the particular content of its experience. Without sensation, which belongs to bodily existence, that experience has no distinctive individual content. What is perceived by means of sensation in its different aspects also involves bodily motility, kinaesthesis, as Husserl refers to it, so that the person as a whole, including his or her lived body, seems to be ineliminable from the reduction.[11] However, it is open to Husserl to respond that an analysis of the sense that we attribute to different experiences need not involve an account of the real constitution of that sense, even though such real constitution is in some sense presupposed.

In pursuing the objection that Husserl must have recourse to the natural attitude to make sense of intentionality, Heidegger overplays his hand, however. For he is not content with establishing that Husserl needs to return to the natural attitude in order to give an adequate account of intentionality. He wants to show that Husserl misinterprets the natural attitude because of the way he divides the universe into real and ideal objects. According to Heidegger, "what is fixed here [in *Ideas* II] as something given by the natural attitude, that namely the human being is given as a living being, a zoological

---

[11] The importance of the body to reduced experience is emphasized by Elizabeth Ströker, *Husserl's Transcendental Phenomenology* (Palo Alto: Stanford University Press, 1993), p. 203.

object, is this attitude as a natural one" (*GA* 20, p. 155). Heidegger's claim is puzzling, since it seems to be so far off the mark. He asserts that thinking of human beings as zoological objects serves to characterize what counts as natural in the natural attitude, as Husserl understands it. Heidegger rightly rejects the idea that the natural attitude to take to human beings is to regard them as zoological objects. But if we look at the manuscript of *Ideas* II, we also find Husserl rejecting the zoological interpretation as unnatural. Far from claiming that the natural attitude is one in which we regard human beings as zoological objects, Husserl insists that this way of looking at things belongs to the unnatural theoretical attitude of the naturalist. This is the way human beings appear to the natural*istic* attitude. Husserl insists that the natural attitude to human beings is the personalistic attitude: "In the natural life of the ego we do not see the world therefore always, indeed nor even predominantly naturalistically – as if we wanted to do physics or zoology ..." (*Ideas* II, section 49, p. 183). Thus Husserl is in complete agreement with Heidegger when the latter complains that "what is thus examined [namely naturalistically] and defined is merely his occurrent being as a thing, *to which* forms of behavior are perhaps 'annexes' but that are not relevant to the determination of the character of the being of this entity" (*GA* 20, p. 156).

We have already seen that Heidegger ascribes to Husserl what the latter regards as a limited *naturalistic* conception of a person in order to argue against the adequacy of Husserl's account of human existence. For it is only according to a naturalistic conception of a human being that Husserl thinks that an individual human being can be regarded as a mere exemplar of a type. Heidegger now suggests that Husserl thinks of persons and states of consciousness as mere annexes to natural things. This is the way persons do appear for Husserl according to the naturalistic attitude. But, for Husserl, the only ultimate access we have to persons is through a realization that they have the kind of experience that is revealed to us in the pure consciousness of the phenomenological reduction. Thus, far from thinking of persons as mere appendages to natural objects, Husserl in fact emphasizes the impossibility of adequately under-standing persons as mere appendages to such objects. Instead he argues that the existence of persons is the condition for the possibility of making sense of natural things and must therefore be regarded as both epistemologically and metaphysically primary.

Husserl denies the possibility of any naturalistic reduction of a person to a causal functional relation between material states.

The difference between Heidegger's position and that of Husserl's cannot be fairly taken to be that Husserl thinks of persons as mere instances of a certain kind, or that he thinks that one can do without the first- or second-person perspective in understanding what it is to be a person. Husserl would be the last to deny that "speaking to *Dasein* must always also say the *personal* pronoun 'I am,' 'you are' according to the for each its ownness <*Jemeinigkeit*> of this entity" (*SuZ*, p. 42). Heidegger falsely suggests disagreement on these points with Husserl. Nor does Husserl deny that dispositions, potentialities to be are significant: "In relation to my centripedal ego acts I have the consciousness *I can*" (*Ideas* II, section 60, p. 257), or that responsibility for one's actions is the key to understanding human existence: "Above all one must distinguish the *'person in a specific sense'*: the subject of acts that are to be judged under the standpoint of *reason*, the subject that is *'self-responsible'* from the universal and unitary empirical subject" (*Ideas* II, section 60, p. 257). However, Husserl never endorses the consequences that Heidegger draws from these insights. The character that a human being has as such ("Dasein") is to be properly understood as nothing but that individual's potentialities. For the idea that a person is nothing but a set of potential or dispositional relations to the world it shares with other persons, goes against Husserl's basic claim that persons are autonomous. Husserl's methodological solipsism commits him to arguing that persons have an individual essence that, in principle, is independent of any real entities. This methodological solipsism leads Husserl to think of the world as a series of levels of experience.

A METAPHYSICS OF LEVELS AND THE PRIMACY OF
PERCEPTION

Heidegger is on much better ground when he criticizes Husserl for the kind of level metaphysics ("Schichtenmetaphysik") to be found in *Ideas* II. Husserl undeniably envisions different levels of constitution. At the most fundamental level, purposely left out of the construction in the *Ideas*, we have time-consciousness. Such time-consciousness is then given a distinctive unity in pure consciousness by means of a transcendental ego. On the basis of what is available to the transcendental ego in pure consciousness, Husserl first constructs bodies, then psyche (sensory experience), and finally spirits. This naturally gives rise to difficult questions about how these different individuals are related, questions for which Husserl never has a satisfactory answer:

Lived body (*Leib*), psyche (*Seele*), and spirit may mark in some way that out of which this entity is composed, but with this composite and its composition the mode of being of this entity remains undetermined from the outset; it can hardly be extracted after the fact from the composite, because I have already put myself in a completely foreign dimension of being by determining the entity in terms of the characteristics of body, psyche, and spirit. (*GA* 20, p. 207)

The only way that Husserl seems to be able to think of constitution is in terms of different levels of being that can be constituted out of individual experiences. But this notion of constitution leaves serious questions when it comes to making transitions from each level of constitution to the next. However, even if Husserl has no satisfactory answer for how body, psyche, and spirit go to make up a human being, it seems to be somewhat misleading for Heidegger to claim that the notion of spirit that Husserl uses fundamentally distorts the nature of human existence.

The personalistic attitude that Husserl describes involves an understanding of one's environment, including other persons, things, and tools, in terms of motivations and beliefs that are inherently holistic because they are based on the way the world as a whole is given for each of us (*Ideas* II, section 50, pp. 185ff.). This seems to leave Heidegger's conception of human existence and its being-in-the-world looking like it is not a genuine alternative to Husserl's view at all. Does Heidegger's position simply collapse into the position that Husserl already defends in *Ideas* II? No. It does not. For Husserl thinks of our environment as having levels. The basic level of our environment is "an egoistic environment" which, in principle, can be pried apart from the "communicative environment" that we share with other persons (*Ideas* II, section 51, p. 193). This reflects a difference in conception between Heidegger's conception of being-in-the-world and Husserl's notion of the environment of persons.

Dasein is not simply identical with the self. For *Dasein*, human existence, includes the whole world in itself: "Self and world are not two entities, like subject and object, or like I and you; rather, self and world are the basic determinations of *Dasein* itself, in the unity of the structure of being-in-the-world" (*GA* 24, p. 422). To think of the self and world as two distinct entities is to fall into an error endemic to the traditional metaphysical conception of a person. The temptation that Heidegger wants to undercut in the tradition of modern philosophy, of which Husserl is the representative example, is to think of being-in-the-world as a relation that a subject has to a world of objects. This suggests that there might be a world of objects without a subject (realism), or a subject without objects (idealism). Heidegger seeks to undercut the skeptical potential inherent in this picture by arguing that we have no freestanding conception of a human being as a subject that could exist independently of the distinctive spatiality that characterizes what it is to be a human being:

> *Dasein* itself has its own "being-in-space" that is in turn only possible *on the basis of being-in-the-world in general.* Being-in can therefore also not be clarified by saying: Being-in in a world is a property of spirit and the "spatiality" of a human being is a character of its lived body that is always also "founded" on its corporeality. Then one is back to the occurrence-together of a spirit thing with a certain character and a corporeal thing, and the being of the composite entity as such remains even more in the dark. The understanding of being-in-the-world as an essential structure of *Dasein* first makes insight into the existential spatiality of *Dasein* possible. The insight saves one from not seeing or erasing this structure which erasure is not ontologically but "metaphysically" motivated in the naive opinion that a human being is first of all a spirit thing, and then is afterwards inserted "into" space ... Human beings "are" not and then have a relation of being to the "world" that they occasionally give themselves. *Dasein* is never "first of all" an entity that is free-of-being-in, that then gets in the mood to take on a "relation" to the world. (*SuZ*, p. 56)

By rejecting Husserl's level ontology, Heidegger also rejects the coherence of the idea of a subject that might have no spatial world to relate to but its own solipsistic, notional world. This idea is ultimately the key to Heidegger's rejection of Husserl's Cartesianism.

On Husserl's view, the world is ultimately constituted in private consciousness through the constitution of objects of perceptual consciousness. Everything else, for instance tools or "objects of use," has an existence that is parasitic on such perceptual objects and our valuations of them. And the perceptual objects are ultimately comprehensible in terms of their position in an environment that can be understood in a methodologically solipsistic way. Husserl insists that "first of all the world according to its *kernel* is a world that sensibly appears and is character ized as 'occurrent' ('vorhanden'), given and sometimes actually grasped in simple intuitions of experience. The ego finds itself related to this world of experience in new acts, for instance in valuing acts, in acts of approbation and disapprobation" (*Ideas* ii, section 50, p. 186).

Husserl insists, to be sure, that "by bracketing the world nothing is lost, but world knowledge is won as something ultimately justified" (*First Philosophy*, Hua 8 (1923), pp. 275, 279). He maintains that the problem that the phenomenological reduction does not allow one to "return to the world" is spurious (p. 479). The difference between our representation of the world and the world itself disappears at the limit of an all-inclusive notion of intersubjectivity (p. 480). Even this account does not alter the basic framework in which Husserl thinks of experience. We begin with private perceptual experiences and work our way out to a world that we share with other subjects, and then, in principle, we are able to work our way back to the private world of our own immediate experience.

It is in this sense that approaching the intentional by means of phenomenologically reduced experience involves a theoretical modification of the original experience of the intentional which amounts to a distortion of the nature of the intentional. To be sure, this objection falls short if it is based on the claim that Husserl fails to recognize that the theoretical take on intentionality is a modification of the more original pre-theoretical way in which we intentionally relate to the world.[12] Heidegger's objection is best understood as the claim that Husserl gives even the pre-theoretical take on the world of original intentionality a theoretical interpretation by thinking of it in terms of a level structure with private perceptual experiences, and even, ultimately, sensations, as its basis.

Against Husserl's basically perceptual and intuitive model of self-presence, he argues that we are present to ourselves "not and never primarily as *object* of intuition and intuitive determination, of mere becoming and having acquaintance, but *Dasein* is *there* (*da*) for itself in

---

[12] Ludwig Landgrebe, *Phänomenologie und Metaphysik* (Hamburg: Meiner Verlag, 1949), notes that Heidegger's tendency to treat Husserl's notion of intentionality as if it consisted merely of theoretical acts that are directed at objects involves an unfair distortion that serves to make Heidegger's own position seem more plausible and distinctive.

the how of its most authentic being (*eigensten Seins*)."[13] Our existence is best understood when we are not explicitly directing our attention at some "object," but rather simply living out our lives in a context in which we move with competence.[14] While many of Heidegger's objections seem to be unfair to Husserl, he is clearly right that, for Husserl, the perceptual object is the original source of all truth. Heidegger maintains that this perceptual object is something that only manifests itself to us in a "certain kind of only-just-looking at the world" in which the "primary given world and experienced world is in a certain way closed out" (*GA* 20, p. 265). It is not just that the perceptual object is presented to us in a way that, in principle, is independent of its actual environment. It is also that when we interpret something as a perceptual object we are already giving it a construal that is highly theoretical. The interpretation of what we experience as an object of perception masks the actual primacy of our interested emotional approach to whatever we encounter in the world. This encourages us to think of emotions, and *pro* and *contra* attitudes as addenda to objects purely perceived, whereas, in fact, the pure object of perception is itself an abstraction from the constitutive set of concerns that make each of our worlds what it is for us.

Heidegger's rejection of the primacy of perceptual presence has not always been recognized even by perceptive interpreters of Heidegger. Thus Frederick Olafson argues not only that Heidegger seeks a "replacement of the traditional psychological apparatus by a concept of presence," but also that "perception is the foundational fact for a philosophical account of presence."[15] Here Olafson falsely assimilates Heidegger's project to that of Husserl and Merleau-Ponty.[16] For, even though Heidegger thinks that some general notion of presence is required in order to make sense of the way we understand the world, he originally rejects the whole idea of a presence-based account of understanding because of the tendency

---

[13] *Ontology: Hermeneutics of Facticity* (Bloomington: Indiana University Press, 1995), *GA* 63 (1923), p. 7.

[14] *The Metaphysical Foundations of Logic Starting from Leibniz* (Bloomington: University of Indiana Press, 1984), *GA* 21 (1925–1926), pp. 146–147.

[15] Frederick Olafson, *What is a Human Being?: A Heideggerian View* (New York: Cambridge, 1995), pp. 14 and 87.

[16] For Merleau-Ponty's advocacy of the primacy of perception, see "The Primacy of Perception and its Philosophical Consequences," in Maurice Merleau-Ponty, *The Primacy of Perception* (Evanston: Northwestern University Press), pp. 12–42.

for it to give pride of place to the kind of momentary snapshot view of reality to be had from visual perception. Heidegger sees this as the underlying difficulty in Husserl's whole epistemology and metaphysics. When he later accepts the importance of presence in understanding being, it is a notion of presence that is neutral with respect to the distinction between past, present, and future.

CHAPTER 6

Heidegger on the nature of significance

This chapter consists of three parts. In the first part, I discuss Heidegger's analysis of language. According to this analysis of language, we are able to articulate our understanding and affectedness by our environment through language. In the second part, I turn to the way Heidegger's account of truth provides the basis for a general theory of significance ("Bedeutsamkeit") that is, in turn, the basis for a theory of non-linguistic and linguistic meaning. Truth is the condition for the possibility of the concerns we have as human beings. These concerns structure our understanding of the world in a way that is incomprehensible independently of the spatial world in which we move as agents. Our concerns provide a holistic pattern of significance that cannot be understood in a methodologically solipsistic manner, although we must engage in a kind of existential disengagement to fully appreciate them. The pattern of significance that governs us as agents in the spatial and temporal world is, in turn, the basis for Heidegger's account of sense ("Sinn") and meaning ("Bedeutung").

In the third part of the chapter, I turn to a discussion of the breakdown of the holistic structure of significance that first reveals to us that very functional structure of significance. The breakdown of significance at the same time leaves a place for an account of nature that is independent of what we care about and provides a way for Heidegger to provide a revised version of Husserl's phenomenological reduction which side-steps Husserl's commitment to methodological solipsism.

LANGUAGE AND SIGNIFICANCE

When, in *Being and Time*, Heidegger describes human beings (or "Dasein") as "being-in-the-world," the relation that obtains between human beings and their world is not an accidental one. As Heidegger makes explicit, the world in which *Dasein* exists is not simply a collection of objects, but a "totality of relations ... [which] we call *significance*" (*SuZ*, p. 87). This totality of relations is "disclosed beforehand with a certain intelligibility [*Verständlichkeit*]" (*SuZ*, p. 86). Elsewhere Heidegger writes that the world which is the background against which humans project their possibilities has *meaning* or *sense* (*Sinn*) and that meaning or sense is "that wherein the intelligibility of anything is sustained" (*SuZ*, p. 151). The world is, from the outset, something intelligible and significant to human beings. It is not, as other philosophical models might have it, something which might turn out to be unintelligible to us. Heidegger is willing to concede that nature might be unintelligible to us, but nature manifests itself in our shared world only as what is intelligible to human beings. The thesis of the immediate intelligibility of our surroundings is crucial to Heidegger's philosophical project.

Heidegger seeks to ground the idea of the immediate intelligibility of our surroundings in the constitutive role of truth in our existence. Like verificationist and truth-conditional analyses of meaning, Heidegger takes the notion of truth to be the primitive term of a theory of meaning. But against the traditional candidates for truth such as the coherence of beliefs, or the correspondence of beliefs to facts about the world, Heidegger maintains that the function of truth is to disclose the world to us (*SuZ*, p. 223). This disclosure of the world to us is a constitutive feature of being human. On this view, to be human is to have at least sufficient understanding to be mistaken about something. To regard oneself as mistaken about something one must have some understanding that a norm applies to oneself. In understanding what is here from what is there and what is now from what is then, as humans do, or rather *Dasein* does, one already has some understanding of the context in which one exists and in which one is able competently to engage in various activities. This understanding of context provides the basis for understanding the application of norms to oneself and to other human beings.

Now a statement is true if and only if it discovers what it purports to discover or rather discloses things as they are themselves. This ability of statements to discover the way the world is depends itself on our ability to understand things in a sense that is not yet articulated in the propositional form of a statement or assertion: "a statement about ... is only true because dealing with ... [*der Umgang mit* ...] already has a certain truth" (*GA* 26, p. 158). In dealing with something, one already understands it in some way. One is thus already giving it some meaning for oneself. This suggests that Heidegger thinks of truth on the pragmatist model of what allows us to get on in our environment.[1] There is some truth to this view, although it would be a mistake to think that truth reduces to what works. Truth is rather the condition for the possibility of recognizing what works. Thus, meaning is not constituted by the evidence that would make a certain statement or mode of behavior true. One cannot take evidence to consist in the necessity of the possibility of recognizing practical activity to be successful or unsucessful.[2] For many forms of activity, such as contemplation, are not strictly speaking practical even though they have some role to play in our self-determination.

Truth extends beyond practical activity to anything that we can understand, be emotionally affected by, or articulate through discourse. Discourse is a basic factor in constituting our world, together with the way we are affected by our moods (and other emotions) and the way in which we develop a project that determines our existence through the way in which we understand our environment and ourselves (*SuZ*, p. 161). Discourse, along with affectedness, and understand ing, are conditions for the very possibility of human existence because they constitute the basic ways in which entities of any kind, and being itself, have truth for us, that is, are disclosed to us. While the way we are affected by our environment reaches beyond the shared domain of public interaction to a more basic experience of nature and of ourselves, discourse is critical in articulating what we understand and how we are affected by nature and by our own sense of who we are.

The earlier Heidegger ascribes a constitutive role in human existence to language, although language does not come fully into its own in his philosophy until after his so-called turn. In the "Letter on Humanism," Heidegger maintains that language is "the house of being" in which human beings dwell.[3] But even in *Being and Time*

---

[1] The priority of this prepredicative dealing with the environment relative to propositional thought is emphasized in particular in his lectures on *Logik, die Frage nach der Wahrheit, GA* 21, pp. 144–152.

[2] This is the way Mark Okrent attempts to establish that Heidegger is a verificationist about meaning in his *Heidegger's Pragmatism* (Ithaca: Cornell, 1988), pp. 127–128.

[3] *Martin Heidegger: Basic Writings* (New York: Harper and Row, 1977), p. 193, *GA* 9, p. 313.

Heidegger thinks that there would be no experience as we know it without language. Language is supposed to be based on discourse ("Rede"). Heidegger makes matters somewhat confusing by giving primacy to "Rede" ("discourse") over "Sprache" (normally "language") in *Being and Time*. This initially suggests that he means to privilege communication relative to understanding *in foro interno*. But his use of the term "Sprache" is actually quite misleading. By "Sprache" he means "speech" not the more general notion of "language": "The outspokenness of discourse [*Rede*] is language [*die Sprache*]" (*SuZ*, p. 161). Heidegger seems to use "Sprache" to refer to externalized speech, whereas discourse or *Rede* is something that need not be uttered: "For the most part, discourse is expressed by being spoken out, and has always been so expressed; it is language" (*SuZ*, p. 167). It would be a mistake to conclude from this that discourse is a form of private language that need not be communicable to others: "speaking *Dasein* speaks *out* not because it is first of all cut off from the outside as something 'inner,' but because as understanding being-in-the-world it is already outside" (*SuZ*, p. 162).

Discourse depends on some prior understanding and emotional response to one's environment that it articulates. As Heidegger puts it, discourse "determines" understanding and affectedness in an equally basic way (*SuZ*, p. 133). This does not mean that there is, in fact, understanding or emotional response in human existence that is not structured by language. For our understanding and emotional responses are themselves grounded in the way in which we interpret what we experience. It is in terms of discourse that we articulate the way things are for us. This includes our emotional responses to our environment as well as any understanding of anything as thus and such. The importance of discourse lies in the articulative capacity that it brings to pre-predicative understanding of the kind involved in our use of equipment and our understanding of what our life is about.

Heidegger thinks that it is a mistake to identify understanding something as thus and such or even discourse with predication. This leads him to distinguish between "hermeneutic" and "apophantic" interpretation (*SuZ*, p. 158). Predication is apophantic interpretation. In predicating some (property) F of some (individual) a, we must have an understanding of the individual and property involved. This is revealed (hence apophansis) by the interpretation. This articulation of understanding in propositional form is, however, only a special case of a more general hermeneutic ability. Predicative interpretation is parasitic on a more general and basic way we have of interpreting things that is not inherently propositional in character. Predication is possible because we are able to interpret our world pre-predicatively in pursuing our projects and in using equipment to realize our ends. Any use of equipment requires an understanding of what is being used. This involves a pre-predicative interpretation of that equipment as being thus and such. This interpretation of what something can be used for can be articulated in propositional form, but need not be so articulated.

Discourse underlies interpretation because it is the articulation of what we can understand (*SuZ*, p. 161). Since Heidegger does not restrict his claim to "apophantic" interpretation, we must assume that he intends to claim that even "hermeneutic" interpretation of the kind that is characteristic of our ability to work with equipment involves competence in discourse. Our ability to articulate things in language thus gives us the capacity to understand and use equipment even though such use of equipment does not involve any explicit use of language or of assertions. It is in terms of this interpretative ability that we are able to then interpret what we encounter in terms of the way it can contribute as circumstances, means, or ends to our projects. This circumstance, means, ends structure is what provides us with a general context of significance in terms of which we can interpret things and in terms of which we can then understand the sense and meaning of linguistic expressions. This suggests the view defended by Charles Guignon that the source of significance is to be understood as language: "What is the source of this most primordial level of intelligibility? Heidegger says that it is 'discursiveness' or 'speech' ('Rede')."[4]

Guignon distinguishes between an instrumental and a constitutive conception of language. He then argues that Heidegger is committed to both of these conceptions and is guilty of inconsistency in virtue of this dual commitment. Heidegger undeniably thinks that language is sometimes an instrument. It is our instrumental use of statements ("Aussagen") that accounts according to his story for the tendency to understand truth as a correspondence relation between two sets of entities (*SuZ*, p. 224). This instrumental use of language presupposes a prior understanding of entities. That understanding may itself be

---

[4] Charles Guignon, *Heidegger and the Problem of Knowledge* (Indianapolis: Hackett, 1983), p. 111.

articulated in language. Guignon does not understand the instrumentalist conception of language in this way. For him, it consists instead in the thesis that "there is a prior grasp of the nonsemantic field of significance of the world which becomes the basis for gaining mastery of the language."[5] This seems to me to be doubly mistaken as an interpretation of Heidegger. It is certainly odd to talk of a nonsemantic field of significance ("Bedeutsamkeit"), if not contradictory. Significance involves an understanding of that in which one moves as what it is (*SuZ*, p. 87). This involves an articulation and interpretation of what one is involved in. While this interpretation need not be predicative, it is based on discourse. Heidegger does not think of language primarily as an instrument. He cannot given his view that language or rather discourse is one of the conditions for the possibility of human existence. He quite explicitly refers to language as having the character of *Dasein* (*SuZ*, p. 167). Heidegger does think that understanding is primarily non-propositional and pre-predicative in nature. It is based on our ability to orient ourselves in our environment. This environment is, however, constituted for us by the significance or meaningfulness of the entities and relations between them in terms of which we orient ourselves. Such significance is based on our ability to structure our environment in terms of the projects that we pursue. The world presents itself to us as a pattern of circumstances and means to the realization of the various projects that contribute to our basic project of living a certain. This understanding of entities and the relations between entities can express itself in terms of statements with a propositional structure.

According to the constitutive view, as Guignon understands it, language gives rise to and makes our full-blown sense of the world possible. Guignon's contrast between the instrument and constitutive views of language is somewhat unclear, since one can acknowledge the possibility that language is responsible for our *full-blown* sense of the world, while arguing that language itself presupposes the ability to understand meanings that are logically prior to language. Moreover, one can deny that all meaning is expressible without remainder in propositions or predicative sentences while still maintaining that meanings are available only to those who understand a language. This seems to me to be Heidegger's actual position. In general,

[5] Ibid., p. 118.

Guignon fails to distinguish a weak from a strong notion of the way in which language may be constitutive of our sense of world. For Heidegger, language is "more than one kind of equipment at our disposal for dealing with the world."[6] Language is a constitutive factor in human existence. This is a weak notion of constitutivity that is sufficient for rejecting the idea that language is a mere instrument. This constitutive role in human experience accrues to speech because it is understood by Heidegger to be the "articulation of intelligibility" (*SuZ*, p. 161). It does not, however, follow from this that language or discourse is the source of intelligibility and significance.

Heidegger thinks of discourse, and indeed of all language, as the expression of meaning and thus of an understanding which is not just articulable, but also actually articulates some interpretation of what is presented to us in our world: "The intelligibility of being-in-the-world – an intelligibility which goes with an affectedness ('Befindlichkeit') – *speaks out as discourse*. The totality-of-meaning belonging to intelligibility is *put into words*. To meanings, words accrue" (*SuZ*, p. 161). Guignon's awareness of this later claim that meanings accrue to words and that discourse cannot be strongly constitutive of meaning and intelligibility leads him to attribute inconsistency to Heidegger. But instead one should reject Guignon's strong constitutivity thesis and its claim that language generates "the template" through which we understand ourselves and the world.[7] The early Heidegger's view on the relation of language and significance is rather the converse of this strong constitutivity thesis. We can understand language, because we are the kinds of beings who exist by projecting a pattern of significance in terms of which we can understand the entities in our world. This view of understanding does not commit one to think that one first has an understanding of pre-linguistic meanings and then associates those meanings with words. There is a priority asserted here, but it is a logical priority, or a temporal priority only in Heidegger own distinctive way of understanding temporality.

We can understand language because we are the kind of creatures who are able to form a sense of what we are doing when we are orienting ourselves in the world: "Language itself has *Dasein*'s kind of being. There is no language in general as some kind of free-floating

----

[6] Ibid., p. 119.   [7] Ibid., p. 120.

nature in which the various individual "existences" would partake. Every language, like *Dasein* itself, is *historical* in its very being."[8] This historicity of language derives from the temporality that is the ultimate source of significance. It tends, according to Heidegger, to be disguised to us because of the uniformity of language engendered by standard linguistic practices in our day-to-day involvements with others. These linguistic practices are themselves but a segment of the totality of practices in which we are involved in everyday existence.

THE STRUCTURE OF SIGNIFICANCE

At a certain level of generality, Heidegger embeds his account of meaning in the framework of the common-sense psychology that governs our everyday understanding of things. We understand human emotions, thoughts, desires, and actions in terms of the way in which they fit together in a coherent account of how they promote the overall ends that makes that person who she or he is. This does not mean that meanings are simply reducible to psychological states. For those psychological states are themselves ones that we ascribe to ourselves and others on the assumption that the human being in question is justified in responding to her environment in the way that she does given the way that environment presents itself to her. This means that where behavior or beliefs or emotions do not seem to be justified in the light of the way that human being views her environment, we look for an underlying explanation that would help us understand and thus to justify that behavior, belief or emotional response.

The ends that a human being pursues, structure the way that individual understands her environment. There is thus no level of meaning for Heidegger that is genuinely independent of our interests and more particularly the end of self-determination. This does not mean that, in principle, it is not possible to engage in disinterested inquiry. But such disinterested inquiry must itself be motivated by goals that a human being has set for herself: "*Dasein* must give itself to understand its own ability-to-be. It gives itself to mean how things stand with its ability-to-be. The totality of these relations, i.e. everything which belongs to the structure of the totality with which *Dasein* can give itself to understand anything, is what we call

---

[8] *History of the Concept of Time*, p. 373.

significance. This is the structure of that which we refer to as *world in the strict ontological sense*" (*GA* 24, p. 419).

One understands one's own emotions, beliefs, and desires and those of others only in terms of the way in which they track the environment in which one pursues one's projects. Because we relate to the world in terms of our own possibilities for self-determination, the way we understand the world is structured by our interests, and these interests cannot be understood in complete abstraction from the actual spatial world to which we belong. The characteristic feature of significance is its irreducibly contextual nature. It displays itself in all of the forms of behavior through which we are able as human beings to understand ourselves in relation to the world, but is not exhausted by any of them. We are supposed to understand what equipment, signs, words, things, and human beings are only in the context of their relations to other tools, signs, words, things, and human beings:

> Since *Dasein* is moreover essentially determined by the fact that it *speaks, expresses itself, discourses, and as speaker discloses, discovers, and lets things be seen*, it is thereby understandable that there are such things as have meanings. It is not as if there were first verbal sounds that in time were furnished with meanings. On the contrary, what is primary is being in the world, that is, concerned understanding and being in the context of meanings ... meanings are to be understood on the basis of significance and this in turn means only on the basis of being-in-the-world. (*GA* 20, pp. 287–288)

Whatever is significant is supposed to be significant in virtue of a certain determinate relation to other possible entities in the world. The context of significance is sufficiently broad that it includes the very meaning of what it is to be.

Heidegger regards his notion of significance as the basis for an understanding of meaning and language. But he does not restrict significance to the understanding of language. Anything is significant for Heidegger that can be understood in some way at all. Thus, not only words, but also things, tools, and persons have their own distinctive form of significance. Anything that is understood as being thus and such at all is significant for us. This reflects Heidegger's conviction that understanding language and linguistic meaning is merely a special case of the kind of know-how we require in order to get around in the world. This notion of sense is not restricted to words, statements, concepts or thoughts. But it does involve an articulable understanding of something as thus and such (*SuZ*, p. 149).

The context of significance is inherently holistic. Heidegger never offers a recognizable argument in favor of such holism, but it can be teased together from his position. We have no sharp way of distinguishing our beliefs about the world from the interests that we pursue, just as our understanding of our own interests reflects our understanding of the way the world is. Any effort to distinguish individual semantic vehicles marks an abstraction from the very conditions in our beliefs and desires that give those semantic vehicles their cognitive significance. The key here is Heidegger's thesis that any kind of know-how involves an implicit understanding of a general context that forms and guides one's interests: "I grasp it so that I have already gone around it, I understand it from what it is used for."[9] He refers to this as one's prepossession ("Vorhabe") of the context. This is then interpreted by one's interests in a certain way (preview – "Vorsicht") according to a certain contextual frame-work (preconception – "Vorgriff") (*SuZ*, p. 150). The idea that interpretation is always guided by this understanding of context leads Heidegger to his famous thesis of a "hermeneutical circle." It is because any understanding of sense or meaning involves the interpretative "pre-structure" of prepossession, preview, and pre-conception that we cannot understand sense or meaning in isolation from a more general context.

To think of sense as constituted by a general context of under-standing that is constitutive of both the self and world is to think of "sense as the formal existential framework of the disclosure belong-ing to the understanding ... not a property attached to an entity, lying 'behind' it, or hovering somewhere as an 'intermediate realm'" (*SuZ*, p. 151). At first, this view seems simply to reproduce Husserl's move toward idealism. In an effort to make our ability to understand sense intelligible, we reject the idea that it is independent of the normative principles governing our interpretations. But Heidegger claims more than this. He argues that we cannot make sense of sense primarily as "the content" of a judgment or the proposition asserted by that judgment (*SuZ*, p. 154). The "content" of a proposition is only intelligible in terms of its relation to a context of interpretation. "The [hermeneutic] 'circle' in understand-ing belongs to the structure of sense" (*SuZ*, p. 153). This context of significance must be supplied by our engagements in the world.

[9] *GA* 21 (1925–1926), p. 147.

These engagements in the world are public from the outset, because they conform to norms of behavior that are rooted in public roles. But they are not merely public. They are also rooted in an affective relationship to nature that transcends even the publicity of social constraints: "Nature is originally revealed in *Dasein* through its existing as affected-attuned *amongst* entities."[10] If this is true, then it is impossible to offer a "purely immanent" methodologically solipsistic analysis of sense.

Heidegger refers to the systematic way in which our interests govern our actions and, indeed, our understanding of anything at all as their referential context ("Verweisungszusammenhang"). This referential context gives us a pre-linguistic understanding of entities as what they are. It also accounts for the holistic character of significance. A context of significance is displayed in and presupposed by our ability to get about in the world and deal with our environment. This context of significance is constituted by the systematic connections between our interests and the different parts of one's environment. These connections exist in virtue of the various aspects of human action. Significance is constituted by the connections between context, goals, means, and ultimate ends that are required for all human action. The referential context is most directly apparent in the way in which we are able pre-linguistically to organize the means of achieving our goals in such a way that we can move in action from one means to another almost without interruption, until there is a breakdown of the normal means–ends relations with which we are accustomed.

One's understanding of meaning, one's understanding of anything in one's environment, is first of all an understanding of what it is useful for. This implicit understanding of something in terms of the use to which it can be put gives that something a reference to something else for which it can be used. This implicit reference to potential uses or goals for which the item in question can serve as a means, also involves an implicit context of use in which that item can serve that purpose. Moreover, the purposes in question are ones that are structured by their relation to the selves that understand the potential uses to which items can be put and are the ultimate ends of their use.

---

[10] "On the Essence of Ground," *The Essence of Reasons* (Evanston: Northwestern University Press, 1969), pp. 80–83, *GA* 9, pp. 155–156n.

Entities that function as instruments or equipment in this means–end relation are ontologically distinctive and irreducible to any other kind of entities. Such tools or instruments are to be understood as being "ready to hand" or equipment in their very being. The connection between ends and means serves to give the instruments which we use to pursue our ends a necessary relatedness to each other. Thus, Heidegger claims that "taken strictly, there 'is' no such thing as a tool. To the being of any tool there always belongs a totality of tools, in which it can be this tool that it is. Tools are essentially 'something in order to' ..." (*SuZ*, pp. 97, 352). As a means to the accomplishment of certain tasks, a tool cannot exist except in relation to other means to the accomplishment of more or less closely related tasks. Any tool or piece of equipment is a potential means to the attainment of one of our goals that is encountered as a tool in a context of potential means to the realization of one's interests. One's natural environment is also included in this pattern of interests, since it is quite relevant to the pursuit of those interests (*SuZ*, pp. 70–71). The goals in terms of which one understands one's environment may, in turn, themselves involve the construction of the means to the attainment of further ends.

Goals together with the means and the circumstances to attain them are structured by the sense of who one is to be. This ground project is what Heidegger refers to as the "for the sake of which." Thus the ground project that is that of forming a certain self is what provides the basis for the holistic significance of the world. There is compelling textual support for this idea of the dependence of the significance on the end of self-determination: "The understanding of significance as the disclosedness of each world is grounded ... in the understanding of the for the sake of which, from which all discovery of a context of use is derived" (*SuZ*, p. 297). Indeed, Heidegger maintains that the "context of reference in significance ... is 'tied' to a for the sake of which" (*SuZ*, p. 192). This is because the context of references in terms of which human beings move in their implicit understanding of how it is with them in the world is determined by how they implicitly or explicitly understand what they want to be: "The for the sake of which has this universal scope as what is constitutive of the selfhood of *Dasein*, in other words: it is that, *in terms of which* <*woraufzu*> *Dasein* as that which transcends, transcends ... In other words: the world, primarily characterized by the for the sake of which is the original totality of that which *Dasein* as free gives itself to understand" (*GA* 26, pp. 246–247).

Both the handiness of tools and the existence of the self are essentially characterized by a holistic pattern of significance structured by our cares. However, this pattern of significance, that allows us to understand language and the world, is subject to breakdown. In this case, we are no longer able simply to deal with whatever we have to in our environment as a matter of course. We are forced to reflect on how things work, because they no longer work as they are wont to. This is what motivates reflection on the pattern of significance in which we normally move unreflectively. Entities may be encountered even where this pattern of significance has broken down. In fact, to understand the nature (being) of the entities with which we are familiar, a breakdown of significance must occur. For it is only in response to an interruption in the pattern of significance that we engage in reflection on the nature of things with which we are otherwise familiar. This is true even of the self that tends to be treated purely instrumentally in everyday life. The self is only apparent to us when the contribution it makes to the structure of experience is disrupted.

In Heidegger's reinterpretation of the phenomenological reduction, the being of entities is revealed to us not by reflection on the data of consciousness, but by a breakdown of the general context of significance in which we move in everyday existence (Husserl's natural attitude). It is when entities fail to behave as we expect them to behave that we are led to attempt to understand what they are. Tools, for example, fail to work and we thus come to reflect on what they are used for and what they are used with (*SuZ*, pp. 73ff.). The failure of entities such as tools to meet our normative expectations leads us to consider the normative context of significance in which we otherwise move pre-reflectively. This is even true of the existence of other human beings. When we are alone, we understand the way in which we are normally together with other human beings in virtue of the very breakdown of this everyday context of significance through the absence of other human beings (*SuZ*, p. 120). But Heidegger takes the idea of a phenomenological reduction a step further when he argues that in experiencing anxiety we come to focus on our own individual existence in the world as everything else that exists in the world is deprived of its significance for us: "Dasein is isolated ("vereinzelt"), but *as* being-in-the-world" (*SuZ*, p. 189). It is through this sequence of experiences that we become aware of the world, and being in general, as a problem. Heidegger replaces Husserl's methodological solipsism with an "existential solipsism" (*SuZ*, p. 188). But both philosophers require a turn inward to attain an authentic understanding of what things mean.[11]

From Husserl's point of view, Heidegger's claims about human existence are only philosophical to the extent that they involve a bracketing of the existence assumptions of the natural attitude. To some extent, Heidegger accepts this interpretation of his fundamental ontology as based on the phenomenological reduction.[12] In taking the meaning of being to be the central topic of the phenomenological reduction, Heidegger remains within Husserl's conception of what counts as a phenomenon. In some more general sense, Heidegger also uses a form of the eidetic reduction. While he rejects the Platonism in Husserl's notion of eidetic, he is committed to providing an account of the most general conditions of human existence (so-called existentials) as well as the most general conditions (categories) governing the being of other types of entities.

Heidegger's revision in the methodology of the phenomenological reduction leads Husserl to the conclusion that Heidegger does not understand the nature of the phenomenological reduction.[13] Although it is debatable whether he fails to understand it, Heidegger certainly rejects the reduction in the Cartesian form in which

---

[11] Some of the parallels between the Heideggerian and Husserlian conceptions of the phenomenological reduction have been noted in an interesting article by Rudolf Bernet, "Phenomenological Reduction and the Double Life," in Theodore Kisiel and John van Buren (eds.), *Reading Heidegger from the Start: Essays in his Earliest Thought* (Albany, N.Y.: State University of New York Press, 1994), pp. 245–268. However, by taking a very late version of Husserl's account of the reduction actually formulated by Fink to respond to Heidegger's objections to the Husserlian phenomenological reduction, Bernet confronts Heidegger's alternative account of the reduction with a version of the reduction that is already revised to meet Heidegger's main objection that Husserl has ignored the proper topic of the reduction, the world itself.

[12] According to Jean Beaufret, *Dialogue avec Heidegger* 3 (Paris: Éditions de Minuit: 1974), p. 125, in 1947 Heidegger told him that the phenomenological reduction frees one's attention to being by bracketing the existence of entities. This claim is consistent with the position that Heidegger develops in the *Basic Problems of Phenomenology*.

[13] In a letter to R. Ingarten of December 26, 1927, Husserl claims that Heidegger, despite his "genius," has not completely understood the reduction, *Briefe an Roman Ingarten* (The Hague: Martinus Nijhoff, 1968), p. 43.

Husserl presents it, especially in the *Ideas*. Like Merleau-Ponty after him, Heidegger maintains that a phenomenological reduction, as Husserl understands it, is, in fact, an impossibility.[14] Heidegger argues that the phenomenological reduction, as Husserl understands it, prevents Husserl from coming to terms with the nature of the intentionality to which the phenomenological reduction is to provide us access. The reduction brackets the very reality of the intentional in order to be able to understand this reality as it presents itself in absolute, immanent consciousness (*GA* 20, p. 149ff.). In the process, it also abstracts from the individuality of my experiences and investigates their nature as act and object types.

In place of the phenomenological reduction as Husserl understands it, namely as a shift from the natural attitude in which we relate to a world of things and persons existing outside of us to the way objects are constituted as objects of a transcendental consciousness, Heidegger suggests that the reduction be understood as the shift from an understanding of particular entities to an understanding of the nature of their being.[15]

While Heidegger rejects Husserl's claim that the world might turn out to be unintelligible to us (*Ideas*, section 49), he introduces a distinction between the world that is constituted by the pattern of significance in which human beings move, and nature that reproduces the Husserlian distinction between bracketed and unbracketed existence at one remove:

Nature is what is in principle explainable and to be explained because it is in principle incomprehensible [*unverständlich*]. It is *the incomprehensible pure and simple.* And it is the incomprehensible because it is the *"unworlded" world*, insofar as we take nature in this extreme sense of the entity as it is disclosed in physics ... As the incomprehensible it is likewise the entity that simply does not have the character of *Dasein* at all, while *Dasein* is the entity that is in principle comprehensible. Since understanding belongs to its being as being-in-the-world, world is comprehensible to *Dasein* insofar as it is encountered in the character of significance. (*GA* 20, p. 298)[16]

[14] "The most important lesson which the reduction teaches us is the impossibility of a complete reduction," Maurice Merleau-Ponty, *The Phenomenology of Perception*, C. Smith trans. (New York: Humanities Press, 1962), p. xiv.

[15] *The Basic Problems of Phenomenology*, GA 24 (1926), pp. 31ff.

[16] The claim that nature is inherently unintelligible may also be found in *SuZ*, p. 337: "All explanation is rooted as understanding discovery of what is incomprehensible in the primary understanding of *Dasein*." Earlier in the same work he also insists that "all entities belonging to a mode of being that is not the kind of *Dasein* must be understood as *nonsensical*, essentially devoid of sense" (*SuZ*, p. 152).

Heidegger extends the phenomenological reduction to the world, but beyond the world there is a nature that transcends the world of our significant engagements and threatens us with the possibility of unintelligibility. This contingency of human existence is the ultimate source of anxiety.

While Heidegger pushes the exploration of significance to our being-in-the-world, he can find access to this being-in-the-world only by a process in which our everyday understanding of ourselves is suspended by the prospect of the very possibility of the insignificance of the world. But where Husserl thinks that the process of reflection is what brings us to the distance from our everyday engagements which makes it possible for us to understand the world and the being of the entities in the world authentically, Heidegger argues that it is anxiety in the face of the possibility that these engagements might ultimately be based on a nature that is inherently meaningless that leads to an authentic understanding of oneself and the world in which one moves (*SuZ*, p. 343). It is this authentic understanding of oneself and others that then paves the way for an understanding of one's own existence and then ultimately of other modes of being. But the question of what it is to be only arises in the face of astonishment at the very existence of a world that is intelligible to us.

Heidegger refers to entities other than the self that can only be encountered through the breakdown of significance as present at hand. These entities are just there, they do not have to have any necessary connections to each other. In this way, they are unlike the entities that we understand in terms of the holistic pattern of significance that makes our world what it is. Presence at hand is the way Heidegger characterizes nature or rather natural entities.[17] The presence at hand of nature has two sides to it. On the one hand, nature is something that is independent of the world. On the other hand, nature is a modification of the way in which we understand what is handy. I shall take up this modification of being ready to hand first. We do not come to regard entities as "things" until the pattern of significance to be found in our instrumental dealings with the world is broken down by a tool that fails to function. Then we

---

[17] An excellent discussion of the status of nature and its relation to presence at hand in Heidegger's thought may be found in Joseph Fell, "The Familiar and the Strange: On the Limits of Praxis in the Early Heidegger," in Hubert Dreyfus and Harrison Hall (eds.), *Heidegger: A Critical Reader* (Oxford: Blackwell, 1992), pp. 65–80.

come to see it as simply there, without connection to other tools, since it is no longer embedded in the functional pattern of significance constitutive of the work-world. At the same time, this breakdown of significance allows us to see that systematic pattern of intelligibility that governs our understanding as such for the first time. We come to be aware of the normativity of the constraints governing our practices precisely through the failure of our responses to satisfy the norms encapsulated in those constraints. It is indeed only the possibility of error that makes it plausible to think of those norms as making it possible for us to understand or recognize tools.

The role of language as a tool is crucial here. Language and speech provide us with the means of articulating truths about the entities in our world in such a way that those truths are communicable to others. We use statements as tools to express our understanding of entities in the world to other persons (*SuZ*, p. 155). These tools are successful in communication to the extent that they depend on an average, context-independent understanding of the world. But therein lies also the tendency for them to replace the perspective that is unique to me or you with this average understanding. Replacement of one's distinctive understanding by an average understanding encourages one to think of the relation between statements and the entities in the world in a different way. This average understanding does not require the presence of the entities about which some truth is to be communicated (*SuZ*, p. 155). One comes to think of the semantic relation between statements and the entities of which they purport to be true as something autonomous from the conditions under which statements and their objects are understood by us.

This tendency to isolate the objects understood from one's understanding of them is encouraged by the breakdown of language as a tool of communication. Communication depends on at least some understanding of shared truths about the environment. Where communication breaks down, one searches for the source of error. This suggests the idea that there are objects to which our statements may or may not correspond. By using statements to refer to individual entities that are in doubt, we come to think that there is a correspondence relation between statements and entities, such that each is what it is in abstraction from the other, and in abstraction from other entities. In the process the "as" structure of interpretation is modified in a direction away from holistic context of significant relations involved in our prepredicative engagement with our environment (*SuZ*, p. 158).

A molecularist theory of meaning is quite appropriate to a description of the propositions expressed by theoretical statements. Theoretical statements abstract from the pattern of interests in which we move in everyday existence. But such statements are highly abstract ways of expressing an understanding that is itself fundamentally non-propositional in character. Heidegger's defense of meaning holism is based on his rejection of the view that understanding and language can be made intelligible primarily in terms of the grasping or entertaining of propositions or of the statements that express them: "Insofar as the statement (the 'judgment') is based on understanding and represents a derived form of the performance of interpretation, it also 'has' a sense. But this [sense] cannot however be defined as what is to be found 'in' a judgment along with the making of a judgment" (*SuZ*, p. 154). Theoretical propositional statements ("theoretische Aussagesätze") interpret things in a way that abstracts from the global context of significance in terms of which we orient ourselves in the world. This leads Heidegger to claim that theoretical propositions interpret the world in terms of objects which have no essential connection to each other. He expresses this idea in his terminology as the interpretation of entities in the world as occurrent or "present at hand" ("vorhanden").

In thinking of statements in abstraction from the conditions of their use, these statements themselves come to be regarded as objects that may or may not correspond to objects in the world. But there is simply no meaningful way of articulating what the objects would be to which our statements should correspond that is independent of one's understanding of the world. The notion of correspondence adds nothing to the claim that we have discovered the way things are. This leads Heidegger to the view that this correspondence relation between statements or beliefs and objects is really an unfortunate way of construing what is, in fact, the discovery of an entity as it is expressed through a statement. This discovery itself can be thought of as successful only against the background of one's understanding of other entities in the world.

The adequacy or correspondence theory of truth models the way in which we come to think of the entities in our world as objects of theory rather than as instruments for dealing with our world. This theoretical stance, and even the idea of correspondence, have a certain legitimacy. This is easily missed in Heidegger's critique of the correspondence theory of truth. It is legitimate to talk of truth as correspondence where the objects in question are ones that must be somehow understood in abstraction from the world and the pattern of significant relations with which the world is endowed. Heidegger thinks that there is a sense in which nature is radically independent of us. The success of theoretical explanation has its basis in the very autonomy of nature. Theoretical explanation is appropriate to natural entities, since those entities do not themselves have either the character of individuals who understand or even the character of being inherently comprehensible.

Heidegger is skeptical whether nature is really a whole which is logically prior to its parts at all, but he seems to be convinced that in order to understand nature we must think of it in terms of the explanatory goal of systematic unification. This gives human existence and its social practices a radically contingent character. The activities in terms of which we make entities intelligible to ourselves are not able to constitute an independent reality on their own, since they depend on nature for the entities which they make intelligible to us. Nature however is not itself necessarily intelligible to us. The very contingency of nature's intelligibility for us provides an important constraint on the way in which we conceptualize what we experience.[18]

Explanation of objects (the present at hand) in terms of theories is possible, precisely because an object as an object (present at hand) is fundamentally independent of *Dasein* and the context of its significance.[19] This suggests that there might be some meaning after all to the notion of truth as correspondence. A statement could be said to be true, if and only if it corresponds to entities as they are

---

[18] *GA* 20, p. 298. A discussion of this passage may also be found in Robert Dostal, "Time and Phenomenology in Husserl and Heidegger," in Charles Guignon (ed.), *The Cambridge Companion to Heidegger* (New York: Cambridge University Press, 1993), pp. 141–169, p. 163.

[19] Heidegger thinks that there is a sense in which social behavior generates the category of objectively present at hand things, as Robert Brandom suggests in "Heidegger's Categories in *Being and Time*," in Dreyfus and Hall (eds.), <u>Heidegger: A Critical Reader</u>, pp. 45–64. The "category" of such things is dependent on the social practices of science and the procedures of justification associated with that set of practices. But Brandom overstates his case when he claims that "pure presence-at-hand is a philosopher's misunderstanding of the significance of presence-at-hand, and a bad idea," p. 62. This may be a bad idea, but it is Heidegger's bad idea. For Heidegger, nature is something more than whatever a Piercean community of scientific inquirers would tell us that it is.

independent of the context of significance (world) in terms of which we must understand them. The trouble with this notion of correspondence is that it is an empty notion for us. We have no way of saying what entities are except in terms of the way they can be made intelligible to us.

We have no way of grasping what entities are like which is independent of the conditions under which we can discover them to be thus and such. This gives rise to a claim of primacy for interpretation and, in particular, self-interpretation, since such interpretation is the key to the explication of any understanding. It is, indeed, impossible to extricate oneself from the hermeneutic circle, since any understanding one has of anything implicitly involves one's own context of understanding: "Only because there is history, because *Dasein* is itself the primarily historical being, can something like nature be discovered, only for this reason is there natural science" (*GA* 20, p. 356). Heidegger does, however, maintain that we have a non-cognitive access to the independence of nature.[20] This independence of the objects of nature (present at hand entities) from the world, from truth which we can discover, and from being (at least *qua* what is intelligible to us), makes itself felt in the uncanniness of nature, in what has often been described as the sublime. This is an experience of the overwhelming power of nature through a mood which takes hold of us. It is thus an access to nature that is not *per se* propositionally articulated. We experience our lack of being at home in nature in a feeling of the uncanny. Nature is not exhausted in our capacity to make sense of it in terms of language which expresses our own being-in-the-world. This is why Heidegger denies that to be present at hand always means to be a thing (*SuZ*, p. 211). This other sense of presence at hand pulls Heidegger away from the idealistic idea that everything must be as we can only understand it to be. Instead, nature emerges as something that could be radically different from our beliefs about it, as the metaphysical realist maintains. This might seem to conflict with Heidegger's rejection of skepticism. But that rejection of skepticism is predicated

---

[20] "'The force of nature' shows itself as such first when it enters into what human beings are in control of, namely [it shows itself] as that whole of which ultimately human beings are *not* in control and which they are yet tied to and carried by, what is overpowering and which as such *attunes* human beings in their essence, that is in their striving to be, necessarily in this particular way or that. In attunement nature is originally there." *Vom Wesen der Wahrheit* (1931–1932), *GA* 34, p. 237.

on the thesis that human existence always involves some understanding of its world and hence of truth. This does not commit him to the necessity of the possibility for us to understand nature as it is independent of us.

This way in which our understanding of the world is limited is ultimately reflected in the way Heidegger reconstructs the relation between self-deceptive (inauthentic) and self-transparent (authentic) existence. The uncanniness of nature is the basis for the anxiety which Heidegger maintains is the way in which each individual may be brought to terms with the individuality of his or her own existence. In the mood of anxiety, the very being of the world, its holistic significance, is ripped away. Each of us is left with his or her own distinctive existence, and decontextualized natural entities in their bare presence at hand. It is then no longer possible to understand oneself from the other entities or typical behavior patterns of one's world, since the very significance of this world is in question (*SuZ*, p. 187). This is the sense in which Heidegger takes self-interpreta tion to be groundless. It is only through our confrontation with the very meaninglessness of nature that we come to form a distinctive understanding of ourselves as we come to understand the limits of the intelligibility with which social patterns of behavior are able to provide us. Thus the decontextualization of experience turns out paradoxically to be necessary for the realization of the very ideal of authenticity that expresses the fundamental truth about human existence, even though this human existence is essentially contextual.

It is a contingent fact, for Heidegger, that nature is intelligible to us at all.[21] This is why he can refer to nature as meaningless. This does not mean that it cannot have meaning for us, but that it is what it is regardless of whether it has meaning for us or not. It is through this contingency of meaningfulness that we are confronted with the contingency and the bare facticity of our own individual existences,

---

[21] "Innerworldliness does not belong to the being of what is present at hand [*zum Sein des Vorhandenen*], of nature, as a determination of its being, but as a *possible* determination of its being, yet a necessary determination for the possibility of the discoverability of nature," *GA* 24, p. 240. This passage supports Dorothea Frede's insistence that "intelligibility" resides as much in the "things encountered themselves as in the understanding residing in us, and this 'fittingness' is not due to any merit of ours," "The Question of Being: Heidegger's Project," in Charles Guignon (ed.), *The Cambridge Companion to Heidegger*, pp. 42–69, p. 66. Frede seems to think that this view also applies to Heidegger's position in the twenties, although she adduces support for it from Heidegger's later philosophy where being is conceived of as being independent of the self.

indeed of our whole "being-in-the-world." For we then discover that our need to postulate an order of nature which corresponds to our demands for the explanability of nature may be no more than a need which we must satisfy. We cannot, as it were, demonstrate that nature must be as we must understand it to be, for we have no way of understanding it which is independent of the constraints laid down by our own project of coming to terms with what makes us who we are.

Heidegger does not seem to regard it as a contingent fact in the same way that we can understand something as a piece of equipment or someone as a human being. For something to be a tool is, in principle, for it to be intelligible as a piece of equipment and thus to belong to our being-in-the-world as a certain means to the achievement of some possible set of goals. A tool is only a tool insofar as it belongs to the functional context of a work-world in which there are other tools with other functions. In the same way, for someone to be a person, we must be able to take that being to belong, at least potentially, to the space of reasons and thus to our being-in-the-world. This means that we must regard that human being as capable of articulating phrases which, in principle, are intelligible to other human beings. In Heidegger's jargon, human beings are characterized in their very being as being with others.

Nature differs from persons and tools in that its connection to the world in terms of which each of us come to have a more or less distinctive conception of ourselves is a contingent one. This says as much about our notion of a world as it does about nature. But, if it is true that nature need not conform to our rationalizing descriptions in the same way that the world of everyday common-sense psychology must do, then this gives us some justification in being skeptical about the possibility of reconstructing everyday human existence in terms of the theoretical model appropriate to the scientific study of nature. Such an account may even prove to be inadequate to understanding nature itself. The important point is that the contexture of significance in terms of which we make sense of ourselves and others is not sufficiently fine grained to allow us uniquely to individuate the beliefs, desires, and emotional responses we experience or even the means that we use to further our ends. These "objects" cannot be isolated from the background assumptions and interests of the interpreter in the way that Husserl, for one, thought was crucial to providing the basis for a scientific study of intentionality and psychology. If this is true, then we cannot accept the claim that propositional understanding supervenes on an understanding that is directly embedded in our engagements with the world and then go on to argue that the "objects" of pre-propositional understanding are themselves ultimately to be understood in the theoretical terms of propositional understanding.

The pattern of significance that makes the world our shared world does not become apparent to us until it faces some form of local breakdown. This reflects the normative character of significance. As reflective agents, we conform to norms that become obvious to us when we are confronted with some violation of those norms. But Heidegger does not believe that a total breakdown of norms is something that we are in a position to understand. This would violate the very conditions under which interpretation in terms of common-sense psychology operates. He must, indeed, deny the very possibility of such a breakdown, if his claim that the true skeptic would have to commit suicide is to be valid (see *SuZ*, p. 229), for that claim depends on the assumption that human existence without any truth disclosed to it is impossible.

Heidegger's reinterpretation of Husserl's phenomenological reduction bears with it some of the idealist implications of Husserl's own conception of reduction. In Husserl's phenomenological reduction, one brackets the existence of objects that transcend consciousness in order to understand objects as they are constructed by consciousness. For, according to Husserl, all objects insofar as they are knowable by us must be thought of as potential objects of our constructions. This is designed to avoid the epistemic circularity of trying to understand knowledge by appealing to objects that are supposed to be somehow antecedently known. Husserl is a transcendental idealist because he thinks that all objects are potential objects of constructions to be performed by consciousness, and have no existence that is independent of the possibility of such constitution by consciousness.[22]

---

[22] The *Cartesian Meditations* and the *Formal and Transcendental Logic* mark Husserl's official move away from the realist interpretation of ontology to be found in the *Logical Investigations* in favor of a form of transcendental idealism. Husserl's transcendental idealism is based on the epistemic claim that consciousness is autonomous while the natural world of objects is dependent on what is posited by consciousness as an object. Husserl sometimes seems to have argued that his transcendental idealism involves a metaphysical claim that the world is somehow dependent on us, but he often argues instead that the world must be intelligible to us: "If transcendental subjectivity is the universe of possible sense, then an outside is

Heidegger rejects the form of mind-dependentness that Husserl attributes to entities constituted by the mind. Heidegger's rejection of the particular form of idealism defended by Husserl is linked to the former's rejection of the primacy of epistemic claims. Such epistemic claims need to be justified through the constitution by consciousness of objects making those claims true. However, Heidegger still maintains vestiges of the distinctive kind of transcendental idealism implied by Husserl's method of phenomenological reduction. These vestiges of idealism emerge in Heidegger's claims that being, time, and truth, but not entities themselves, are given only so long as human beings exist (*SuZ*, p. 230).

In the next chapter, I take up the suggestion that Heidegger's theory of significance should be understood on the model of average everyday practices. I argue that everyday practices do have an important role to play in structuring intelligibility, but that, for Heidegger, the ultimate source of intelligibility is not to be sought in average everyday practices, but in temporality itself. Temporality is ultimately, for Heidegger, the source of the truth or rather of the disclosure in terms of which we are able to understand anything.

precisely nonsense" (*CM, Hua* I, section 41). Husserl notes that "no ordinary 'realist' has even been as realistic and as concrete as I, the phenomenological 'idealist' (a word which by the way I no longer use)," Letter to Abbe Baudin in 1934, cited from Iso Kern, *Husserl und Kant* (The Hague: Martinus Nijhoff, 1964), p. 276n.

CHAPTER 7

Temporality as the source of intelligibility

In this chapter, I discuss the claim that average everyday social practices serve as the condition under which anything is intelligible to us.[1] Against a widely held interpretation of Heidegger, I argue that the average everyday social practices to which one conforms as a member of society do not provide the unique source of intelligibility. Heidegger does think that there is an ultimate source of all intelligibility, or rather of all disclosure and significance. This is his notion of temporality. Temporality is supposed to make our ability to understand language and everyday social practices themselves intelligible to us. Only a very rich notion of temporality is up to this job. This notion of temporality already contains an essential relation to space, language, understanding, social roles, and moods in itself, so Heidegger's claim about temporality as the source of intelligibility is less exciting than it first seems to be. But temporality still has an important unifying function to play in connecting the various dispositions that are fundamental to human existence together in a human life.

Heidegger's grounding of knowledge claims and practical engagements in everyday experience has suggested to many philosophers that his position should be assimilated to that of Wittgenstein and pragmatists such as Dewey.[2] There are, indeed, important resemblances between Heidegger's critique of the philosophical tradition,

---

[1] I am indebted to important contributions by David Weberman in this chapter.
[2] Recent work by Karl-Otto Apel, "Wittgenstein und Heidegger. Die Frage nach dem Sinn von Sein und der Sinnlosigkeitsverdacht gegen alle Metaphysik," in Otto Pöggeler (ed.) *Heidegger* (Königstein: Athenäum, 1984), pp. 358–396; Robert Brandom, "Heidegger's Categories in *Being and Time*," *The Monist* 66 (1983), 387–409; Hubert Dreyfus, *Being-in-the-World* (Cambridge, Mass.: MIT Press, 1991); Charles Guignon, *Heidegger and the Problem of Knowledge* (Indianapolis: Hackett, 1983); John Haugeland, "Heidegger on Being a Person," *Nous* 16 (1982), 15–26; Mark Okrent, *Heidegger's Pragmatism* (Ithaca: Cornell, 1988); John Richardson, *Existential Epistemology: A Heideggerian Critique of the Cartesian Project* (New York: Oxford University Press, 1986); and Richard Rorty, "Heidegger, Contingency, and

and those developed by Wittgenstein and Dewey. According to a view that is generally ascribed both to Wittgenstein and pragmatists such as Dewey, meanings do not exist independently of the practices and institutions that give structure to the beliefs of particular individuals. Institutions in society provide the standards against which the grasp of meanings is measured. Any justification of our beliefs also depends on the context in which we find ourselves. There is no way to provide a justification of our beliefs that transcends all context whatsoever, as traditional philosophers such as Descartes and Husserl think, who seek to identify beliefs that have a certainty that is completely independent of any particular context of justi- fication. A person who cannot use expressions as they are used according to the conventions established by such institutions simply does not understand the expressions in question and has also failed to grasp their meaning. Such institutional conceptions of meaning are usually thought to involve strongly social commitments, i.e., a commitment to the actual existence of other persons. It is not clear, however, that even Wittgenstein thought that an individual who had never socially interacted with other individuals who have a language would be incapable of speaking a language or understanding meaning.[3] But it is clear that, for both Dewey and Wittgenstein, and Heidegger as well, there are no significant beliefs that we can identify and ascribe to individuals independently of any particular social context. In Heidegger's case, this is, to be sure, far from immediately obvious, since his project in *Being and Time* is that of identifying conditions that are necessary to any human existence as such (existentials). But this seems to be the ultimate upshot of his position.

The social character of meaning, as Heidegger understands it, raises a question about the source of all significance and intelligibility that I shall address in this chapter. Two candidates suggest them- selves within the framework of Heideggger's conception of being-in- the-world: (1) the one, the they, the anyone as Heidegger's "*das Man*" is variously translated, (2) temporality. I shall argue against the now popular "pragmatist" interpretation according to which either

---

Pragmatism," in Dreyfus and Hall (eds.) *Heidegger: A Critical Reader* (Oxford: Blackwell, 1992), pp. 209–230 are representative of this interpretation.

[3] Colin McGinn, *Wittgenstein* (London: Blackwell, 1987) interprets the passage in the *Philosophical Investigations* to be consistent with an extreme Robinson Crusoe existence, in which, unlike Crusoe, the individual had no prior contact with other language speakers.

language or the anyone is the unique source of intelligibility, although it seems to me to be important to acknowledge and to stress the importance of language and average social identity of the anyone in constituting intelligibility. Against this view, I wish to argue for a less reductionist conception of intelligibility. Intelligibility has the other existentials as enabling conditions as well. Thus moods, understanding, spatiality, an anticipatory experience of death, and much much more are equally necessary to making ourselves and other entities intelligible to us.

"DAS MAN"

"Das Man," which has been variously translated as "the they," "the anyone," or "the one" plays an important, albeit ambiguous, role in *Being and Time*. On the one hand, it appears as a way we have of understanding ourselves which deceives us about the world and ourselves by leading us uncritically to accept the identity and beliefs we have in virtue of our socialization according to certain roles we have in society. It thus forms the basis of a critique of society. On the other hand, the one is responsible for the publicity and shared character of our experience. The first aspect of the anyone has been influenced by those who see Heidegger primarily as an existentialist thinker. The second aspect has been championed by those who have thought of him as a form of pragmatist. It seems to me that there is truth in both views, and one need not see them as mutually exclusive alternatives or currents in Heidegger's thought which pull in different directions. To do so, is to do violence to the distinctiveness of Heidegger's own position which views both existentialist and pragmatist themes as grounded in his concerns with ontology.

Heidegger emphasizes the idea that the anyone plays a constitutive role in making for a shared public world. This has led Guignon to argue that it is in fact the anyone (presumably including discourse within it) which is the source of all possibilities for the self and, hence, also of anything which is significant where he originally argues that it is language: "There can be no exit from the Anyone to discover my 'own' possibilities precisely because the Anyone is the source of all possibilities, both authentic and inauthentic."[4] As an existential, the anyone is a constitutive condition of human exist-

<hr />

[4] "Heidegger's 'Authenticity' Revisited," *Review of Metaphysics* 38 (1984), 321–339, see p. 333.

ence. But it is not *the* sole condition for the intelligibility of entities, including my intelligibility to me and your intelligibility to you. According to Heidegger, it is as basic as such other fundamental structures of existence as being with others, being-in-the-world, understanding, and language, but it is not the source of intelligibility.[5] This claim that the anyone is the source of intelligibility implicit in Guignon's account is explicitly defended by Hubert Dreyfus.

Dreyfus claims that the anyone is *the* condition for intelligibility: "For both Heidegger and Wittgenstein, then, the source of the intelligibility of the world is the average public practices through which alone there can be any understanding at all."[6] Dreyfus identifies the anyone with average public practices. This is itself somewhat problematic, since Heidegger thinks of the one as the neutral "who" involved in everyday activities, rather than those activities themselves (*SuZ*, p. 126). In engaging in a social role, I have an identity that is circumscribed by that role. To the extent that I fail to transcend that role, my identity is reduced to that of being the individual who plays that role. But I am still a self and not a mere role.

In sections entitled "The Positive Function of the One: Conformity as the Source of Intelligibility" and "The One as the Source of Significance and Intelligibility," Dreyfus argues:

For both Heidegger and Wittgenstein, then, the source of the intelligibility of the world is the average public practices through which alone there can be any understanding at all. What is shared is not a conceptual scheme ... [but] simply our average comportment. Once a practice has been explained by appealing to what one does, no more basic explanation is possible ... [T]he constant control the one exerts over each *Dasein* makes a coherent referential whole, shared for-the-sake-of-whichs, and thus, ultimately, significance and intelligibility possible.[7]

The argument has two steps. The first step consists in Dreyfus' claim that, according to *Being and Time* (or at least Division I of that work), *Dasein*'s understanding is essentially and fundamentally social or shared in nature. The second step comes with the claim that the

---

[5] Martin Heidegger, *The History of the Concept of Time* (Bloomington: Indiana University Press, 1985), p. 421.
[6] Hubert Dreyfus, *Being-in-the-World*, p. 155 (see also "The One as the Source of Significance and Intelligibility," ibid., p. 161).
[7] Dreyfus, *Being-in-the-World*, pp. 154f., 161.

shared or social nature of *Dasein*'s understanding constitutes *the* source of the intelligibility of *Dasein*'s world and the objects of its understanding. I shall argue that, while the first step is plausible and important (though mistakenly aligned with another claim about average everydayness), the second step is not warranted.

Let me first examine Dreyfus' claim that *Dasein*'s understanding is essentially a matter of the ways of *das Man* and hence "social" and "average" in nature.[8] As mentioned above, this interpretation departs from most earlier German and Anglophone Heidegger readings, especially those inspired by existentialist themes. In this context, it is worthwhile to consider Frederick Olafson's recent critique of Dreyfus' interpretation. Olafson writes:

[A]lthough the word "social" is ubiquitous in Dreyfus's rendering of Heidegger's relevant views, there is only one occurrence in all of *Being and Time* of each of the two German words for "social" (*sozial* and *gesellschaftlich*). It should also be pointed out that although Dreyfus treats it as the master concept for explicating *Dasein*, the place of the concept of *Das Man* in Heidegger's thought appears to have been less secure. In *The Basic Problems of Phenomenology* ... there is no mention at all of *Das Man*.[9]

Olafson is right about this much: Heidegger is not fully explicit about the social nature of understanding in *Being and Time*.[10] But, as Olafson himself goes on to concede, there certainly is a social dimension to Heidegger's analysis of *Dasein*.[11] The difference between Dreyfus and Olafson, then, has to do with the extent and exact nature of the social character of *Dasein*'s existence. As it turns out, for Olafson, it is Heidegger's "being-with" ("Mitsein") and its negative conformism as *das Man* which make up *Dasein*'s social dimension. For Dreyfus, however, *Dasein*'s social nature is also very much dependent on a positive, constitutive role played by *das Man* in the emergence of *Dasein*'s understanding. I shall argue that Dreyfus is right about the constitutive role played by *das Man*, though wrong about some further claims about its role.

---

[8] I argue below that "shared" and "social" are not equivalent to "average" and "everyday."
[9] Frederick Olafson, "Heidegger à la Wittgenstein or 'Coping' with Professor Dreyfus," *Inquiry* 37 (1994), 45–64, here p. 55. See also the ensuing discussion in Taylor Carman, "On Being Social: A Reply to Olafson," *Inquiry* 37 (1994), 203–223, and Frederick Olafson, "Individualism, Subjectivity, and Presence: A Response to Taylor Carman," *Inquiry* 37 (1994), 331–337.
[10] This dimension is much more pronounced and explicit in Heidegger's 1925 lecture *History of the Concept of Time*, GA 20.
[11] See Olafson, "Heidegger à la Wittgenstein," p. 55.

BEING-WITH

In a short, but centrally located chapter of *Being and Time* (Division 1, chapter 4, sections 25–27), Heidegger introduces the existential or invariant structure of human existence called "being-with" ("Mitsein"). Being-with refers to the character of existence as always lived along with and shared with other human beings or *Daseins*. This, Heidegger insists, is immediately given to us. On Heidegger's account, our understanding of ourselves, of physical objects, and of the world as such is *always* "shot through" with the awareness that there are other human beings like us that populate our environment. This is why being-with is an existential structure. As Heidegger maintains that "'[w]ith' ... [is] to be understood *existentially* ... By reason of this *with-like* [*mithaften*] being-in-the-world, the world is *always* [our italics] the one that I share with others. The world of *Dasein* is a *with-world*. Being-in is *Being-with* others" (*SuZ*, p. 118). Thus, *Dasein*'s being-with is unavoidable. Even a shipwrecked Robinson Crusoe does not represent a break from the being-with character of human existence. Heidegger writes: "Even *Dasein*'s being alone is being-with in the world. The other can *be missing* only *in* and *for* a being-with. Being-alone is a deficient mode of being-with" (*SuZ*, p. 120). This means that the social character of our existence penetrates our experience to such an extent that the physical absence of others fails to erase that character.[12]

The structure of being-with is linked to and presented in the same chapter with another existential structure, namely, "the anyone." Olafson is willing to acknowledge the social nature of being-with, but he overlooks the added social dimension played by *das Man*. According to Olafson, *das Man* is merely a "distorted modality of *being-with*," i.e., our being-with others when we are in an inauthentic and conformist mode.[13] The problem is not however that *das Man* is not conformist (it is!). Olafson's claim is wrong because *das Man* adds something *positive* to the notion of world which is not contained in the notion of *Mitsein* or being-with, to wit, the fact that *Dasein*'s place in the universe is not only shared with other *Daseins*, but its understanding is shaped and made possible by an anonymous,

---

[12] On Heidegger's "deficient modes," see Klaus Hartmann, "The Logic of Deficient and Eminent Modes in Heidegger," *Journal of the British Society for Phenomenology* 5 (1974), 118–134.
[13] Olafson, "Heidegger *à la* Wittgenstein," p. 59.

shared "take" on the world.[14] This is the positive feature of *das Man* that is so important to Dreyfus' interpretation and that is overlooked by Olafson and many other commentators. In a passage from Heidegger's 1925 lecture cited by Dreyfus, we find a confirmation of Dreyfus' reading. In the section entitled "*Das Man* as the who of the being-with-one-another in everydayness," Heidegger writes: "First of all and everyday, one's own world and own *Dasein* are precisely the farthest. What is first is precisely the world in which one is with one another. It is out of this world that one can first more or less genuinely grow into his own world. This common [*gemeinsame*] world, which is there primarily and into which every maturing *Dasein* first grows, governs, as the public [*öffentliche*] world, every interpretation of the world and of *Dasein*."[15] So, Dreyfus is quite right that *Dasein*, *Dasein*'s understanding, and *Dasein*'s world is *first of all* and, in a sense to be specified below, *always* formed by social or shared ways of the anonymous public.[16]

But *das Man* is not only a positive condition for our social or shared understanding of the world. It also plays the negative role of describing our inauthentic and conformist mode of existence.[17] Of course, this point is not lost on Dreyfus. He is well aware of the conformist theme in Heidegger. But Dreyfus fails to recognize that the conformism of *das Man* coexists with ways of being that *surpass das Man*. And this means that there is more to *Dasein*'s understanding and existence than just what the ways of *das Man* deliver. In what

[14] The concept of *das Man* also adds something else, namely, the description of *Dasein* as first and for the most part (largely) indistinguishable from other *Daseins*: "*First of all* I 'am' not 'I' in the sense of the authentic self, but the others in the mode of the anyone" (*SuZ*, p. 129). Though this notion of the indistinguishability of *Daseins* is briefly mentioned in Heidegger's discussion of being-with (*SuZ*, p. 118), it is really only justified by his concept of *das Man*.

[15] See *GA* 20, pp. 339f. For further evidence in support of this interpretation, see the Heidegger passages quoted in Dreyfus, *Being-in-the-World*, pp. 142–146.

[16] Olafson clearly misses this constitutive and positive role played by *das Man* when he writes in his earlier book *Heidegger and the Philosophy of Mind* (New Haven: Yale University Press, 1987), p. 146: "[T]he promise of the strong theory of *Mitsein* to which Heidegger commits himself in *Being and Time* is simply not realized when being as such is under discussion. Although it is understood that it is an essential feature of *Dasein* that the entities it uncovers are, at least in principle, the same entitities in the same world that other like entities uncover... there is no real account of the way in which *my* uncovering an entity as an entity depends on someone else's doing so as well." But, as Dreyfus correctly argues, the connection between *my* uncovering and someone else's uncovering lies in the fact that we initially and usually are *das Man* and have its understanding.

[17] In fact, Heidegger's early discussion of *das Man* in his lecture from a summer semester, 1923, characterizes that notion wholly in negative terms of conformism and not in its positive role as a constituent of shared meaning, see *Ontology: Hermeneutics of Facticity*, *GA* 63, pp. 31ff., 85ff.

follows we shall argue that *das Man* is not, as Dreyfus suggests it is, universal and unsurpassable in the same way that being-with and other existential structures are. Nor is it the case, as Dreyfus also seems to suggest, that *das Man* is coextensive with the social and shared nature of *Dasein*'s understanding.

The function of *das Man* is ambiguous in more ways than one. As we have seen, it plays both a positive, constitutive and a negative, inauthentic role. Furthermore, its very existential status is tricky in a way different from that of other existential structures. What is tricky (or perhaps simply inconsistent on Heidegger's part) is that Heidegger says (1) quite emphatically, that *das Man* is an existential and primordial structure (*SuZ*, p. 129) and hence a feature of our experience that always obtains.[18] But, on the very same page, he also says (2) that *Dasein* only first ("zunächst") and for the most part (i.e., usually) ("zumeist") remains in the mode of *das Man*, and hence that *das Man* is not a feature of our experience that always obtains.[19]

This difference between, on the one hand, primordial or existential features and, on the other hand, first and for the most part ("zunächst und zumeist") features of *Dasein*'s existence, though systematically neglected by Dreyfus and others, is crucial for understanding *Being and Time*. A few examples might be in order here. When Heidegger writes that "[f]irst and for the most part, *Dasein* is captivated by [*benommen*] its world" (*SuZ*, p. 113), he means decidedly that *Dasein* is *not always* in such a state. Likewise, the claim that *Dasein first and for the most part* denies and resists its thrownness in the world contrasts with the claim that *Dasein primordially* or *existentially* (hence *always*) is in some sort of mood that reveals to it its dependence on a world that is not of its own making. Most importantly, as we see below, *Dasein*'s average everyday patterns of existence are, despite Dreyfus' repeated assumptions to the contrary, not primordial, but rather patterns which obtain only some or most of the time.[20] The

---

[18] There (*SuZ*, p. 129), Heidegger says: "*Das Man is an existential; and as a primordial [ursprüngliches] phenomenon, it belongs to Dasein's positive constitution.*"

[19] In the original German (*SuZ*, p. 129), part of which was quoted above, Heidegger says this: "*First of all* I 'am' not 'I' in the sense of the authentic self, but the others in the mode of the anyone. From this anyone and as this anyone I am first of all 'given' to 'myself.' First of all *Dasein* is anyone and for the most part it remains so."

[20] Admittedly, there are instances when Heidegger himself seems to conflate what is first and foremost and what is primordial. A prime example of this is exactly his attribution, at *SuZ*, p. 129, of first the one and then the other status to the concept of *das Man*. But Heidegger's identification of two different roles for *das Man* is not a mere conflation of these two roles. There is no evidence that Heidegger attributes primordiality to everydayness or, for that

question as to whether *das Man* and other social categories are primordial and exceptionless or only first and for the most part is essential to evaluating Dreyfus' interpretation because Dreyfus seems to assume that not only *das Man*, but also the averageness of everyday practices are primordial and unsurpassable. This leads him to restrict Heidegger's analysis of *Dasein* to that aspect of *Dasein*'s experience. If *Dasein*'s understanding can surpass averageness, even if only in a piecemeal and temporary fashion, then a different understanding of *Dasein* and, indeed, the overall argument of *Being and Time*, results.

Is *das Man* primordial and without exception or only first and for the most part? As we have seen, one page alone (*SuZ*, p. 129) offers evidence for both interpretations. There are also further pieces of evidence for each side. In favor of the primordial status of *das Man* is the following argument. While *das Man* always obtains because our understanding is always rooted in a common, public language and culture, what *Dasein* sometimes breaks with or surpasses is not *das Man*, but the anyone-self ("das Man-selbst"). An interpretation that puts weight on this distinction is supported by the following passage:

> The self of everyday *Dasein* is the anyone-self, which we distinguish from the *authentic self* – that is, from the self which has been taken hold of in its own way ... *Authentic being-one's self* does not rest upon an exceptional condition of the subject, a condition that has been detached from the 'anyone'; *it is rather an existentiell modification of the 'anyone' – of the 'anyone' as an essential existential structure.* (*SuZ*, pp. 129–130)[21]

On this interpretation, *das Man* always obtains and is always essentially neutral with respect to authenticity and inauthenticity. What changes is the self. It is sometimes and usually an inauthentic anyone-self, and sometimes but rarely an authentic self, i.e. a self whose self-understanding is individual and distinctive. While Heidegger states explicitly that *das Man* is what we are only "first and for the most part" (*SuZ*, p. 129), this refers to our self-identity. We are first and for the most part anyone-selves. This is why Heidegger often speaks of *das Man* as something which we can

---

matter, that Heidegger regards *das Man* as the most primordial structure in experience. Indeed the addition of "first" or "initially" ("zunächst") to the expression "for the most part" suggests primacy in the order of appearance in contrast to ontological primacy.

[21] While Dreyfus does not distinguish between the anyone and the anyone-self, Guignon's later analysis in "Heidegger's 'Authenticity' Revisited" strongly relies on this distinction. Further passages which seem to support a distinction between *das Man* and *das Man-selbst* can be found at *SuZ*, sections 54–56, pp. 267–274.

"bring ourselves back from" (*SuZ*, p. 268) or out of which we can be summoned (*SuZ*, p. 299). At least two passages in which Heidegger treats the authentic self as basic and the anyone-self as derivative reveal what Heidegger takes to be the primacy of our own distinctive sense of self over the sense of self that we have first of all and for the most part.[22]

Das Man is the common, and hence inauthentic (because not specific to the individual) "take" on the world with which we are temporally first familiar and in which we exist most of the time. It is also *always* operative just in the sense that, even when we develop a different perspective on this or that bit of reality, the common, anonymous take continues to operate as a sort of background, common-sense understanding about those things peripheral to our focus of attention. Thus, when we become authentic and resolute, we do not cease to comprehend the way others think about things. In fact, authentic being-in-the-world is not at all an erasure of the common, anonymous understanding of *das Man*, rather it is a surpassing of that common understanding which consists in reappropriating it in a way that is distinctively one's own.[23] Thus, it is one thing to say that there are no possibilities which we can understand independently of *das Man*, it is quite another to say that *das Man* is itself the source of all possibilities. For example, our socially gained understanding provides us with certain possible social roles, but this does not imply that social roles are the only source of possibilities. Even where possibilities are provided by *das Man*, authentic existence gives them its own distinctive interpretation and thus makes them its own. Self-appropriation is what makes them genuine possibilities. This is strongly suggested by a passage Guignon appeals to for support for his view: "The resolve does not withdraw from 'reality,'

---

[22] In one passage (*SuZ*, p. 317), noted by Olafson, Dreyfus, Carman, and others, Heidegger states that the authentic self is derivative on the anyone-self. In another passage, not noted by these authors (*SuZ*, p. 259), Heidegger writes: "Inauthenticity has possible authenticity as its foundation." The two claims are not inconsistent as has often been thought. The first claim asserts that we have an anyone-self "first and for the most part." The second claim asserts that we could not have an anyone-self if we could not have an authentic self, i.e., a sense of what is genuinely distinctive about our individual lives.

[23] See *SuZ*, pp. 268, 308, but especially *SuZ*, pp. 297f.: "To this lostness [in *das Man*] one's own *Dasein* can appeal, and this appeal can be understood in the way of resoluteness. But in that case this *authentic* disclosedness modifies both the way in which the 'world' is disclosed and the way in which the *Dasein*-with of others is disclosed. The 'world' which is ready-to-hand does not become another one 'in its content,' nor does the circle of others get exchanged for a new one; but both ... are now given a definite character in terms of their ownmost potentiality-for-being-their-selves."

but instead discovers for the first time what is factically possible, in a way which grasps itself as it is possible as authentic (*eigenstes*) ability-to-be in *das Man*" (*SuZ*, p. 299).

What is important here is this: first, the understanding of *das Man is* inauthentic, concealing, and hence "inferior" to authentic understanding. It is not the case that *das Man* is a neutral description which can simply take on either authentic or inauthentic guises. To become authentic is, to some extent, to reappropriate and, hence, undo the anonymous, levelled-down understanding of *das Man*.[24] Our possibilities of thought and action are circumscribed by the intelligibility supplied by the public sphere, but they are not uniquely determined by it. Unlike *das Man*, Heidegger never classifies the phenomena of average everydayness as an existential structure, but only as *Dasein*'s mode of existence *first and for the most part* (*SuZ*, p. 43). It too is "ontologically determinative in every kind of being of factical *Dasein*" (*SuZ*, p. 17), but only insofar as it is a kind of permanent background which nevertheless can be modified in a positive way such that it is effectively surpassed (in important respects) when special dispositions such as authentic resoluteness and anxiety are engaged, and, in a different sense, when one is involved in theoretical contemplation.[25] Thus, when Dreyfus locates the source of intelligibility in our *average* public practices, he is overlooking the fact that there is much meaningfulness outside of *Dasein*'s average everyday understanding. Indeed, for Heidegger, any fundamental understanding must get behind average everyday understanding.

This brings me finally to the second step of Dreyfus's argument: his claim that *das Man* and average, everyday public practices are the source of intelligibility for human beings. As Dreyfus states it most strongly: "[Heidegger's] description of the phenomenon of everydayness in Division I affirms the one [*das Man*] as *ens realissimum* – as the end of the line of explanations of intelligibility."[26] My rejection

---

[24] Dreyfus and other like-minded interpreters seem to deny or neglect this point. Thus, Carman in "On Being Social" (p. 219) argues that *das Man* is an "anonymous normative background" against which authenticity or inauthenticity can "emerge," thus implying that *das Man* is a neutral description.

[25] Authentic resoluteness and anxiety are linked; theoretical contemplation, on the other hand, is a different kind of modification of everydayness.

[26] Dreyfus, *Being-in-the-World*, p. 353. Dreyfus qualifies this statement by pointing to Heidegger's discussion of originary temporality in Division II. He thinks that Division II is incompatible with Division I and that Division I takes everydayness to be "the end of the line." Yet, as we have demonstrated, the limitedness of everydayness is already clearly indicated in Division I of *Being and Time*.

of this step follows from the above argument. There is much that is intelligible (if not, more truthful) that lies beyond *das Man* and average everydayness. *Das Man* cannot be even the deepest source of intelligibility since its understanding is flawed by its association with inauthenticity. And *das Man* cannot be *the* source of intelligibility because it is only one of a number of existential structures, all of which are necessary and equally basic conditions for making the world intelligible as we know it. So, in the end, Dreyfus and Olafson are both wrong in taking the pragmatist, neo-Wittgensteinian and the existentialist dimensions in Heidegger to be mutually exclusive. The social shared world of *das Man* and the possibility of a more authentic understanding do not involve a contradiction. They coexist and are equally central to Heidegger's analysis of human existence or *Dasein*.

NEGLECTING HISTORY

I have argued that Dreyfus rightly rejects Frederick Olafson's claim that the earlier Heidegger failed to develop the essentially social character of all understanding.[27] But Dreyfus seems to share Olafson's view that Heidegger does not develop the essentially historical character of meaning in *Being and Time*. This is difficult to reconcile with the whole plan of the work which was to give a central role to the "destruction" of the history of ontology in order to arrive at a more adequate ontology. It also ignores the account of the historicity of the self in Division II. This neglect of the historical dimension of the social reflects an unwillingness to accept Heidegger's own candidate for the source of significance, the temporality of human existence.

Dreyfus draws a distinction between the provisional hermeneutics of everydayness in Division I of *Being and Time* and the hermeneutics of suspicion that he identifies in Division II. The hermeneutics of everydayness is based, at least in part, on the anyone, while the hermeneutics in Division II is supposed to provide a more truthful account of human existence and being in general based on temporality. It is because the hermeneutics of historical temporality is to correct the dominant interpretation of everyday life that it may be

---

[27] Olafson, *Heidegger and the Philosophy of Mind*, pp. 144ff.; Dreyfus, *Being-in-the-World*, pp. 142–143.

called a hermeneutics of suspicion. In this context Dreyfus admits that, for Heidegger, "*Dasein*'s way of making sense ... and all other ways of being could be understood in terms of temporality."[28] This seems to conflict with Dreyfus' claim that the anyone is the source all significance and intelligibility. Dreyfus also concedes that Heidegger thinks that the kind of conformity to norms required by the average everyday practices of the anyone can lead one to a form of self-deceptive conformism. Everyday practices are average or levelled practices that disguise the differences between individuals. All this suggests that if the anyone is the source of intelligibility it can only be a provisional source for Heidegger. But Dreyfus does not accept this conclusion. He maintains that, even in Division II, Heidegger says nothing to displace the anyone as the source of significance.[29] On the face of it, it is hard to see how average or shared everyday practices can be the ultimate source of significance and intelligibility and yet also what obscures such significance.

Heidegger thinks of the anyone as a condition for the possibility of experience, in part, precisely because a tendency to misunderstand oneself and other entities is a constitutive feature of our experience. The average and levelled form of intelligibility characteristic of the anyone tends to disguise the very nature of what is understood. The understanding of the anyone is supposed to be characterized by ambiguity precisely because it no longer allows one as such to distinguish between what one has genuinely understood and what one has simply appropriated in a non-understanding way from other persons' talk:

The identification with the anyone means the dominance of public interpretation. What is discovered and disclosed stands in the mode of distortion and closure through idle talk, curiosity, and ambiguity. Being [in relation] to entities is not erased, but rootless. Entities are not completely hidden, but barely discovered, yet also distorted; they show themselves – but in the mode of dissemblance [*Scheins*]. At once that which was previously discovered falls back into distortion and hiddenness. *Dasein is, because it is essentially fallen, in "untruth" according to the nature of its being.* (*SuZ*, p. 222)

Dreyfus can concede that the averaged-out understanding provided by the anyone is an "uprooted" understanding that displays the fundamental character of untruth and fallenness in human existence.

---

[28] Ibid., p. 156, p. 38.   [29] Ibid., p. 156.

In this levelled understanding, we understand things in terms of repeatables rather than in their uniqueness.

Dreyfus' considered opinion seems to be that there is no underlying intelligibility that might be obscured in everyday life. From this, he concludes that there can be no higher source of intelligibility for Heidegger than the anyone. Thus, the anyone is to be regarded as the unique source of all intelligibility. Quite surprisingly, given his willingness to ascribe a hermeneutics of suspicion to Heidegger in Division II, Dreyfus contrasts Heidegger's position with that of philosophers such as Descartes, Leibniz, and Marx who have argued that error is endemic to human existence. He cannot, he claims, otherwise account for Heidegger's emphasis on everydayness.[30]

Dreyfus ascribes to Heidegger a hermeneutics of suspicion that replaces the everyday interpretedness of the anyone and denies that there is an interpretation of our existence that could replace the anyone. Dreyfus has a response to the charge of inconsistency that suggests itself. On his view, the ultimate form of the hermeneutics of suspicion is suspicion of the very idea of a deep interpretation that could supplant everyday interpretation.[31] Dreyfus maintains that all understanding is essentially "groundless." This is probably a reference to Heidegger's view that *Dasein* has nothing as a ground (*SuZ*, pp. 284–285). We are never able to get behind the conditions for our own existence, since these conditions are never fully up to us. However, how we respond to such conditions is a matter of a choice. Moreover, this capacity to choose what we are to be is what makes us the kind of creatures that we are, namely creatures that have selves that they ascribe to themselves. This choice of self that makes us who we are is groundless in the following sense: we cannot in making the choice of how to respond to the conditions governing our existence take ourselves to be merely determined by such conditions. For this would undermine the very idea that we are making a choice of who we are to be. In this sense we are also

[30] Ibid., p. 156.

[31] "What gets covered up in everyday understanding is not some deep intelligibility as the tradition has always held; it is that the ultimate 'ground' of intelligibility is simply shared practices. There is no *right* interpretation. Average intelligibility is not inferior intelligibility; it simply obscures its own groundlessness. This is the last stage of the hermeneutics of suspicion. The only deep interpretation left is that there is no deep interpretation." *Being-in-the-World*, p. 157. Here Dreyfus suggests that Heidegger gets beyond the hermeneutics of suspicion that finds us caught in the grip of a pervasive form of self-deception, but elsewhere Dreyfus maintains that the discussion of temporality in the second half of *Being and Time* (Division II) turns into a hermeneutics of suspicion, pp. 37–38.

groundless. There are no specific facts for Heidegger to which we can appeal in our search for an adequate self-understanding. The desire to identify such facts leads to self-deception that is endemic to human existence. But, on the other hand, the groundlessness of our interpretations is ultimately based, for Heidegger, on the fact that they depend on a nature that is independent of us. It is therefore always a contingent matter that our interpretations are adequate.[32]

Dreyfus, by contrast, seems to think that there is no right interpretation to be had of anything. This is most charitably interpreted as a denial that we can identify a uniquely correct interpretation. But it is still odd to premise a claim that the anyone is the source of intelligibility on a thesis that there is no uniquely correct interpretation. For then there will not be a uniquely correct interpretation of what makes intelligibility possible. The appeal to shared practices as what makes things intelligible to us would be pointless if they did not help us to distinguish correct from incorrect behavior and incorrect from correct interpretation. While Dreyfus is right that shared practices provide the initial standards for accept-ability and intelligibility, he fails to show that they cannot be replaced by more adequate standards.

Dreyfus rejects the traditional solution to the problem of standards of intelligibility. This would be to look for a "source for the anyone." But this is only because Dreyfus regards Heidegger's search for a basis of significance in temporal science of ontology to be a distortion of his basic insight that one cannot attain to self-evidence.[33] If true, this would tell against the view that the anyone could be the source of intelligibility. It is hard to see why replacing one source of intelligibility with another would help one to avoid any appeal to self-evidence. It is one thing to claim that temporality is constitutive of human existence and understanding, it is quite another to claim that there is something self-evident about it. Temporality is no more a *certain* foundation for ontology than are the average social practices Dreyfus prefers.[34] Perhaps Dreyfus means

---

[32] There is a useful discussion of groundlessness of *Dasein* in Joseph Fell, *Heidegger and Sartre: An Essay on Being and Place* (New York: Columbia University Press, 1979), pp. 108ff.

[33] *Being-in-the-World*, pp. 38, 162.

[34] Even in the late twenties, Heidegger argues that the temporal interpretation of existence is as subject to error as any other, *The Basic Problems of Phenomenology, GA* 24, p. 459. By the end of his career, he even came to reject the term "fundamental ontology" because of the implication of a Cartesian "unshakeable foundation" ("fundamentum inconcussum") as opposed to a shakeable and hence revisable one ("fundamentum concussum"), "Summary

something weaker with the notion of "self-evidence" such as "correctness." But the interpretation of intelligibility in terms of average social practices must at least purport to be correct.

Dreyfus defends the social character of meaning by assigning a monopoly on meaning to the practices in which one participates. These practices of the anyone are average practices precisely because they disguise the distinctions between the ways different individuals participate in a practice. This gives too much weight to the anyone, which is never assigned any primacy with regard to other existentials by Heidegger himself. From Heidegger's own point of view, emphasis on the anyone distorts the provisional character of the investigation of everydayness. Everydayness gives us a way in to an understanding of the context of significance in which we always move: "But it never occurred to me to assert and prove through this interpretation that the essence of being human consists in dealing with spoons and forks and driving on the streetcar" (*GA* 29–30, p. 263).

To compensate for Heidegger's own tendency to reject the ultimate character of everydayness Dreyfus ascribes some confusion to Heidegger.[35] He notes that Heidegger combines a discussion of conformation to social norms with conformism. Dreyfus finds confusion because he identifies the social (being-with) with what anyone does and hence with *das Man*. Heidegger regards this conformism as an inauthentic form of being with others that is, however, endemic to human existence.

Dreyfus largely ignores Heidegger's later treatment of authentic social relations.[36] Heidegger argues that one can only be truly or authentically oneself by taking control of one's destiny. This destiny involves an essential relation to the other persons who belong to one's community and generation: "In being-together in the same world and in resoluteness for certain possibilities destinies are already directed from the outset."[37] The possibilities of relating to

of a Seminar on the lecture on 'Time and Being'," *On Time and Being* (New York: Harper and Row, 1972), p. 32; *Zur Sache des Denkens* (Tübingen: Max Niemeyer, 1969), p. 34.
[35] *Being-in-the-World*, pp. 143–144.
[36] See however ibid., pp. 329–331.
[37] While Frederick Olafson is clearly right that this account of the role of being- with in one's understanding of one's own historical situation is not as worked out as it might be, in conjunction with the account of socialization by means of the anyone-self it does provide a way of seeing how all the possibilities which present themselves to a person could be said to have an essentially social meaning.

oneself and other entities are, for Heidegger, irreducibly social. These possibilities make for the significance of entitities to us. They do not depend exclusively on conformity to the impersonal principles that anyone would accept. Indeed, Heidegger maintains that thinking of modes of behavior in conformist terms hides their character as possibilities to be as opposed to actualities of behavior. This is consistent with his view that our standards of behavior are derived "first of all" and "for the most part" from everyday delegable involvements. By downplaying authentic social relations in favor of those dominated by the anyone-self, Dreyfus captures only the non-reflective dimension of "the line of thought that leads from Hegel's notion of ethical practice or *Sittlichkeit*, to Dilthey on the objectifications of life, to Heidegger, and on to the later Wittgenstein's forms of life."[38]

Even the passage which Dreyfus regards as Heidegger's "crucial formulation" of the thesis that the anyone is the source of significance really suggests that Heidegger does believe that there is such a "deep intelligibility": "When *Dasein* is familiar with itself as the anyone-self, then that means also that the anyone prefigures the initial interpretation of world and of being-in-the-world. The anyone-self for the sake of which *Dasein* is daily articulates the referential context of significance" (*SuZ*, p. 129). Dreyfus takes the second sentence of this passage as support for the thesis that "the constant control the one exerts over each *Dasein* makes a coherent referential whole, shared for-the-sake-of-whichs, and thus, ultimately, significance and intelligibility possible."[39] I think that this thesis is correct. But this only shows that the anyone is a necessary and not a sufficient condition for intelligibility. The first sentence (which Dreyfus does not quote) suggests, by contrast, that the anyone-self offers a particular *interpretation* of the referential context of significance, rather than being the very source of all significance. The distinction between significance and the articulation of significance in terms of a certain interpretation of what is significant is a crucial distinction for Heidegger. This does not mean that we do or even could approach the pattern of significance except in terms of a certain interpretation of it. Our interpretation of what is significant is initially dominated by the anyone and its publicly accepted interpretation of things (*SuZ*, p. 129). This extends even to our

---

[38] *Being-in-the-World*, p. 144.   [39] Ibid., p. 161.

interpretation of our emotional responses (*SuZ*, p. 169). But this does not mean that the anyone is itself the source of that significance. It is merely the dominant way in which we interpret whatever has any kind of meaning for us.

I am initially not myself in the sense of my authentic self, but rather in the sense of the others, as a one. This does not imply that there is something inherently non-social about the way the world really is, for Heidegger distinguishes between being-with and the anyone. The averageness of one's experience makes being-with others possible, but this does not mean that I cannot ever truly appreciate what is distinctive about myself and other individuals. There is an authentic as well as an inauthentic form of being-with other human beings. The anyone is the inauthentic mode of being-with other human beings, but it is such a pervasive feature of existence that it is a condition for its very possibility. It would, however, be equally mistaken to assume that even being-with is the source of intelligibility.

Dasein is not first of all only a being-with-others, in order then to get out of this being-with-each-other to an objective world, to things ... Instead, as originally as *Dasein* is being-with-others, it is as originally being with what is ready to hand and present to hand ... Only because *Dasein* is previously constituted as being-in-the-world can a *Dasein* factually communicate something to another in its existence, but this factual communication in existence does not first of all constitute the possibility that a *Dasein* has a world with another.[40]

The categories that apply to things in nature apply to them only in virtue of the way in which those things display themselves to us in our spatial and temporal experience. However, it is significant that Dreyfus ignores the role of spatiality in Heidegger's argument against Cartesianism. Dreyfus suspects that *Dasein* does not need to be embodied at all, and also argues that one should distinguish the spatial and existential senses of "in" (as in Being-in-the-World), where Heidegger himself is careful to include the spatial in the existential sense, but to exclude the vulgar notion of the "spatial."[41] and instead claims that the anyone provides "the last nail in the coffin of the Cartesian tradition."[42] His idea is that taking the anyone as the source of intelligibility "blocks the Cartesian claim

[40] *The Basic Problems of Phenomenology*, p. 421.
[41] Dreyfus, *Being-in-the-World*, pp. 41–43.
[42] Ibid., p. 144.

that meaning is grounded in the activity of an individual subject and thereby undermines the traditional claim that meaning is grounded in an absolute source."[43] But it is unclear why anonymous social practices should be favored here over all the other potential sources of significance that are independent of the individual subject.

TIME AS THE SOURCE OF ALL INTELLIGIBILITY

Part of my reasoning for holding that neither language nor *das Man* can be considered the source of intelligibility derives from Heidegger's insistence that there are a plurality of necessary and equiprimordial existential structures which underlie and make possible the intelligibility of the world. It would seem to follow, then, that there can be no encompassing *Existenzial* that could possibly serve as *the* source of intelligibility. Yet I shall argue now that there is one, or rather three piggy-backed, notions that do, in fact, fit that bill. The existential structures that I have investigated, such as being-with, language, and the anyone, are ways in which the world is disclosed to us (*SuZ*, pp. 132–133). Disclosure ("Erschlossenheit"), which Heidegger regards as constitutive of *Dasein*, is the closest thing in his own terminology to the notion of intelligibility. It is the understanding we have of the entities that are now in terms of the entities that are then, of entities that are here in terms of what is there, that makes human existence being-in-the-world. Heidegger identifies such disclosure somewhat problematically with truth in order to indicate that disclosure is the condition under which it makes sense to talk of things or statements being true (*SuZ*, pp. 221).[44]

Now Heidegger is not content to claim that human existence is what it is because a world is disclosed to it. He goes on to argue that the "full disclosure of the there [of being-there: *Dasein*] is grounded in it," where it refers to care ("Sorge") and "this lightedness

---

[43] Ibid., p. 158.

[44] Under the influence of critics who argued that Heidegger had not done justice to the normative dimension of truth, Heidegger came eventually to distinguish disclosure or unconcealment from truth and then to argue that unconcealment or disclosure is the condition for the possibility of truth rather than truth itself: "it [unconcealment] first grants truth as *adaequatio* and *certitudo*, because there can be no presence and presenting outside of the realm of the opening," M. Heidegger, "Das Ende der Philosophie und die Aufgabe des Denkens," in *Zur Sache des Denkens* (Tübingen: Niemeyer, 1969), English trans. by Joan Stambaugh, *Heidegger on Time and Being* (New York: Harper, 1972), p. 69.

[provided by disclosure] first makes all lighting and illumination, every grasping, 'seeing' and having something possible" (*SuZ*, pp. 350–351). "Care" itself has a special status because it is the unifying concept underlying and embracing all the other existential structures. Furthermore, Heidegger holds that temporality is the deeper, enabling condition underlying the phenomenomen of care: "Ecstatic temporality originally lights the there" (*SuZ*, p. 351). So the source(s) for the intelligibility of the world should be understood as indicated by the following diagram which indicates the extent to which different structures are more fundamental than others:

> language *das Man* (other existential structures such as affectedness, talk, understanding, spatiality, etc., etc.)
> disclosure
> care
> temporality

"Care" is *not* just *another* existential structure. Heidegger refers to it as the being, meaning and ontological structure of *Dasein*: "[T]he being of *Dasein* itself is to be made visible as care ... when understood *ontologically Dasein* is care" (*SuZ*, p. 47).[45] Furthermore, Heidegger explicitly states that care is the basis of "reality" as we know it[46] and of all understanding of being (*SuZ*, pp. 212, 230). What makes care special is that it is (i) a description which, unlike the other existential structures, embraces the totality of *Dasein*'s existence (*SuZ*, pp. 182, 193, 196, 209) and (ii) a description that is more primordial than other phenomena (*SuZ*, pp. 192, 193, 196, 206). Why does care have this special comprehensive and primordial character? Heidegger defines care as "being-ahead-of-oneself-in-already-being-in-the-world as being-alongside intra-worldly entities" (*SuZ*, p. 192). As its length indicates, there are a number of things contained in this definition. There is (1) our thrownness or our having found ourselves in a world without our having chosen to be there (being-already-in) as well as (2) our capacity for inauthenticity or becoming transfixed by the things around us (being-alongside). But perhaps even more central to the definition of care is (3) that we are ahead of ourselves, i.e, that we are goal-oriented agents concerned about our future being (which need not exclude our altruistic concern for others). As

---

[45] See also *SuZ*, pp. 41, 121, 182; *GA* 20, pp. 406ff. At *SuZ*, p. 230, Heidegger speaks of care as "the primordial structure of the being of *Dasein*" ("die ursprüngliche Seinsverfassung des Daseins").

[46] *SuZ*, p. 211: "*Realität* ist ... *auf das Phänomen der Sorge zurückverwiesen.*"

Heidegger says early on in *Being and Time, Dasein* is that entity for
whom "in its very being, that being is an issue for it" (*SuZ*, p. 12).
Heidegger returns to this agency-oriented character of *Dasein* in
elucidating his notion of care (*SuZ*, p. 191). To be a human being is to
be concerned or care about one's existence. But to care about one's
own existence is also to be concerned about everything else that may
bear on one's existence in some way. Heidegger thinks that agency is
a basic and general feature about *Dasein* in regard to which the other
existential structures are only aspects.

Though Heidegger does not present such an argument, his special
treatment of care implicitly suggests something like the following
position: care is more basic and general than say one's moods, or
what anyone does, because, while one cannot imagine the former
without the latter, it would make no sense to think that we could
have moods, at least in the specifically human sense, or have the
possibility of losing and finding ourselves unless we cared about what
is to become of us. Thus, it is care that underlies what we are and
care that makes possible the world as we know it and its intelligibility.
While more could be said about the uniquely primordial position of
care, it is important to note that other basic existentials cannot be
derived from care in any interesting sense. Instead, the care-
structure of human existence serves rather to indicate the underlying
root ("Verwurzelung") of the different equally basic structures of
human existence, such as being-in-the-world, the anyone, being
together with others (*GA* 20, p. 421). The next and last point of the
chapter will consist in showing that the role of temporality is that
which underlies and makes possible care and thus, in turn, that
which serves as the deepest source of the intelligibility of *Dasein*'s
world.

The evidence for the connection between temporality and care in
Heidegger's theory is quite explicit. Heidegger writes: "[T]he primordial ontological basis for *Dasein*'s existentiality is *temporality*. The
articulated structural totality of *Dasein*'s being as care can only
become intelligible existentially in terms of [temporality]" (*SuZ*,
p. 234). More briefly, temporality is the "ontological meaning of
care" (*SuZ*, pp. 301, 323, 326) and that which "makes possible" care
in its composite unity (*SuZ*, p. 324).[47] But why does he think of
temporality and care as linked in this way such that the former

---

[47] See also *GA* 20, p. 442.

conditions and is the deeper sense of the latter? Now his definition of care is "being-ahead-of-oneself-in-already-being-in-the-world as being-alongside intra-worldly entities." This is a definition of care that is already unmistakably and essentially temporal. As a first approximation we can say that "already-being-in-the-world" refers to what Heidegger calls our thrownness. Thrownness is a way of expressing the idea that we have an experience that cannot coherently abstract from its dependence on our past environment (as Cartesian skepticism suggested that we might). "Being-alongside ..." refers to our absorption in the present (this absorption in the present gives solipsism of the present moment whatever initial plausibility it has). Most importantly, since Heidegger says that the future is primary (*SuZ*, pp. 327, 329), "being-ahead-of-oneself" is about our future and the manner in which the goal-directedness of our interests structures the way our past environment is understood in the present.

Put together, *Dasein* is care insofar as *Dasein* is a creature that inherits the past, is preoccupied with the present, and able to act on its future by understanding its past and its present in terms of its concern for what it can come to be. This explains what care is and what it is to be a *Dasein*. But this is only a first approximation to *Dasein*'s temporality because, as Heidegger insists, his conceptions of the past, present, and future are not to be understood according to the common-sense or "vulgar" conceptions of these notions. Temporality is also essentially tied up with spatiality and publicity. Spatiality is important to our understanding of ourselves as distinct human beings, and hence to our experience of our own temporal experience as having a point of view from which it organizes time within a larger shared whole of time. This shared time expresses itself as the publicity of time. We care not only about ourselves, but about others. Indeed, in our care for ourselves, there is an implicit understanding of our differences from others. This leads to a concern about the mutual implications of the interests that we individually and collectively pursue.

For Heidegger, temporality is not a matter of the past as the "not any longer now – but earlier," the present as a "now point," and the future as a "not yet now – but later" (*SuZ*, p. 327). Time is not a series of now-points. The key to Heidegger's account of temporality is the way in which past, present, and future coexist and co-determine each other as ways in which human existence understands itself and the particulars in its world. In *Being and Time*, Heidegger argues that one can meaningfully say of any disposition that characterizes a human being that it is future in the past, present in the past, as well as future in the present, etc. But this "temporalizing does not mean a one after the other of the ecstasies. The future is *not later* than having beenness, and having been is *not earlier* than the present" (*SuZ*, p. 350). Past, present, and future are "ecstasies." They exist only by including an essential relation to the other tenses from which they are distinguishable. In this sense, they are literally what they are by being "outside" of themselves. So far, Heidegger appropriates Husserl's conception of the distinctive intentionality of temporality. They are, however, also supposed to take us outside of ourselves. They are structures in terms of which we relate to ourselves as possibilities of being thus and such by relating to entities that are distinct from ourselves. It is here that Heidegger goes beyond Husserl, and it is here that his notion of "care" takes on significance. Unlike Husserl's conception of temporality, Heidegger's does not allow for a completely disinterested – careless – temporal experience. We are always already somehow involved in our world.

Heidegger actually eschews the terms "past," "present," and "future" because of their misleading connotations (*SuZ*, p. 326). But he has little to say about what distinguishes past, present, and future when properly understood. Yet we need to be able to draw an interesting distinction between them in order to be able to find the claim that they each include the other at all illuminating. He notes that "past" temporality, or what has been, has the structure of coming back to oneself. "Present" temporality has the structure of presenting. It is the way in which what one has been and what one is to be expresses itself in what one does. "Future" temporality has the structure of coming towards oneself. It is the way in which what has been is taken up in what is to be (*SuZ*, pp. 325ff.). These characterizations of time help us to see how the past, present, and future could be interdependent, yet distinct. Each involves the other, but in each case the primacy goes to one of these dimensions of time over the other. This also suggests that the various aspects of one's life and the lives of others may well be temporally connected in a manner which defies any straightforward sequential structuring.

Heidegger regards temporality as the deeper and enabling structure of care, and, as I have indicated, care is the primary candidate for the source of the intelligibility of *Dasein*'s world. *A fortiori*, then, temporality is that which is the deeper, if not the deepest, source of the intelligibility of our world. This only confirms what Heidegger says elsewhere about the role of time and temporality (the difference between these two terms in Heidegger is that the former is a general ontological concept, while the latter is an existential structure of *Dasein* that Heidegger thinks is the basis of the general ontological notion of time). Thus, toward the beginning of *Being and Time*, Heidegger writes that *"time needs to be explicated primordially as the horizon for the understanding of being and in terms of temporality as the being of Dasein which understands being"* (*SuZ*, p. 17).[48] Note the connection between temporality and the understanding of being and hence the intelligibility of *Dasein*'s world.

Heidegger does not say, in so many words, that temporality is the source of intelligibility, but this is only because "intelligibility" and "source of intelligibility" are not the technical and oft-occurring terms in Heidegger that they have become in recent commentary. The idea of intelligibility is one that is, indeed, potentially misleading from Heidegger's perspective. If intelligibility is understood as the way the world is disclosed to human beings in their very existence, then intelligibility is central to *Being and Time*. But intelligibility is not, in this case, restricted to theoretical understanding. Disclosure is always, for Heidegger, more about emotional attunement and practical know-how than it is about theoretical understanding of the kind suggested by the Platonic and Kantian heritage of the notion of intelligibility. This is true of the Heideggerian term that can be rendered in English as "intelligibility" ("Verständlichkeit") which he interprets as being able to understand in the sense of having know-how. Heidegger thinks of such know-how as expressing possibilities for one to be. And he regards time as the source of all possibility: "Because the original possibilizer, the source of possibility itself, is time, time temporalizes itself as the absolutely earliest."[49] Time is, indeed, the source of the a priori conditions of experience as Heidegger understands them.

Further evidence for the connection between temporality and intelligibility is supplied by Heidegger's claims that temporality grounds understanding, articulation and the "hermeneutic as-structure" (*SuZ*, p. 360), the "intentionality" of consciousness (*SuZ*,

---

[48] See also *GA* 24, p. 274: "Temporality [*Zeitlichkeit*] is the condition for the possibility of understanding being at all. Being is understood and conceptualized from time."

[49] *GA* 24, p. 463.

p. 363n.), and the unity of significance of *Dasein*'s world (*SuZ*, p. 365). These claims are not immediately obvious, but they are defensible. Our ability to understand entities *as* being thus and such is parasitic on our ability to distinguish different aspects of those entities. We are able to do this, in turn, because we are able to shift temporal perspectives and to connect those different perspectives together in one experience. The capacity to distinguish and connect different temporal perspectives is also involved in all intentionality, that is, in all understanding of entities as being distinct from our understanding of them. Such intentionality involves the capacity to understand entities from different perspectives and, in the process, to distinguish an entity from one's particular perspectival understandings of it.

We can only understand things as thus and such, and as independent of our own understanding of them, because our own understanding of ourselves as particular individuals involves the ability to distinguish our own particular spatio-temporal situation, with its own distinctive perspective, from other different possible spatio-temporal situations with their own distinctive spatio-temporal perspectives. These other situations with their distinctive perspectives are ones that any of the others might be in who are implicit in our everyday understanding of ourselves. Not only human beings, but also animals and any kind of entity that might be of interest to us will have to be understood in terms of their relation to these spatio-temporal situations. The totality of these spatio-temporal situations expresses what is of potential significance to us.

The argument I have given so far for the temporality of intentionality is very much in the spirit of Husserl's view that temporality is involved in all synthesis of the different perspectives that are constitutive of our intentional relations to objects.[50] Heidegger modifies Husserl's view in three important ways. First he gives up the primacy of perceptual perspectives that characterizes Husserl's approach in favor of the kind of pre-theoretical selectivity that marks our concerns. Second, he argues that these concerns have a distinctive care-structure. They involve a temporality that is literally ecstatic, not just in the sense that the present includes the future and the past in it, but also in the sense that temporal relations include

---

[50] An explicit development of this thesis in Husserl may be found in *Cartesianische Meditationen und Pariser Vorträge, Husserliana: Edmund Husserls Gesammelte Werke* (The Hague: Martinus Nijhoff, 1950), vol. 1. English: *Cartesian Meditations*, trans. Dorian Cairns (The Hague: Martinus Nijhoff, 1973), sections 17–18.

ineliminable *pro* and *contra* attitudes to one's environment. Instead of thinking of intentionality as a primitive property of consciousness, as Husserl does, Heidegger argues that the intentionality of consciousness is to be understood in terms of our ability to make entities present to us as creatures with concerns. Third, Heidegger understands creatures with concerns neither as minds, nor bodies, nor as a synthesis of minds and bodies, but rather as creatures whose spatio-temporal existence in the world is constitutive of their behavior. Such behavior is directed, in part, at what is spatially and temporally present to them. But this capacity to relate to entities as present, is itself just a special case of our general ability temporally to relate to entities in our behavior. Even our behavior towards what is present involves the past in the form of information and the future in the form of the ends in terms of which we interpret the present.

The circumstances in which we move, the ends we pursue, and the means by which we pursue those ends are linked together in our ground project. This ground project, in terms of which we understand whatever we do understand, is structured by the past, the present, and the future. We come at what we understand from the way it involves what we are to be against the background of what has been: "The unity of significance, i.e. the ontological constitution of the world, must then also be grounded in temporality" (*SuZ*, p. 365). This claim must be read in the light of other more forceful claims which he makes. "The 'as,' like understanding and interpretation in general, is grounded in the ecstatic-horizonal unity of temporality" (*SuZ*, p. 360). This means that, whenever one understands or interprets anything, one interprets it in terms of certain background assumptions that one makes. These assumptions are supposed to interpret the way the world is in the light of information provided by one's immediate and less immediate causal past. It is, thus, only because the self is temporal that it can understand or interpret anything at all.

The idea here is that, in order to interpret anything as thus and such, one must first be able to situate it in a context and interpret it in terms of what one wants to do with it. In this sense, interpretation presupposes a context of significance which is itself formed by the structure involved in human agency. Heidegger thinks that our projection of a context of significance can be explicated in term of temporal notions. We come at what we understand from a context of beliefs, emotions, and desires that are supplied by our past; we interpret that context on the basis of the interests that are supplied by what we want to do and how we understand what we are to be; and the interpretation of the context of our experience in terms of our interests expresses itself in present action. This is why Heidegger can claim that the intentionality of "consciousness" is grounded in temporality (*SuZ*, p. 363n). Intentionality is the directedness of the mind toward objects. Language and understanding are "about" objects only because we are able to relate to those objects through the context provided by our past and the interests that form our understanding of what our goals are and what it is to be the human beings that we are. Heidegger argues that, in order to understand the way in which intentionality is constituted, one must look to the distinctive temporality of human existence: "Since my being is continually such that I am ahead of myself, I must come back to what I encounter from my being ahead of it in order to grasp it. Here an immanent structure of simply grasping, of *as* behavior displays itself that proves on closer analysis to be *time*" (*GA* 21, p. 147). Time itself provides the structured context of interpretation that is constitutive of meaning.

Heidegger takes the fundamental character of temporality so seriously that he thinks he can use the notion of temporality to explicate what is going on in the traditional notion of the a priori. Here Heidegger seems, above all, to have Kant's conception of the a priori as conditions for the possibility of any experience in mind. Temporality becomes the condition under which all the conditions of the possibility of human existence and of at least any experience of other entities is possible. Temporality makes the existentials and categories possible which are, in turn, the conditions under which human existence, on the one hand, and the being of other kinds of entities, on the other hand, are possible. "Because the original possibilizer, the source of possibility itself, is time, time temporalizes itself as the absolutely earliest" (*GA* 24, p. 463). The priority referred to in the term "a priori" is construed as its dependence on temporality. Temporality allows Heidegger to make sense of the priority involved in logical priority without commitment to the idea that what is prior is actually earlier "in" time. The source of all possibility cannot be any of the individual existentials or categories, although these existentials and categories do give necessary structure to possibilities. The source of all possibilities can only be found in what makes the totality of these structures possible. This is why

Heidegger refers to time as "the basic existential of existence." It is only because time is the basic existential of existence that it can provide the horizon or context in which being in general is to be understood.

In the next chapter, I begin developing Heidegger's own full notion of a human being as the kind of being whose very nature it is to exist spatially and, especially, temporally. I articulate Heidegger's alternative both to the conception of time-consciousness articulated by Husserl and defenders of the primacy of tense and temporal becoming, and to those theorists who favor a theory of time based on physical theory. I show how Heidegger responds to relativity theory by criticizing the primacy of present experience, while rejecting the claim of physical theory to provide the most fundamental description of time.

CHAPTER 8

Heidegger's theory of time

Heidegger claims that the traditional theory of time is based on a failure to understand the nature of time. In this chapter I develop and evaluate this thesis. As an account of temporal experience, Heidegger's conception of temporality is avowedly revisionist. It depends on rejecting the intuitive claim that time is fundamentally now-centered. Heidegger offers an interesting rationale for the thesis that what exists now should not be taken to be as fundamental to experience as we tend to take it to be. This amounts to a critique of the traditional manner in which time is interpreted in terms of tense. The notion of tense is generally thought to involve a now relative to which a present, and then a past and future may be defined. Heidegger argues that this notion of time as a succession of nows is highly derivative. It can only be adequately understood in terms of a notion of tense that is based on a quite different notion of presence. Heidegger's work also suggests a rather subtle critique of the most obvious alternative to the conception of time based on tense. This alternative theory of time based on physical theory construes time as the tenseless existence of events at certain clock-times.

In articulating Heidegger's conception of time I shall proceed as follows: first I discuss what he refers to as the "vulgar" notion of time. This is the notion of time that has dominated the philosophical tradition and the natural sciences. It is based on the assumption that time, regardless of whether it is identified with tense or not, is something that is essentially measurable by clocks. From Heidegger's point of view, the vulgar notion of time is a distortion of temporality.

I then explicate this notion of temporality and its relation to the interpretation of human existence as constituting by care. I show how temporality may be understood as the non-sequential tensed structure underlying tensed discourse. I argue against any straightforward reduction of this tensed structure and the direction of time to physical occurrences. I next discuss the manner in which the systematic illusion of temporal sequence is due to the way our expectations express themselves in the selectiveness of demonstrative language. The selectiveness of demonstrative discourse provides the basis for Heidegger's critique and reconstruction of time understood as tensed discourse about things. This requires a discussion of the way temporality manifests itself in the language of demonstrative discourse. I argue that Heidegger's skepticism about the identification of what is real with what exists now is due to his appropriation of the relativity of simultaneity from special relativity. His interpretation of physical theory also leads him to the thesis that time is presupposed but not completely analyzed in physical theory. I then discuss Heidegger's response to the conception of time as a tenseless sequence of events that occur without any necessary relation to the experience of persons.

My discussion of Heidegger's response to the conception of time as tenseless sequence involves a critical discussion of his reasons for maintaining that truth and being are essentially temporal as well as his reasons for maintaining that time, truth, and being cannot exist independently of us. I conclude that Heidegger's analysis gives us some basis for thinking that his own notion of temporality is built into an understanding of temporal experience. But his initial thesis that time cannot exist independently of us in nature proves to be indefensible, and he first wavers about the status of time *vis-à-vis* nature and is then eventually forced to give up the implausible claim in favor of the view that time is necessary to the very being of nature.

CARE AND TEMPORALITY

Against the Husserlian idea, also defended by B-theorists in the philosophy of time, that there is a form of tenseless existence that characterizes individuals, Heidegger argues that "If the expressions 'before' [*vor*] and 'already' [*schon*] were to have *this* tensed [*zeithafte*] signification, which they can also have, then one would be saying with the temporality of care that it [care] is something which is 'earlier' and 'later,' 'not yet' and 'no longer' all at once. Care would then be conceived of as an entity which is found and runs its course 'in time.' The *being* of an entity with the character of *Dasein* would become something *present at hand*" (*SuZ*, p. 375). Heidegger also wants to avoid an A-series of time according to which temporal process would be understood as a "*becoming* of the ecstasies (thus the present becomes the past, the future becomes the present, etc.)"[1] He thus also rejects the Husserlian idea that experiences are in time in the sense of being past, present, and future. While there is a sense in which one can say that experiences are past, present, and future in virtue of their being picked out demonstratively, he wants to reject Husserl's idea that past, present, and future are constituted by a sequence of experiences that have a kind of consciousness of themselves.

However, Heidegger takes over two important ideas from Husserl's analysis of time-consciousness. The first idea is that time is not to be understood fundamentally in terms of what can be measured by clocks. For Heidegger, as for Husserl, this has to do with the claim that any account of time in terms of what is measurable by clocks would have to depend on some knowledge of physical processes which cannot be presupposed any longer when we reach the fundamental level of temporal experience. He also takes over from Husserl the idea that the interconnectedness of past, present, and future involves a distinctive form of intentionality that is the key to understanding all other experience. However, Heidegger wants to show how the presencing involved in Husserl's notion of intentionality, consciousness's directedness at objects, involves an understanding of spatio-temporal context that undercuts any prospects for achieving the methodological solipsism to which Husserl is attracted. This involves a reinterpretation of the whole notion of experience (away from the interiority of "Erlebnisse").

Heidegger wants to reinterpret the nature of the distinction between past, present, and future away from the model of a series regardless of whether we interpret it as what McTaggart would call an A-, B-, or even C-series. In this way he hopes to articulate a conception of temporality that abstracts from the prominence of clocks in the philosophical interpretation of tense. In order to articulate his response to the A- and B-series conceptions of time I need to develop his own conception of temporality. The most distinctive feature of Heidegger's conception of time is the way in which he links time to human existence. Human beings are char-

---

[1] Piotr Hoffman, "Death, Time, and History," in Charles Guignon (ed.), *The Cambridge Companion to Heidegger* (New York: Cambridge University Press, 1993), p. 208. Thus Heidegger rejects not only the existence of a metric intrinsic to temporality, as Hoffman claims, but the fundamental character of becoming and succession, as well.

acterized by Heidegger as *Dasein* to express the way in which they must situate themselves spatially and temporally in order to exist. "Da-sein" literally means "to be here," but also "there," and "now" and "then." As Heidegger interprets *Dasein*, it is to be here and now only in virtue of also having an understanding of what it is to be there and then. To exist in this sense involves some understanding of truth, some disclosure of one's spatio-temporal world (*SuZ*, p. 132). Temporality (including spatiality) constitutes the very disclosure (understanding of some truth) that is constitutive of human existence. Temporality is supposed to be what constitutes human beings as individuals who care about each other, their own projects, and the world in general. Care is Heidegger's way of characterizing the distinctive kind of being that distinguishes those beings that have an understanding of entities as being thus and such. This goes with an understanding of being in general. We are who and what we are because of the things, animals, and human beings who matter to us. They can matter to us because we have some understanding of what and who they are and what and who we are.

The way in which we are formed by already being in the world, while structuring our heritage in terms of the way we will be, is expressed in Heidegger's definition of care as "being-ahead-of-oneself-in-already-being-in-the-world" (*SuZ*, p. 192). The three modes of temporality, to have been, to be present, and to be about to be, corresponding to the everyday notion of tenses, are built into the definition of care. This is certainly not the everyday meaning of care. But there is some plausibility to the idea that we can make sense of our cares, what matters to us, only in terms of what has been, is, and will be true of its relation to us. These temporal distinctions also involve an essentially spatial dimension that is reflected in the way we understand what we care about.

As we have seen, Heidegger's definition of care is "being-ahead-of-oneself-in-already-being-in-the-world as being-alongside intra-worldly entities." Of course, this is a definition of care that is already unmistakably and essentially temporal. As a first approximation we can say that "already-being-in-the-world" refers to what Heidegger calls our thrownness. Thrownness is a way of expressing the idea that we have an experience that cannot coherently abstract from its dependence on our past environment (as Cartesian skepticism suggested that we might). "Being-alongside ..." refers to our absorption in the present (this absorption in the present gives solipsism of the present moment whatever initial plausibility it has). Most importantly, since Heidegger says that the future is primary (*SuZ*, pp. 327, 329), "being-ahead-of-oneself" is about our future and the manner in which the goal-directedness of our interests structures the way our past environment is understood in the present.

Put together, *Dasein* is care insofar as *Dasein* is a creature that inherits the past, is preoccupied with the present and able to act on its future by understanding its past and its present in terms of its concern for what it can come to be. This explains what care is and what it is to be a *Dasein*. But this is only a first approximation to *Dasein*'s temporality because, as Heidegger insists, his conceptions of the past, present, and future are not to be understood according to the common-sense or "vulgar" conceptions of these notions.[2] Temporality is also essentially tied up with spatiality and publicity. Spatiality is important to our understanding of ourselves as distinct human beings, and hence to our experience of our own temporal experience as having a point of view from which it organizes time within a larger shared whole of time. This shared time expresses itself as the publicity of time. We care not only about ourselves, but about others. Indeed, in our care for ourselves there is an implicit understanding of our differences from others. This leads to a concern about the mutual implications of the interests that we individually and collectively pursue.

The key to Heidegger's account of temporality is the way in which past, present, and future coexist and codetermine each other as ways in which human existence understands itself and the particulars in its world. In *Being and Time*, Heidegger argues that one can meaningfully say of any disposition that characterizes a person that it is future in the past, present in the past, as well as future in the present, etc. But this "temporalizing does not mean a one after the other of the ecstasies. The future is not *later* than having beenness and the latter is *not earlier* than the present" (*SuZ*, p. 350). Past, present, and future are "ecstasies." They exist only by including an essential relation to the other tenses from which they are distinguishable. In this sense, they are literally what they are by going "outside of" themselves (ec-static).[3] They are also supposed to take us outside of ourselves. They are structures in terms of which we relate to

---

[2] An earlier and somewhat different version of this chapter is to be found in Pierre Keller, "Critique of the Vulgar Notion of Time," *International Journal of Philosophical Studies* 4, 1 (1996).

[3] See the discussion of temporal transcendence and intentionality in Françoise Dastur, "La

ourselves as possibilies of being thus and such by relating to entities that are distinct from ourselves. Heidegger avoids at least any obvious contradiction in his notion of temporality. As temporality, pastness, presentness, and futurity are not mutually exclusive determinations as are past, present, and future in time conceived of as a sequence of successively real states. In Heidegger's view, the tenses are not mutually exclusive properties of a thing or an event, but rather different ways in which the world exists for human existence. From this point of view, it makes sense to talk of the past, present, and future of the past, present, and future. Each of these is a distinctive temporal perspective.

Heidegger eschews the terms "past," "present," and "future" because of their misleading connotations having to do with passage (*SuZ*, p. 326). But he does not have much to say about what distinguishes past, present, and future when they are properly understood in terms of temporality. Yet we need to be able to draw an interesting distinction between the tenses in order to be able to find the claim that they each include the other at all illuminating. He notes that "past" temporality, or what has been, has the structure of coming back to oneself. "Present" temporality has the structure of presenting. It is the way in which what one has been and what one is to be expresses itself in what one does. "Future" temporality has the structure of coming towards oneself. It is the way in which what has been is taken up in what is to be (*SuZ*, pp. 325ff.). These characterizations of time help us to see how the past, present, and future could be interdependent, yet distinct. Each involves the other, but in each case the primacy goes to one of these dimensions of time over the other. This also suggests that the various aspects of one's life and those of others may well be temporally connected together in a manner which defies any straightforward sequential structuring.

Reference to what has been, what is, and what will be as coming back to oneself, presenting, and coming towards oneself depends heavily on metaphors from human action.[4] This is no accident.

constitution ekstatique-horizontale de la temporalité chez Heidegger," *Heidegger Studies* 2 (1984), 97–110, esp. 100.

[4] Paul Edwards suggests that Heidegger's notion of a temporal stretch is incoherent: "If I am in the front-row of a procession I can run ahead and thus be in advance of the position I would be occupying if I had stayed in line. Heidegger believes that in the same way I can stretch or run into the future while I am still in the present. If this were possible then I *could* now be my not-yet and I could also get my death into the present. But this is not possible," *Heidegger and Death* (La Salle: Open Court, 1979), p. 25. These absurdities follow only if one

Entities are disclosed to us primarily in our ability as agents to deal with our environment. The distinction between what has been, what is, and what will be is supposed to reflect what it is to be a human being. We find ourselves in a world that is not completely of our own making (facticity). This is the basis for what has been, or pastness. We come to terms with facticity by developing a way of existing that determines who we are (project). Our different projects are bound together in a fundamental project of understanding the world in terms of our interest in what we are to become. This interest in what we are to be is the basis for our experience of the future and its futurity. Our projects are, in turn, the basis for our appropriation of the way we have been thrown into the world. In the way that our past informs our projects, the past is future. In interpreting ourselves in terms of our origins, we also tend to identify ourselves with what we experience in our world (fallenness). This is the presence of the past and the future.

The way in which the facticity of what has been, the fallenness of what is, and the character of what will be as project constitute time can be elucidated by the role they play in our understanding of the direction of time. Heidegger argues that the irreversibility of the time-series of earlier and later resists complete mathematical analysis. This alludes to the time-order invariance of the fundamental laws of physical theory and the difficulty of identifying anything in nature that is fundamentally time-order invariant.[5] Only the second law of thermodynamics involves a preferred temporal direction, and the second law is a phenomenological law based on the inherently probabilistic laws of statistical mechanics. Entropy or disorder in a system is accounted for by relative frequency of the number of microstates consistent with any given macrostate divided by the total number of possible microstates. Macrostates of higher entropy, and hence a direction of time that favors increase in disorder, are more probable since a system tends to develop to those macrostates that involve relatively more microscopic arrangements of particles. Boltzmann's H-theorem demonstrates that a closed system which is in a state of non-maximal entropy will very probably be in a state of higher entropy at some later time. But, if we apply the same

---

already assumes the notion of time as a succession of presents each of which is independently real.

[5] Martin Heidegger, *The Concept of Time*, English–German edition (Oxford: Blackwell, 1992), pp. 18, 18E.

considerations to a time t_0 prior to time t_1, we find that the system will have the same probability of being at a higher entropy level at t_0 as the level of entropy it had at t_1. However, the assumption that the past has a higher level of entropy than the future contradicts the second law and our experience.

The entropy increase required by the second law is usually introduced by appeal to some hypothesis concerning the frequency of low entropy starting states in a particular region of the universe. But these hypotheses must make some assumption to the effect that processes develop only in a future direction.[6] Boltzmann, for instance, postulates that the universe as a whole is in thermal equilibrium, but that there are pockets of low entropy the size of galaxies due to statistical fluctuations in the ensemble of molecules in the universe. The problem with this suggestion is that it is much more probable that the present, with all its information about the past, is itself a thermal fluctuation, than that the past with an even lower entropy ever existed.[7] Improbable states count as documents which provide us with information about the past only if we are able to assume that they were preceded by still more improbable states. The Big Bang origin of the universe may be appealed to in order to account for low initial entropy. The temporal direction of the universe is then accounted for by the return of the universe to thermodynamical equilibrium. Unfortunately, this still fails to show the universe cannot have been preceded by a state of higher entropy. It thus fails to establish a direction to time. There have been attempts to account for the asymmetry by appeal to weak coupling and chaotic background noise, but these strategies are all rather *ad hoc*.

An account in the spirit of Heidegger's conception of temporality promises to close this gap. It would understand probability as the *prediction* of the relative frequency of an event of a certain type. Such a future-oriented understanding of probability allows one to explain the irreversibility involved in the second law, by excluding the possibility, suggested by the probabilistic nature of the laws of statistical mechanics, that there has been a decrease of entropy in the past. Thus, the H-theorem yields irreversibility if and only if one can make predictions about the future based on thermodynamical

---

[6] The alternative ways in which one might introduce some time-asymmetrical assumption are well canvassed by Paul Horwich, *Asymmetries in Time* (Cambridge, Mass. MIT Press, 1991) and Huw Price, *Time's Arrow and Archimedes' Point* (Oxford University Press, 1996).

[7] M. Bronstein and L. Landau, *Soviet Physics* 4 (1933), 114.

probabilities and not about the past.[8] The future is available to us
only through our projections based on the way the facticity of the
past manifests itself in the present. In a situation in which we know
what happened in the past, this knowledge will affect our probability
judgments.[9] And, in a situation in which we do not know what
happened in the past, we will make our probability judgments based
on what was in the past of that past of which we are ignorant. We
can then, of course, regard the present, and the past itself as a past
future.

From this point of view, the second law provides a criterion of
temporal priority, but not a reductive analysis of the direction of
time. For we are only justified in interpreting the direction of
entropy increase as the direction of time by a prior appeal to the
assumption that we have information, present documents from the
past, but not from the future. Progress can then be made in
explicating the notions of what has been, what is, and what will be,
in terms of the way information discloses itself to us. It is tempting to
think of the reality of the past as a mere trace in the present of what
no longer exists. Here a trace is an event that provides information
about its causal antecedents. If we abstract from the idea that only
the present is actual, we can, however, understand the reality of the
past in a different way. The past is in the present and the future in
the form of information about what has been. This information is
embedded in the structure of things as a trace, that is, as information
about the causal antecedents of the event. This trace might be found
in the geological record, or in memory, or on a computer diskette. As
information for us, it is always information about what has been.
The trace expresses Heidegger's idea of the facticity of what is past.
For something to be future, by contrast, there can be no traces of it.
For the future is the domain of things of which we can have an
understanding only through the way in which we can extrapolate
from the traces of what has been. This expresses the connection

---

[8] Carl Friedrich von Weizsäcker, *Aufbau der Physik* (Hamburg: Hanser, 1985), esp. pp. 136–139,
and "The Second Law and the Difference between Past and Future," in *The Unity of Nature*
(New York: Farrar, Strauss, Giroux, 1980), pp. 138–146.

[9] "It should not be forgotten, when our ensembles are chosen to illustrate the probabilities in
the real world, that while the probabilities of subsequent events may often be determined
from the probabilities of prior events, it is rarely the case that probabilities of prior events
can be determined from those of subsequent events, for we are rarely justified in excluding
the consideration of the antecedent probability of the prior events," J. Willard Gibbs,
Elementary Principles in Statistical Mechanics (New York: Dover Publications, 1960), p. 151.

between the future and the notion of a project or projection. The present is itself just the interface of that for which we have traces, what has been, with that for which we have no traces, that which will be.

DEMONSTRATIVE DISCOURSE AND THE VULGAR NOTION OF TIME

Heidegger argues, as do most B-theorists, that the passage of time is an illusion generated by our use of demonstrative language. This is a very attractive picture of why the "myth of passage" has had such a grip on us. However, Heidegger agrees with A-theorists, as I have argued, that the tenses displayed in demonstrative discourse are fundamental to our understanding of time. This goes beyond recent concessions by B-theorists. For, according to Heidegger, even the metalanguage, in terms of which we understand the distinction between past, present, and future, and, indeed, between earlier, later, and simultaneous, is inherently tensed. To fully articulate Heidegger's response first to the A- and then later the B-series theories of time, I need to articulate the conditions for demonstrative discourse. This will allow me to show how he proposes to derive both the A- and B-series theories of time from degenerate cases of demonstrative discourse.

Demonstrative discourse about time, talk of time in terms of "today" and "tomorrow," "now" and "then," builds on the context supplied by our public engagements with the world and our dependence on a nature that is radically independent of us. Heidegger refers to demonstrative or indexical expressions as "adverbs of *Dasein*." Spatial and temporal demonstratives express various systematically connected ways for human beings ("Dasein") to be who and what they are.[10] Such self-locating demonstratives presuppose but do not themselves constitute the spatiality and temporality that makes human existence what it is. As expressions of alternative ways for a human being to be, they tacitly involve the

---

[10] "Adverbs of *Dasein* with their pronominal sense of 'I' and 'you' make my own being-in as *Dasein* and the other as with-*Dasein* evident only as a 'here' and an 'over there'. 'Here' and 'over there' are only possible insofar as there is something like a 'there' (*ein 'Da'*). This 'here' is our being toward being-with-one-another insofar as the possibility of a totality for use ('Bewandtnisganzheit') in orientation obtains at all," *The History of the Concept of Time*, GA 20, p. 253.

totality of relationships in which each person's existence is situated. This leads to the claim that demonstrative or indexical expressions can only be adequately understood in terms of a conception of human existence (of self, spatiality, and temporality) that is radically different from the one that one arrives at when one thinks of what these expressions refer to in isolation. Thus, the now sequence of disconnected presents is an abstraction from the "world-time" of public engagements in terms of which particulars are initially intelligible to us (*SuZ*, p. 419). This abstraction leads to the idea that the semantical properties of indexicals can be treated in isolation from the conditions under which they can be used and understood. This means that indexical discourse in general and more particularly temporal indexical discourse can be described adequately only in terms of instrumental reason and a broad notion of practical reason. This self-determination is based on information provided by a person's environment.[11]

Situatedness in a world consisting of a set of external circumstances is tacitly expressed in the contextual meaning of indexical expressions, thus Heidegger can say that: "*In saying I Dasein expresses its being-in-the-world*" (*SuZ*, p. 321). The same remark applies to saying *here* and *now*. This being-in-the-world is the way the world as a whole presents itself to a certain human existence with a standpoint within the world. The notion of time, like that of the self, develops out of one's performance of social functions. This time is also extended, that is, it consists essentially of intervals, since it is conceived of in terms of the performance of tasks in the world. Time is "datable" because such temporal intervals are understood with reference to the occurrence of specific events in one's world. Heidegger thus emphasizes four aspects of the "use" of time which are constitutive of what he refers to as "world-time": its significance

---

[11] See especially the discussion by Gareth Evans, *The Varieties of Reference* (Oxford University Press, 1982), "a demonstrative identification of an object is part of a scheme of thought which also allows for a place to be identified as *here*, and ... both must be explained in terms of the position of the subject in a spatial world; hence both are connected with the subject's identification of himself," p. 176. One might find reference to demonstrative or indexical discourse in this context anachronistic. But Heidegger devoted seminars to Husserl's analysis of "essentially subjective and occasional expressions" in the *Investigations* I, section 26, p. 313. The evidence for this may be found in Theodore Kisiel, *The Genesis of Heidegger's Being and Time*, p. 556. Not only is the term "now" discussed in the *Investigations*, but this discussion can be related to Husserl's interpretation of time and consciousness in terms of presencing ("Gegenwärtigen," see *SuZ*, p. 363n).

or meaningfulness ("Bedeutsamkeit"), its datability, its extension, and its publicity (*SuZ*, p. 414; *GA* 24, pp. 369ff.). These four features of world-time underwrite the way in which we use the expression "now" and engage in discourse about time in general. They must, indeed, be regarded as constitutive features of time in general.

Indexicals do not have meaning in isolation. They presuppose a context of significance. Heidegger's notion of significance is holistic. Nothing is supposed to have meaning in isolation from everything else. The general idea is that any characterization of what one understands in terms of discrete beliefs, emotions, and desires, with a sentential or propositional structure is an abstraction from the way one orients oneself in one's engagements with the world. This idea applies not only to our beliefs, emotions, and desires but also to the structure of time as it presents itself in our engagements with the world. Time is "meaningful" or "significant" because the specific events in one's world are understood only in relation to each other. What is now has its meaning only relative to what is then. Thus, time itself is understood only in terms of the relations between different temporal intervals and the different events that take place during those intervals. These intervals may be distinguished and expressed in terms of language.

Although they may be used to pick out individual spaces, times, objects, and persons, indexicals do so against the background of an understanding of what space, time, objects, and persons are in general. This understanding is not itself based on any descriptive knowledge, but expresses an immediate ostensive understanding of the objects involved. This is best seen with respect to their type meaning. Occurrences of an indexical may agree in type meaning but express a different token meaning if used in different circumstances. "Now" uttered on two different occasions is an example. Conversely, indexicals can have different type meaning and yet express the same content when uttered in different circumstances. This is a function of the interchangeability of spatio-temporal standpoints. It gives rise to reciprocal perspectives each of which is intelligible from the standpoint of the other. The present may be defined as what is happening now, the past may be defined as what has already happened or what has happened earlier than now, and the future may be defined as what has yet to happen or what is happening later than now. These contextual relations are sufficiently systematic to be formalizable in a logic for indexicals.

Indexicals have token meaning that is determined by the circumstances of their use. In specifying the circumstances of a particular use of an indexical we "date" its use (more or less effectively). We say "then when ..." This datability can best be explained by assuming that indexical discourse interprets the relational character of time and space. The type meaning of indexicals would seem to be an abstraction from their token meaning. Token meaning is a function of the particular natural and historical circumstances in which a certain indexical type is tokened. By abstracting from such circumstances and focusing only on the type meaning of indexicals, space and the subject take on the appearance of being disconnected from particular circumstances.

Time interpreted as a sequence of nows is time conceived of in abstraction from the conditions under which the demonstratives can be used in terms of which that now sequence is articulated. The time expressed in these nows is actually public, since it depends on affective relations to our environment that are expressible in terms of a public language, even though it presents itself as if it might belong only to the experience of a single individual. This illusion of privacy derives from the tendency in discourse to privilege what is immediately present to the consciousness of the user of demonstrative or indexical terms such as "this," "I," "here," and "now." It is in terms of the discriminating powers of intentionality, together with descriptions of situations and objects, that we come to understand what we are referring to when we use these interdefinable demonstrative expressions. In using our capacity to distinguish individual objects by means of the intentionality of discourse and language, we isolate individual occurrences and objects from their overall context of significance.

As one concentrates more and more on the accuracy of tools to measure temporal relations between objects of use, one can come to regard time itself as something that is an object measured. Moreover, increased accuracy leads one to become more and more concerned with ever smaller units of time. The now distinguished by discourse is transformed into a knife-edged now as language is regimented by the desire for greater precision in measurement. The use of temporal indexicals as expressions that pick out temporal regions encourages the idea that time can be divided up into regions with no essential connection to other temporal regions. The conception of a sequence of disconnected moments is encouraged by the use of indexicals to isolate particular times. Its effect can be seen through the influence of Aristotle's emphasis on time (in *Physics* IV) as a now sequence. Every temporally extended present can be further divided into nows which converge to a now of no extension. Once the unextended now becomes the basic unit of time, time seems to fall apart into disconnected and successively real moments. These nows become the disconnected epistemological presents of the theoretician and the Cartesian skeptic with his or her solipsism of the present moment. The appearance of succession arises from the continual replacement of one now and its specific experiential content by another now with a different experiential content. The different contents of experience are selected by means of the demonstrative power of discourse. This demonstrative power derives from the presencing that is characteristic of intentionality.

In pursuing our projects there is a tendency to lose track of the underlying meaning that one gives to one's life and thus of the way in which the basic project of living the life we do structures all of our particular immediate goals. In focusing on the achievement of the goals set by the roles we have in our social interactions, we tend to focus on particular accomplishments or failures in isolation from the meaning that they have for the project of our life as a whole. The accomplishments or failures that we have within our social roles encourage us to think of our existence as human beings on the model of a sequence of person-stages each of which is ontologically independent of the other, rather than as the unity of a certain human existence that is not yet complete until death. This tendency is encouraged by the capacity of language to order events and objects in a sequence. What is present is then distinguished by particular failures or accomplishments that stand out against the general background of our overall interests.[12]

RELATIVITY AND THE NOW

The theory of special relativity has been particularly influential in calling into question the assumption that time should be understood

[12] It is sometimes argued that Heidegger cannot account for temporal passage by means of his theory of temporality, for instance by Peter McInerney, *Time and Experience* (Philadelphia: Temple University Press, 1991), pp. 136, 147. But these remarks should be sufficient to respond to the claim that Heidegger does not have the means for explaining our belief in passage. This criticism ignores the way in which temporality expresses itself demonstratively in the different nows of consciousness.

on the model of the A-series and its now sequence. According to special relativity, different observers do not, in general, observe the same things to be simultaneous. A may be simultaneous with B relative to one observer, and B simultaneous with C for another observer, but A may not be simultaneous with C for either observer. Simultaneity is therefore no longer a transitive relation. It must be relativized to the reference frame of a given inertial state of motion. Since observers at different positions in the universe observe different things to be simultaneous with each other, the traditional notion of successive slices of the universe as a whole becomes problematic.[13] Indeed, to maintain conformity with special relativity theory, one must relativize what is real to a particular reference frame. Not only is there no unique meaning to simultaneity in special relativity, but intervals are not perceived in the same way by observers who are undergoing acceleration relative to one another. Thus, different observers no longer can be taken to agree about which events belong to the same time or even about the properties that those events display. They may disagree about such basic properties of objects as the mass and length of those objects, although the physical laws governing such objects are themselves invariant between different reference frames.

Heidegger's interest in special relativity is documented in a very early article of his on time from 1918.[14] It is thus quite plausible to ascribe a seminal influence to special relativity in the development of his theory of time. In the 1924 talk on time in which he first presents his early mature philosophy, Heidegger notes that special relativity is incompatible with absolute simultaneity.[15] Once one rejects the notion of absolute simultaneity, one is forced to relativize the now to

[13] McTaggart anticipated the objection from alternative time-series in his 1905 *Mind* article, "The Unreality of Time," reprinted in his *Philosophical Studies* (London: Edward Arnold Press, 1934), p. 122: "No doubt in such a case, no present would be *the* present – it would only be the present of a certain aspect of the universe. But then no time would be *time* – it would only be the time of a certain aspect of the universe." The compatibility of temporal becoming with special relativity is argued convincingly by Howard Stein, "Minkowski Space-Time", *Journal of Philosophy* 65 (1968), 5–23 and also Lawrence Sklar, *Space, Time, and Spacetime* (Berkeley: University of California Press, 1974), 272–275. For a defense of the view that special relativity is incompatible with temporal becoming, see Hilary Putnam, "Time and Physical Geometry," *Journal of Philosophy* 64 (1967), 240–247 and C. W. Rietdijk, "A Rigorous Proof of Determinism Derived from the Special Theory of Relativity," *Philosophy of Science* 33 (1966), 341–344.
[14] Martin Heidegger, "Der Zeitbegriff in der Geisteswissenschaft," *GA* 1, pp. 413–434, esp. p. 424.
[15] Heidegger, *The Concept of Time*, pp. 3, 3E.

the position of a certain observer. The assumption that the now is what is fundamental to time, and indeed for an understanding of reality in general, loses much of its force. The interpretation of what is real as what is present is then much less plausible. Worries about the relativity of simultaneity would have provided Heidegger with good reason to be skeptical about the primacy traditionally given to succession in understanding. For succession presupposes a now sequence that no longer has the observer-independent status it was traditionally thought to have.

Heidegger also interprets special relativity as eliminating time and space in favor of interactions between physical events. This, together with the difficulties of identifying a basis in physical law for the direction of time, lead him to deny an ultimate status to time and space in physics: "The current state of this [physical] research is set down in Einstein's relativity theory. Here are some principles derived from it: Space is nothing in itself; there is no absolute space. Space exists only through the bodies and energies contained in it. (An old principle of Aristotle's.) Time is also nothing. It consists only in the events which occur in it. There is no absolute time, and also no absolute simultaneity."[16] The time of physical theory is understood as a reductive relational view that gives no reality to time independent of physical relations between events.

The view that relativity theory commits one to a relational theory of space and time, was prevalent even among experts in the field during the 1920s. Since the relationist view dominated the interpretation of physical theory at the time Heidegger was formulating his views about the nature of physical reality, he concluded that the absolute theory of space and time was incompatible with physical theory. The absolutist maintains that space and time have a reality independent of the physical objects that have spatial and temporal relations to each other. The relationist, by contrast, insists that time and space are, at best, the spatial and temporal relations between real things or events, or perhaps only the physical basis for such spatial and temporal relations. The relational theory of space and time continues to have defenders, although the general theory of relativity gives considerable prima facie support to the absolute theory of space and time. The Machian goal of accounting for spatial and temporal relations purely by means of the distribution of

[16] Ibid.

matter and energy in the universe was an important inspiration to Einstein in formulating the general theory. But this goal has proved to be elusive. There are solutions to the field equations that ascribe a topology and metric to space and time in the absence of all matter. There are also models of the general theory that appear to allow for the possibility of global rotations.[17] If all the matter in the universe is rotating, it is difficult to account for rotation in terms of purely relative motions of matter. This means that the relationist must work very hard to account for the structure of space and time purely in terms of the non-temporal relations between physical events.

Heidegger affirms the existence of physical occurrences that are independent of time, but not the existence of a physical time that is independent of the way in which such occurrences are disclosed to us. Were he to assume an ultimate ontological difference between time and events or things with changing states that holds independently of human understanding, he would be committed to an absolute theory of time. Because he identifies time with the basic condition under which entities exist *for us*, he is led to deny an independent reality to time: "There is no nature-time, insofar as all time belongs essentially to *Dasein*" (*GA* 24, p. 370). There are "motions" ("Bewegungen") in nature that do not occur in time when time is taken in abstraction from the existence of human beings. These changes are nevertheless "in time" insofar as they present themselves to us in the form of occurrent objects, insofar as "they are discovered as pure nature" (*GA* 20, p. 442). There is thus a sense in which motion or change do not presuppose time, as well as a sense for Heidegger in which they are in time. We can, indeed, make sense of motion or change in terms of tenseless relations between different events, even though those events present themselves to human experience as tensed and will have to be cashed out in a metalanguage that is irreducibly tensed. Heidegger can thus acknowledge the existence of time as an independent physical

---

[17] Even if one rejects empty models of theories about space and time as devoid of empirical significance, one will have to contend with models in which space and time are almost devoid of matter. For all we know all the matter in the universe might be aggregated very close to its center. A discussion of empty and almost empty models of the universe may be found in Stephen Hawking and George Ellis, *The Large Scale Structure of Space-Time* (Cambridge University Press, 1973), pp. 117ff. In the Kerr solution, we are concerned with what amounts to an isolated rotating mass. This is easier to regard as a description of our space-time than Gödel's solution which involves the possibility of closed loops through time, ibid. pp. 162–170.

parameter. But, for him, time and motion as objects of physical and mathematical theory are our temporal interpretations of motions in nature that are not intrinsically temporal.

TIME AND NATURE

Skepticism about the feasibility of analyzing temporal notions in purely physical terms is an important reason for Heidegger to reject the B-series theory of time. The notion of time as a series of point events "existing" tenselessly at particular clock-times and ordered according to earlier and later is, for Heidegger, an abstraction from the most fundamental conception of temporality.[18] Temporality is tied to human existence. The thesis that we have no intelligible conception of time that is independent of human existence provides the basis for his rejection of the B-series theory of time. The B-series theory assumes that the self-referential structure displayed by demonstrative discourse has only epistemic priority in our under-standing of time. In principle, it is eliminable in favor of an objective account of time that makes no implicit reference to human existence. Heidegger agrees with the A-theorist that this contextual dimension of time cannot be eliminated from discourse about time without replacing time with mere changes in states or events. Physical *time* exists only relative to possible measurements, predictions, and theories which we might come up with.[19] It involves the necessity of the possibility of something being measurable and hence repeatable.

---

[18] Thus, in his paper of 1918, Heidegger maintains that the "indication of quantity collects the time-points that have flowed by until then together into one. We make, as it were, a cut in the time-scale, thereby destroying actual [*eigentliche*] time in its flow and freezing it. The flow freezes, becomes a plane and can only be measured as a plane. Time has become a homogeneous order of positions, a scale, a parameter," *GA* 1, p. 424. In the same paper, Heidegger insists that historical time is inherently heterogeneous, consisting of qualitatively different social structures that "cannot be expressed mathematically through a series, since there is no law determining how the *times* succeed each other," p. 431.

[19] The independence of physical reality has a place in an ultimate description of the world, as Heidegger understands such a description, but the reality described by physical science is just one mode of being among others. The task of understanding the various basic senses of being would fall to a metaontology. This metaontology is based on differences in what are traditionally regarded as tenses, between something having been, something being present, and something coming to be. In a lecture of 1928, Heidegger promises a metaontology as the ontology for which fundamental ontology merely paves the way. This metaontology must take up the question of the status of entities insofar as they are independent of human existence. *Metaphysical Foundations of Logic*, *GA* 26, p. 199: "The possibility that there is understanding in being has the factual existence of *Dasein* as a presupposition and this in turn the factual presence at hand [*Vorhandensein*] of nature."

This accessibility to measurement leads Heidegger to identify such being with presence to perceptual, logical, or mathematical intuition. Physical time, like physical reality in general, derives its intelligibility for us from the possibility for us of being acquainted with entities through information from observations. The information from these observations is the basis for predictions. The connection to observation and prediction gives time (and the same thing applies to space) an essentially demonstrative dimension.

The claim that the B-series is an abstract representation of reality must ultimately depend on Heidegger's critique of the most basic underlying assumption of the B-series theory. This is the assumption that there are tenseless or timeless truths. Heidegger attributes the assertion of "eternal truths" to the residual effects of theology in philosophy (*SuZ*, p. 229). They are truths that one can only make sense of by assuming the possibility of a God's-eye point of view, a point of view that can survey the whole of time. He argues that even the being of atemporal truths and abstract objects has been traditionally understood on the model of presence, namely as persistence through all time. This way of understanding eternity emphasizes the idea of omnipresence or sempiternity, that is the idea behind the scholastic notion of the standing now ("nunc stans"), or the now that does not involve succession.[20] Interpreting eternity as the omnipresence characteristic of an eternal life leads Heidegger to the dubious thesis that the notion of atemporal truth and atemporal existence in general is a privation of temporal truth and existence and hence parasitic on temporal existence. In thinking of something as outside of time, one is thinking of it as not "in" time. But, according to Heidegger, this does not mean that one's understanding of truth or existence is independent of temporality, since temporality is not exhausted by what is in time (see *GA* 26, p. 182). Thus, in formulating mathematical statements such as "two plus two is equal to four," we make use of a timeless present. The timeless present is itself based on temporality insofar as it involves presence.

The fundamental ontologist insists that the formulation of puta-

---

[20] "... even 'eternity', taken, for instance, as 'nunc stans,' is only comprehensible through and through as the 'standing' 'now' from time." Martin Heidegger, *Kant and the Problem of Metaphysics*, *GA* 3, p. 240. Eleanore Stump and Norman Kretzmann, "Eternity," *Journal of Philosophy* 78 (1981), 429–458, distinguish eternity as atemporal duration from time, but this is because they identify time and the temporal with succession. Heidegger's point is that the putatively atemporal notion of eternity involves a notion of omnipresence that is temporal, although it does not involve succession.

tively atemporal facts requires us to take a God's-eye perspective that we cannot have. Even the idea of such a perspective is a mere abstraction from the particular temporal perspective which we all have in virtue of being human. This is ultimately based on the assumption that any theory of reference would have to involve some way of making objects present to one. For, in order for us to be able to legitimately claim that such objects exist, we must be able to provide an account of how we could know them to exist. To be sure, this might involve an intuitive understanding of logical principles, plus whatever other principles are required in order to establish whether the objects in question are indeed present in the domain in which they are supposed to be. It does not, therefore, demonstrate that the objects in question cannot be said to exist radically independently of us.

On the basis of his conception of truth as "disclosure," that is, what is revealed to us, as opposed to the correspondence of our beliefs to reality, or the coherence of those beliefs amongst themselves, Heidegger came to maintain that truth is given only so long as there are persons for whom there is a world. For only then is there something that can be revealed to them. To use his term of art, there is truth only so long as there is *Dasein*. This leads him to maintain that truth is itself essentially historical in nature. He relativizes being, time, and truth to what exists relative to human beings and their distinctive histories.[21] Heidegger insists somewhat paradoxically that, while being, truth, and time "are" only so long as there are human beings, entities themselves are independent of the existence of persons: "Being – not entities – 'is given' only insofar as there is truth. And truth *is* only, insofar as and as long as *Dasein* is" (*SuZ*, p. 230). This suggests that there could be entities without being, a notion which seems to make nonsense of the very notion of

---

[21] The fundamental role of a shared historical community in the constitution of the most basic level of time is emphasized by Heidegger in his discussion of authentic historicity and the idea of a shared fate (*SuZ*, p. 384). This shared history presupposes not only the distinction between what has been, what is, and what will be, but also the four constitutive features of world-time (significance, datability, extension, and publicity), and is not indeed fully comprehensible in abstraction from world-time. The appeal to historical community as the basis for the constitution of a shared public time provides the beginnings of a response to the rhetorical question posed by Paul Ricoeur in his analysis of Heidegger's conception of time: "We may first ask ourselves whether history is not itself constructed on the fault line between phenomenological time and astronomical, physical, and biological time – in short, whether history is not itself a fracture zone," *Time and Narrative*, University of Chicago Press, 1986, vol. 3, p. 95.

being. A more charitable reading of Heidegger's position is that only
so long as human beings (or other beings with a sense of self) exist is
there a distinction to be drawn between being, truth, and time, on
the one hand, and entities, on the other.[22] In denying that being is
given independently of us, Heidegger wants to reject the idea that
being (or, for that matter, truth or time) is an entity at all: "Since
being is not and hence is never some entity-along-with [other]
entities, the question what the being of an entity in-itself is, has no
sense or legitimacy" (*GA* 26, p. 195). While other entities may be
independent of us, the very notion of independence is something
that depends on the contrast with what is dependent on us. There
can be no independence without a self to whom such independence
is intelligible: "When *Dasein* does not exist, 'independence' 'is' not
either, nor 'is' the 'in-itself.'"[23] Being, time, and truth are the most
fundamental ways in which entities are given, but being, world,
truth, and time are not given as such unless a being is capable of
distinguishing them from particular entities. It is thus arguable that
world, truth, being, and time depend on the necessity of the
possibility of being distinguished from entities. This still construes
these notions as expressions of the intelligibility of entities.

The apparent contradiction in Heidegger's view can be dissolved
by distinguishing between being and being's givenness to us. Being is
given ("gibt es") as something distinct from entities only for human
beings who understand what it is to be, but this does not mean that
entities have no being that is independent of us. Once one has made
this move there seems to be little reason to deny to time the same
kind of independence from us. For time is supposed to be the
horizon of being, the condition under which being is intelligible to
us. The pressure to draw the distinction between being and its
givenness to us forces Heidegger to a more robust independence

[22] Karsten Harries notes in "Truth and Freedom," in Robert Sokolowski (ed.), *Edmund Husserl and the Phenomenological Tradition* (Washington, DC: Catholic University of America Press, 1988), pp. 150ff., that by thinking of things that are independent of us as stripped of their connection to our world ("entweltlicht"), Heidegger simultaneously strips them of his notion of being which is tied to the world. After his reversal ("Kehre") in the forties, he gives up the Dasein dependence of being and time and with it the distinction between world and nature.

[23] For an articulation of this view, see Hubert Dreyfus, *Being-in-the-World*, pp. 254ff. Dreyfus' reconstruction of Heidegger's position as a "hermeneutical realism" which is opposed to ontological reductionism is, in general, quite plausible. But he cannot get around Heidegger's dual commitment to a notion of being which is identical with what is intelligible to us and a notion of being which is independent of what is intelligible to us.

claim for being, in general, and a conception of time and truth that has more of a place for the independence of time from human existence. Only a theory of time that can also provide a place for time in nature can claim to provide a plausible account of time.

Heidegger eventually maintains that the only understanding we have of being is in terms of the temporal notion of presence. In *Being and Time*, he still seems to think of presence solely in its contrastive role to what has been and what will be.[24] He thus comes to accept what he diagnoses to be the philosophical tradition's tendency to interpret being in terms of presence. But he continues to reject what he takes to be its tendency to identify being with what exists now, and thus with a certain conception of presence. This leads him to search for a new way of understanding presence. As Heidegger puts it in one of his last essays, "Time and Being," past, present, and future are not simultaneous with each other. They are not copresent in the sense of presence that is characteristic of the present as opposed to the past and the future. Rather, they are copresent ("anwesend") in a sense that is common to all three of these aspects of time.[25] There is no present or now which shifts along the time axis with the occurrence of different events (and consciousness perhaps) toward ever later events leaving a trail of states of things which have become past behind it. In "Time and Being," Heidegger tries to explicate this idea by describing time as four-dimensional,

[24] Frederick Olafson, *Heidegger and the Philosophy of Mind*, maintains "that being is to be understood as presence remains the basic postulate that it is throughout Heidegger's thought," p. 174. This is true for Heidegger's later thought. But it runs counter to the contrast he draws in *Being and Time*, between the presence orientation of theory and our understanding of equipment and the future directedness of the authentic temporality of human existence (*SuZ*, p. 329). In *Being and Time*, Heidegger was still trying to break away from any model of time based on presence. He later seems to have realized that even the future orientation of authentic temporality interprets time and being according to the way entities present themselves to us. Jacques Derrida has helpful remarks on the shift in Heidegger's position concerning presence in his papers "Ousía and Grammé," and "Différance" in *Margins of Philosophy* (University of Chicago Press, 1982). Derrida is skeptical about whether Heidegger can articulate an actual alternative to the vulgar notion of time and its present-orientation, because Derrida thinks that the concept of time in general is inherently metaphysical. This presupposes Heidegger's identification of the metaphysics of time with presence, but it also applies Heidegger's later critique of metaphysics to *Being and Time*. In this period, however, Heidegger still regarded the happening of *Dasein* as itself inherently metaphysical. Derrida's own notion of *différance* is an attempt to articulate the absence or rather the temporal deferral of presence that he takes to be involved in the Heideggerian distinction between being and entities and in the system of differences that underlies all intelligibility.

[25] "Zeit und Sein," *Zur Sache des Denkens*, pp. 10ff., "Time and Being," *On Time and Being*, pp. 9–14.

thus contrasting it with the one-dimensional model of time to be found in clock-time.[26] The present, past, and future are each dimensions of time. Every event in our shared public world is an event which is present, past, and future, and intelligible to us on the basis of the way it unifies the past, present, and future. The unity of this intelligibility, that is, the possibility of truth, is the fourth dimension of time. The whole of time is thus logically prior to any of the tenses on this model. Such philosophers as Aristotle, Kant, and Hegel, who were criticized by Heidegger for situating their account of time in the context of their philosophies of nature rather than primarily in their psychologies (or better, in their ontologies of human existence), have turned out to have been right after all. We should be suspicious of the very distinction between the most general temporal conditions under which entities are given to us and natural time.

In the next chapter I look at Heidegger's theory of temporality from the perspective of the connection of the self to its persistence over time. I emphasize the spatiality of human existence against time-slice conceptions of the self which take the self to consist of a series of successively occurrent episodes that, in principle, may exist independently of each other. Here, in his theory of spatiality of human existence, Heidegger presents a position that is more in keeping with a generous version of naturalism. In the final chapter, I then use the spatial dimension that characterizes human identity over time to develop a forensic conception of temporality as responsibility for self.

[26] "Zeit und Sein", pp. 15–16, "Time and Being," pp. 14–15.

CHAPTER 9

Spatiality and human identity

In recent metaphysics, a growing consensus has emerged that a revision of the traditional and common-sense conception of personal identity is required.[1] Common-sense would have it that we are individuals characterized by a certain distinctive identity. This numerical identity makes each of us who we are over the entire period of our lives. The revisionist view finds our intuitions about our own identity to be ill-founded. Personal identity is reduced to mere relations of similarity between certain sets of mental and physical events. Instead of thinking of persons as characterized by strict numerical identity over time, the reductionist about personal identity takes mental or physical states to be numerically distinct person-stages. These person-stages are then regarded as ontologically more basic than persons who have identity over time. The psychological continuity that holds between person-stages may not always be one to one or transitive. This means that each person-stage may have more than one set of past and future person-stages of which it is the continuant and which are its continuants. Thus, persons or, rather, person-stages may coalesce and divide in a manner analogous to the fusion and fission of protists (such as amoebae).

Heidegger offers a critique of reductionist tendencies in the traditional metaphysics of personal identity that anticipates some of the basic assumptions of the new theory. His discussion of personal identity has generally been ignored, even by scholars of Heidegger's thought. This may be due, in part, to the fact that Heidegger prefers the idiom of "self-sufficiency" or rather of "self-persistence" ("Selb-

---

[1] The revisionist conception of personal identity that would reduce personal identity to similarity relations between mental or physical states has been persuasively defended by Derek Parfit, "Personal Identity," *Philosophical Review* 80 (1971), 3–27, and *Reasons and Persons* (New York: Oxford University Press, 1984). Parfit's reductionism has been widely influential.

ständigkeit": *SuZ*, pp. 316ff., 375), to that of personal identity; it also may be due to the fact that where Heidegger's conception of self-identity has been discussed it has been assimilated to the reductionist model, as will become apparent from my critical discussion of John Haugeland's institutional interpretation of Heidegger on personal identity.[2] The lack of attention given to Heidegger's account of self-identity is unfortunate, since his account can be quite helpful in identifying what is problematic in the new reductionist account of personal identity and in suggesting a positive alternative to the conception of a person presupposed by the reductionist view. Thus, Heidegger's conception of self-persistence can contribute to the defense of a robust conception of personal identity that appeals to the role of self-identity in ascribing responsibility for one's actions.

In this chapter, I develop Heidegger's conception of self-identity as a way of articulating what I take to be a plausible account of personal identity, or, rather, of human identity. For I take Heidegger to deny that there is any interesting distinction between human identity and self-identity, or personal identity. I provide reasons to resist the Lockean distinction between persons and human beings. This involves a rejection of the idea that a human being or self could exist in disembodied form or be transferred from one body to another. I argue that the key to the identity of the self is an understanding of self that is able to express the unity of a human existence from birth to death. This unity is not best described either in terms of an abstract theoretical conception of persistence over space and time or in terms of everyday social roles. The key is rather the way in which we take responsibility for our histories in coming to terms with our existences as individuals who are what we are only by the manner in which we relate to the spatio-temporal context of the world to which we belong. Although the notion of a self has developed out of our practices of ascribing responsibility to individuals, I argue that some metaphysical conception of the identity of an individual must underwrite our practices of attributing responsibility to individuals either for their actions or for their character. I defend this claim against the now dominant idea of individual existence as a series of temporal slices or person-stages with relations of psychological or physical continuity but without strict diachronic numerical identity for the self. To do so, I call into question attempts

---

[2] John Haugeland, "Heidegger On Being a Person," *Nous* 16 (1982).

to ascribe beliefs, emotions, and desires or physical states to individuals that could support a case for the fission or fusion of individuals over time.

THE INSTITUTIONAL INTERPRETATION OF THE SELF

Heidegger's conception of self-identity has recently been given a reductionist interpretation according to which a person is an entity that supervenes on some more basic set of entities. For John Haugeland, the Heideggerian notion of a self or a person is to be understood as a "primordial institution," a subpattern of *Dasein* that has accountability.[3] "Dasein" is Heidegger's term for human existence. Haugeland is careful not to directly characterize *Dasein* as a mass term. He also avoids the assertion that *Dasein* is not to be understood in any sense as an individual person.[4] But Haugeland does think that personal identity and agency can be explicated in terms of institutional identity. The institutional interpretation of *Dasein* ascribes *Dasein* to anything which can bear responsibility. Instead of attempting to illuminate the notion of responsibility by appeal to what it is to exist in the way in which we do, the institutional interpretation appeals to responsibility to explain the identity of *Dasein*. This interpretation has the merit of emphasizing the notion of responsibility, or rather of accountability, in understanding *Dasein*. But it ignores the specific role that being a human being plays in Heidegger's account of self-identity.

In order to contrast institutions with persons, Haugeland seems to drop the interesting point of the analogy between institutions and persons. He distinguishes people from other institutions, such as General Motors and marriage, by their accountability. But the analogy between persons and institutions is only plausible so long as one thinks of institutions as agents which bear responsibility for what they do. This is why it is easier to see an analogy between my identity and yours and that of General Motors than it is to see the analogy between our identities and that of marriage. While General

---

[3] Ibid.

[4] Hubert Dreyfus in his *Being-in-the-World*, p. 14, notes that Haugeland regards "Dasein" as a mass term that does not apply to individuals at all. However, even though Haugeland thinks that "Dasein" is a term that is used somewhat like a mass term, he does not actually construe "Dasein" as a mass term, or deny that *Dasein* refers to individuals.

Motors may be said to pursue certain goals and projects for which it
may be held legally accountable, it would be odd indeed to say this
of the institution of marriage. Marriage may play a significant causal
role in some outcome, for instance, marriage may be said to be of
some harm or help to individuals. But it does not seem to make
sense to distinguish between effects brought about by marriage that
are voluntary or involuntary. This distinction between the voluntary
and the involuntary needs to be drawn wherever there is a notion of
responsibility for action of the kind that applies to persons. Persons
may be praised or blamed for actions for which they are held
responsible. The extent to which a course of action is voluntary or
involuntary is of crucial significance in assigning praise or blame.

There is also a significant distinction to be drawn between a
person who is a human being and an institution such as General
Motors, an institution which may be regarded as a legal person in
the sense that it is capable of bearing responsibility for its actions.
But an institution like General Motors is nothing but the complex of
social roles of those who make up that institution. A human being,
by contrast, has an identity that is not exhausted by its social roles.
This is true for human beings and for other non-collective language
users, possible extra-terrestrial intelligences like Mr. Spock in Star-
Trek, who are persons. While collective entities may be said to have
a concern for their own being, their identities seem to be previously
fixed by the set of roles which make them what they are. Institutions
are also capable of modifying and transforming themselves, so that
they do not really have a fixed nature. But the very flexibility of
institutions suggests a more interesting distinction between human
beings and institutional agents. Unless we think of human beings at
a dubiously high level of abstraction, their behavior cannot be
detached from the fact that they are distinct human beings with
certain capacities and dispositions. Institutions are most plausibly
regarded as entities that supervene on other more basic entities.
Thus, it only seems plausible to regard human beings as institutions,
if we think of human beings as entities that supervene on sequences
of physical or mental events or on some more basic physical objects.

Haugeland maintains that selves and agents are not "self-subsis-
tent entities," but, rather, mere institutional frameworks, comparable
to language, that are instituted within concrete behavior.[5] Heidegger

[5] Ibid., p. 35.

treats language or rather discourse ("Rede") as an existential, i.e. as a condition for the possibility of human existence, but he never treats the self itself as an existential, as the institutional interpretation suggests he would. Thus, *Dasein* is not an anonymous "concrete behavior" that only takes on the identity of a self as a supervenient feature. The converse is true; the anonymous subject of day-to-day existence is itself an existential that depends on an underlying discreteness of persons or, rather, of human beings. This discreteness is expressed in what Heidegger takes to be a fundamental feature of all human existence ("Dasein"). This is the feature of being in its each case my own ("Jemeinigkeit").

In his more recent work, Haugeland has tried to compensate for some of the problems posed by his institutional interpretation of personal identity by introducing the notion that persons cast themselves into roles. This self-casting accounts for the distinctive continuity of persons.[6] This is possible, according to Haugeland, because *Dasein* is essentially a being that makes sense of itself. This allows him to understand the distinctive way in which we come to terms with our different roles. He characterizes *Dasein* as "a living way of life" of which there may well be distinctive individual instances, "idio-ways-of-life."[7] This view provides no account of how one could distinguish between Dasein making sense of itself as what that *Dasein* truly is and *Dasein* making sense of itself in a way that fails to express what that *Dasein* truly is. Thus, although Haugeland talks of a "reidentifiable who" that connects various social roles together, he leaves it a mystery how one could reidentify a who in the different ways in which roles might be connected together.[8]

It has sometimes been suggested that the notion of a person might be grounded in the notion of a person or self as bearer of responsibility. In this way, one could simply side-step the need to explicate the notion of responsibility in terms of some prior metaphysical conception of the person or self. Heidegger does not directly address the criteria for identifying or distinguishing selves at a time. Nor does he discuss the criteria to be used to reidentify a self and its behavior over time. This makes it rather plausible to ascribe a conception of human responsibility to Heidegger that is not underwritten by any metaphysical conception. This interpretation has the

---

[6] "Dasein's Disclosedness" in H. Dreyfus and H. Hall (eds.), *Heidegger: A Critical Reader*, pp. 39–40.

[7] Ibid., p. 36.   [8] Ibid. p. 39.

merit of avoiding the ascription of a metaphysical account of the self to Heidegger. In his later philosophy, he chastises the whole of traditional philosophy for adopting such an account.[9] But, if pressed, this rejection of metaphysics would leave Heidegger without any obvious way of determining for which actions a particular self should be held responsible. A purely forensic, or responsibility-based, notion of a person only postpones the question of what the criteria are for personal identity. For one still needs to address the question of what the criteria are according to which behavior and dispositions to behave are to be correctly ascribed to a certain self either by that self or by another self. Moreover, in *Being and Time*, Heidegger is not yet committed to the rejection of a metaphysical conception of human existence.[10]

One does not avoid questions about the relation between different phases of a person or questions about the relation between the mental and the physical by framing questions of personal identity in terms of a person's or self's responsibility for his or her actions. It is true that persons and actions do not seem to fit well into a complete disjunction between mental or physical entities. Nor does the relation between the mental and the physical seem to be particularly tractable. It is thus tempting to attempt to circumvent these problems by reconfiguring one's ontology in such a way that they no longer arise. But it is not clear how one can then determine which actions are to count as actions for which a specific person or self is responsible. For this seems to require a prior conception of what are to count as the actions of a specific self. The appeal to a conception of personal identity or self-identity based on one's responsibility for one's character and one's actions does not itself settle the problem of ontology. It leaves the matter open as to what the metaphysical nature of persons in fact is.

It might be thought that one can articulate what it is to be me simply by presupposing the existence of a body that makes me distinct from other individuals. But, even if one accepts some form of bodily identity as criterial for personal identity, the bodies in question cannot be things upon which institutions supervene, for

[9] The criticism of metaphysical conceptions of persons and what it is to be a human being is explicit in his 1946 "Letter on Humanism," *GA* 9, pp. 321ff.; *Martin Heidegger: Basic Writings* (New York: Harper and Row, 1977) (henceforth *BW*, pp. 202ff.).

[10] This may be seen from the 1929 lecture "What is Metaphysics?" This paper claims that "metaphysics is the basic happening in *Dasein*. It is *Dasein* itself," *GA* 9, p. 122; *BW*, p. 112.

then one will have given up the idea that *Dasein* is a basic particular. By thinking of human beings as things with properties, or persons as that notion is often understood, one is encouraged to divide those properties into ones which are mental and physical. Human beings, as Heidegger understands them, are not psychophysical beings in the end any more than they are beings whose identity is exhausted by either mental criteria of identity, such as memory of past states, or physical criteria of identity, such as the spatio-temporal continuity of a body. Even to refer to human beings as psychophysical beings is misleading. For it suggests that human beings could be understood as a synthesis of the mental and the physical. This is a view that plays a crucial role in the traditional conception of personal identity.

Heidegger explicitly rejects any account of personal identity in terms of psychophysical identity (*SuZ*, p. 117). His immediate target is Husserl's account of a person in *Ideas* II in which an intersubjective world is constructed out of the take that each individual has in virtue of representing the world from the standpoint of a certain body. Heidegger's desire to distance himself from the Husserlian double-aspect conception of a person accounts for his tendency to eschew talk of persons in favor of talk of human beings or selves. A human being may be thought of with some abstraction as an object occupying a certain route through space and time, but, from Heidegger's perspective: "*Dasein* is, however, not merely and not primarily intratemporal, occurring and extant [*vorhanden*] in a world, but is intrinsically temporal in an original, fundamental way. Nevertheless, *Dasein* is also in a certain way in time, for we can view it in a certain respect as an extant entity" (*GA* 24, p. 384). The same remark could be applied by analogy to space.

Heidegger avoids reference to "embodiment" in *Being and Time*, although he does insist that human beings "literally take up space" (*SuZ*, p. 368). To think of a human being as embodied is already to think of a human being as a psychophysical being, that is, to think of human beings in terms of a metaphysics that generates the problem of how the mind relates to the body. In the early thirties, Heidegger explicitly acknowledges that "the body belongs to the *Dasein* of human beings."[11] But he also insists that "the human body is something essentially different from an animal organism" (*GA* 9, pp. 321–322; *BW*, p. 204). A human being is spatial, but does not

---

[11] Heidegger, *Vom Wesen der Wahrheit* (1931–1932) *GA* 34, p. 236.

have a body in the same sense in which other creatures and things do. In *Being and Time*, Heidegger expresses this point by arguing that spatiality is an existential, a constitutive feature of human existence, and not an occurrent property or relation of things as it is traditionally conceived to be.

The spatiality of human existence is not to be understood on the model of an "extended body-thing" (*SuZ*, p. 368). This does not mean that it is possible for a human being to exist in a disembodied form or that space exists only in the representations of human beings. Heidegger is skeptical about the idea that we exist in space in the way that we are accustomed to thinking of embodied existence, but he is committed to the general idea that we must exist spatially. In fact, he thinks that thinking of persons as non-spatial is driven by concerns about immortality. This leads one to assume "an I that is non-spatial and that then has effects in space through some hocus pocus."[12] Against this Cartesian and Husserlian view of the self, he insists that the human being who has an understanding of itself as self, cannot be said to be sufficiently independent of its body to "have" a body. For us to be spatial is not optional, but a condition for the possibility of our existence. Spatial orientation is so basic for him that one cannot exist as a human being without taking up space. But, as a human being, one takes up space and time in a different way than a thing or even than an animal. Both of these ideas are direct implications of his conception of human existence as *Da-sein*, being-there.

The conception of a human being as essentially situated in a spatial environment might seem to be threatened by recent developments in brain science. Recent brain research, particularly concerning the separation of the two hemispheres of the brain through commissurotomy, seems to support speculations about the possibility of fusion or fission of the self which go back to seventeenth-century discussions of personal identity. But, on closer inspection, work with the corpus callosum so far fails to show that the brain of a person may be divided in such a way as to preserve two distinct centers of self that are not physically connected. In the case of commissurotomy of the corpus callosum, parts of the cortex are divided, but the subcortical area and spinal cord remain intact. In hemispherectomies, half of the cerebral cortex of one hemisphere of the brain is removed, but not the whole of the half-brain. There is no evidence

---

[12] *GA* 21, p. 292.

that it is physically possible to preserve brain function while also removing or dividing the subcortical regions and spinal cord.[13]

The phenomena associated with commissurotomy have seemed to provide scientific legitimacy to the recent tendency to replace the notion of personal or self-identity with a weaker notion of survival, that does not require transitivity or a one-to-one and all-or-nothing relation between different person-stages as the notion of identity requires. In such extreme cases, there seems to be nothing left of personal identity but some form of continuity or similarity between person-stages that is weaker than genuine identity. This would be true regardless of whether the self is thought of as identical with a body, or with one of the body's constitutive organs (for instance the brain), or with some form of psychological continuity.

First impressions notwithstanding, we do not have enough evidence to tell whether the scenarios involving fission or fusion of selves are, in fact, theoretically possible. They clearly are logically possible, but this does not seem to be enough to make us seriously consider such possibilities as possibilities for us as the kind of selves we are. It is thus far from clear that we have any basis for denying the tacit assumption which is the basis of Heidegger's conception of self-identity. This is the idea that we have an implicit understanding of our identity as human beings from birth to death. Such an understanding can be, and often is, distorted by an inauthentic self-understanding. This accounts for instances in which our consciousness seems to divide or fuse. For Heidegger, the key is that this implicit understanding of self-identity essentially involves the occupation of a spatial and temporal region. The existence of the self cannot be taken in abstraction from this unity of human existence without distortion of what it is to be a self. This identification of the self with a certain unique spatio-temporal history may yet turn out to be mistaken. But the evidence required to seriously challenge this conception of the self has yet to be adduced.

THE LOCKEAN CONCEPTION OF A PERSON

The reductionist conception of a person has generally conceived of the metaphysical nature of persons in terms of psychological as well

---

[13] There is a very useful discussion of this point in Kathleen Wilkes, *Real People* (Oxford: Clarendon, 1988), esp. pp. 132ff.

as physical continuity. John Locke is the philosopher most identified with the notion of psychological continuity as the criterion of personal identity. In Locke's classical defense of the forensic concept of a person, the primary bearer of responsibility is consciousness rather than the human being who has that consciousness. From Locke's perspective, consciousness of one's past and future is what gives diachronic unity to oneself as a bearer of responsibility. The unity of consciousness is what Locke calls a person. The Lockean notion of personal identity depends heavily on consciousness and thus on psychological continuity. It seems that individuals can make identity statements about themselves by appeal to statements expressing their memories about their past histories. Such memory statements seem to bypass any knowledge concerning the identity of one's body, and indeed any appeal to the kind of evidence that persons make use of to make such identity statements about other persons.

The Lockean theory of personal identity has problems wherever such psychological continuity is in doubt. Locke advertised as a merit of the theory his desperate expedient of absolving one of responsibility for those actions of which one had no consciousness. He found support for this view in the practices of the law courts which do not assign responsibility to one for actions performed in madness. In madness one is then, quite literally, not oneself. Fugues in which one is in a prolonged state of amnesia, as well as multiple-personality disorders, force one, as a Lockean, to accept the idea that many human beings are different persons over the course of their lives and even simultaneously.

Locke does not deny that there is a bearer of responsibility that we characterize metaphysically. Instead, he thinks that the bearer of responsibility may turn out not to be identical with a particular human being. A particular human being is the functional identity over time of a living organism belonging to the human species. In general, persons are identical for Locke with the functional unity of a human organism, but there are cases where a person may cease to be identical with that functional unity. Locke uses the example of a prince whose soul (or person) and its beliefs are put in the body of a cobbler to support his claim that the identity of a person does not necessarily coincide with that of a human being.[14] This example

---

[14] John Locke, *An Essay Concerning Human Understanding* (New York: Dover, 1959), Book II, ch. xxvii, section 15, p. 457.

depends on the Cartesian idea that beliefs could be what they are independent of the human being who has them in a certain environment. The idea that different persons could have the same beliefs even though they are in different physical states and different environments does seem plausible. This independence of beliefs from a particular context encourages the idea that it might be possible to transfer the beliefs of a person as whole from that person to another person.

In more contemporary examples, it is customary to imagine transfer of mental states between two bodies by means of some science-fiction mechanism. This leads to the idea that our beliefs about our past might, in principle, be based on quasi-memories of what had, in fact, been experienced by some other human being rather than genuine veridical memories of our own actual past.[15] The possibility of quasi-memories raises serious doubts as to whether our beliefs about our own psychological continuity are sufficient to support knowledge of personal identity. This suggests that some form of bodily criterion of personal identity will be required after all. However, a bodily criterion of personal identity cannot stand on its own. For, in considering the identity of the self, or person, we are concerned not just with the persistence of a body, but with that of a living organism that has emotions, beliefs, and desires, in short, some understanding of its past and future.

From Heidegger's point of view, there is a problem with assuming, as neo-Lockeans do, that our memories might, in fact, be delusive quasi-memories. Our understanding of quasi-memories is parasitic on our understanding of memories that disclose truths about our past. One can undoubtedly have pseudo-memories. But one cannot have quasi-memories that are systematically disconnected from one's environment, without undermining the link between belief and the environment that is the basis for ascribing beliefs to oneself at all. In order to conceive of someone implanting delusive quasi-memories in a human being, I need to assume that a human being has mental states that do not depend on the environment for their very capacity to present anything to that human being. This assumption is not one that one can make so long as one conceives of a human being in Heideggerian terms as *Dasein*.

Heidegger rejects the Cartesian and Lockean notion of conscious

---

[15] Sidney Shoemaker, "Persons and their Pasts," *American Philosophical Quarterly* 7 (1970), 271.

states that could be what they are independently of the environment that they represent.[16] As Heidegger conceives of the self, it derives its identity from the way in which it understands its environment. Indeed, it is what it is only insofar as that spatio-temporal environment has a certain truth for it. The ascription of beliefs and desires to a human being both by that human being and by other human beings occurs against the background of beliefs and desires about the world. It is this role of the world as the shared background against which beliefs, desires, and emotions are meaningfully ascribed that is denied by the Cartesian when he suggests that we could have beliefs and desires that were systematically misleading. This leads Heidegger to claim that Descartes "jumped over" the phenomenon of world in his analysis of the mind and nature (*SuZ*, p. 95).

Heidegger does not have a direct argument against the claim that what one takes to be a shared public world of experience is, in fact, a private world of my subjectivity. He does maintain that we can articulate our beliefs and desires through the normative constraints of discourse "not because *Dasein* is first of all something 'inner' that is cut off from an outer, but because as being-in-the-world it already understands 'outside'" (*SuZ*, p. 162). While Heidegger protests that Kant's very search for an argument to refute psychological idealism is based on a mistake, he needs an argument very much in the spirit of Kant's refutation of idealism in order to establish his thesis that being-in-the-world is a condition for the possibility of the very distinction between the inner and the outer. He needs to show that one cannot ascribe beliefs, moods, and desires to a self except on the basis of spatial regularities that preclude one from providing an autonomous internal account of beliefs and desires. This would allow one to articulate a conception of a human being that does not involve one in the same skeptical difficulties about such matters as personal identity and psychophysical interaction. This alternative conception calls into question the extent to which we can, indeed,

---

[16] Descartes' allegiance to the independence of beliefs and the mental in general from any particular physical environment is mitigated somewhat by his thesis that the soul is not in the body like a pilot is in a ship. The soul is connected to the body so as to make one thing (C. Adam and P. Tannery [eds.], Sixth Meditation, *Oeuvres de Descartes* [Paris: Leopold Cerf, 1987–1913], VII, p. 81). The role of embodiment in Descartes's conception of a human being is controversial. Paul Hoffman, "The Unity of Descartes' Man," *The Philosophical Review* 95 (1983), 339–370, and Daisie Radner, "Descartes' Notion of the Union of Mind and Body," *Journal of the History of Philosophy* 9 (1971), 159–170, have emphasized the unity of mind and body in Descartes, but even such accounts must allow for some substantial distinction between the mental and the physical.

make sense of our beliefs, desires, and emotions in abstraction from the environment in which we are situated as human beings.

Now Heidegger cannot simply dismiss the phenomena of psychological disunity that form the basis for Locke's claim that we are sometimes quite alienated from ourselves. It is, indeed, an important part of Heidegger's conception of self-identity that we have an inherent tendency as human beings to misinterpret ourselves. Our tendency to interpret our existence in terms of some aspect of our existence that cannot do justice to the unity of our lives as wholes is what Heidegger designates as inauthenticity. An adequate conception of one's whole life is an authentic one. Those states which the Lockean thinks of as evidence for a breakdown in personal identity will be states which the Heideggerian will regard as inauthentic understandings of one's self-identity. They involve forms of self-loss in the sense that the individual fails to understand the underlying unity of his or her own existence.[17] But they provide evidence for a misinterpretation of what gives unity to one's spatio-temporal existence rather than providing evidence for an absence of spatio-temporal unity in one's existence.

RECONSTRUCTING THE LOCKEAN CONCEPTION OF PERSONAL IDENTITY

Heidegger does not accept the Lockean distinction between persons and human beings. He prefers to think of personal identity in terms of the teleological unity of one's life. This means that my self is construed as a unity of capacities structured by the meaning I give to my life. In focusing on the means to the achievement of the goals that have been set for one by one's social roles, one comes to think of one's history as something that is preserved only through the present conscious states which are memories of the past. One then also comes to think of one's future as something which exists only in and through present anticipations. Taking this view seriously leads one to a conception of self as a successive becoming of different states of

---

[17] As the psychiatrist Ludwig Binswanger develops Heidegger's position, schizophrenic cases of-self-understanding have a common feature: "In all these cases, the Dasein can no longer freely allow the world to be, but is, rather, increasingly surrendered over to one particular world-design, possessed by it, overwhelmed by it," "The Case of Lola Voss," in *Being-in-the-World* (New York: Basic Books, 1963), p. 284. From this point of view, schizophrenia is an extreme form of the normal daily tendency to self-loss in what one does. But here the averaging out of different social constraints no longer works as it normally does.

consciousness which are linked together only by the fact that some of those successive present states of consciousness are anticipations and some are memories.

The performance of daily tasks has its own form of temporality. Here the present dominates through a modification of my past and future to correspond to my expectations of the success or failure of my individual projects. Our everyday identity as persons is determined by the responsibility that we have for the social roles we occupy. This everyday understanding of oneself is characterized by a sense of who one is that is structured by forgetting oneself, presenting, expecting corresponding to the traditional notions of past, present, and future (*SuZ*, pp. 338–339). The future is manifest to me in the form of whatever tasks my social roles and day-to-day life set for me to do. In performing these tasks, I must respond to the success or failure which goes with my ability to satisfy the demands placed on me by my social roles. This notion of the future thus takes the form of waiting or expecting one thing or other to happen. It involves a forgetting of who I am and have been as distinct from the demands placed on me by my social roles. It thus presupposes a certain conception of the past and the present.

The way I relate to my past, my memory with respect to my social obligations, is determined by my forgetfulness of my own distinctive self. I forget my past and the very fact that I have forgotten it (*GA* 24, p. 411). This forgetting of the past is then the basis for my efforts to retain and remember it. The past is forgotten by me and hence available to me only through memory which retrieves what has been forgotten. Memory thus construed is a negative rather than a positive phenomenon. It presupposes a suppression of the inherent identity of my history which is then retrieved through memory. The suppression of information about my past and the world I live in has a useful function. It allows one to react more spontaneously to different situations, a capacity which is apparently less developed in mnemonists of unusual ability.[18]

The repression of information presupposed by memory provides a way of reconstructing the Lockean memory criterion of personal identity as an expression of forgetfulness of self. Memory is taken to presuppose a prior understanding of one's identity as a human

---

[18] A classic discussion of the limitations of those with fantastic mnemonic abilities may be found in Alexander Luria, *The Mind of the Mnemonist* (New York: Basic Books, 1968).

being. The problem with the memory criterion of personal identity does seem to be that it presupposes the ability to distinguish genuine from merely apparent memories. This distinction can only be drawn by appeal to some further criterion of personal identity, such as the persistence of one's body.

The "everyday fleeting saying I–I" is characteristic of one's self-interpretation according to the demands of one's social roles (*SuZ*, p. 322). One is moved from one demand to the next, without any need for a developed sense of who one is. One does have an abstract understanding of oneself and of spaces and times that one can express in demonstrative language, "I," "here," "now." This linguistic articulation of oneself and one's concerns allows one to focus on very restricted intervals of one's experience. This leads to the idea that times and spaces might be constructed out of punctual entities. It is plausible to claim that belief in the existence of punctual moments that successively replace one another ultimately stems from the articulation of temporal relations in speech. Daily existence and its anonymous self has a temporal structure that is not fully articulatable in terms of a now-succession. But everyday existence already relates to time as sets of intervals to be calculated for the success of one's engagements. The articulation of daily business in demonstrative language then encourages a conception of a self that exists as something present "in time," that is, as a sequence of experiences each of which is successively present or real. One can abstract in turn from the succesive replacement of nows. This leads to an abstract conception of the self as a tenseless sequence of events ordered according to relations of earlier and later. Heidegger does not deny that the self can be modelled this way. But what he does claim is that one has in the process abstracted away from what it is to be a self.

The tendency to lose track of who one is in contrast to the demands of one's various social roles marks everyday existence. This self-loss is the basis for the kind of temporality presupposed by the Lockean conception of self as a sequence of successive temporal phases. But, from the Heideggerian point of view, this notion of self is based on a concept of time and the self that abstracts even from the everyday temporality of our engagements. As truth comes to be understood more and more in terms of what corresponds to statements or assertions that we make about the world, the self and the spatio-temporal intervals that constitute it come to be understood in terms of objects corresponding to such statements. These objects need no longer be conceived in terms of the everyday spatio-temporal engagements with the world. They come to be understood as the objects out of which the everyday conception of time, the self, and human existence is to be constructed. We think of time and the states of the self as a sequence that is based on the articulation of experience in terms of the model of precisely individuating theoretical assertions about objects in the world. From the standpoint of our theoretical assertions and disinterested observations, it is hard to see why any phase of a person, or moment of time needs to have any essential connection with any other.

Heidegger's challenge to the received conception of personal identity concerns one of ontological priority. The Lockean, or neo-Lockean, can readily accept the claim that our everyday notion of personal identity is quite different from the way in which we theoretically conceptualize personal identity. The distinction between the everyday conception of personal identity in terms of which we ascribe praise and blame to actions based on character, and our theoretical notion of personal identity as a construct from momentary experiences, is indeed an important part of Hume's account of personal identity.[19] And Hume's account of personal identity is itself a critical response to the Lockean conception of personal identity. But, unlike Hume, Heidegger wishes not only to raise worries about the adequacy of our theoretical conception of personal identity, but also to resist its claim to ontological priority.

From Heidegger's perspective, it is a misunderstanding of the ontology of human beings to think of them as sequences of momentary particulars or phases that can branch or merge together. Such an interpretation of human existence is suggested by thinking of responsibility for action in terms of individual choices. Like Hume, Heidegger does not think that an adequate conception of human responsibility can be articulated in abstraction from the standing

---

[19] Although Hume regards the self as "a bundle or collection of different perceptions," *A Treatise of Human Nature*, Selby-Bigge (ed.) (New York: Oxford University Press, 1978), p. 251, he also distinguishes between personal identity with respect to our thought and with respect to the passions and the concern we take in our past and future, p. 253. It is the latter notion of personal identity that is presupposed in Hume's account of moral responsibility. "Actions are by their very nature temporary and perishing; and where they proceed not from some cause in the characters and disposition of the person, who perform'd them, they infix not themselves upon him, and can neither redound to his honour, if good, nor infamy, if evil," p. 411.

dispositions of a person that express the unity of that person over time. The important point is that one can only be responsible for actions that one has performed voluntarily. This means that there must be some way of distinguishing the performance of the action by choice from the mere accidental occurrence of the action in question. But one can only draw this distinction if the action is one that conforms to a pattern of behavior that is based on the standing dispositions of the agent. The agent must be able to interpret the action that he or she has performed or will perform as conforming to a normative principle that applies to him- or herself and that the agent accepts as a principle governing his or her action. This does not mean that one must be conscious of performing or having performed the actions in question. It does mean, however, that the actions must be mine or yours, that is, ascribable by me or you to a particular human being to whom behavior conforming to a normative principle of action can be ascribed.

Traditional theories of personal identity, regardless of whether they take bodily or psychological continuity or identity to be the basis for survival, are based on the conception of time as a sequence in which the states of a person have a certain position. According to the sequential model of human existence, "*Dasein* measures its way through the span of time provided for it between both limits [birth and death], in such a way that it, only 'real' in each instance of the now, jumps through the now sequence of its 'time,' as it were" (*SuZ*, p. 373). The problem of personal identity is then construed as the problem of how to determine the identity or continuity of the self through this sequence of experiences. Heidegger insists that this approach treats the self as something which is "extant in time." This means that the self is treated as if it were a thing rather than as a self-interpretive process. Interpreting the self as a thing prevents a "genuine ontological analysis of the *stretch* of *Dasein* between birth and death" (*SuZ*, p. 374).

To inquire into the identity of the self on the basis of the physical states or states of consciousness that the self has is to treat the self as a thing which has properties at a time, or states (in Heidegger's jargon, something extant or present-at-hand, "ein Vorhandenes," *SuZ*, p. 117). Heidegger's most basic objection to this way of thinking about persons is that the whole idea that a person is a kind of thing is based on a mistake. The mistake lies not in the corporeality of things, but in a more fundamental feature of what it is to be a thing.

Human beings are unlike things in that they can only be understood by actually being human beings who have a self.

Regardless of whether one thinks of a person in terms of strict identity over time or some weaker notion of continuity, the sequential notion of time does indeed seem to be presupposed in contemporary discussion of personal "identity." The notion of time as a sequence of events which are successively present, past, and future has considerable justification in experience. Thinking of personal identity in terms of such a now sequence encourages a certain skepticism about whether one is the same thing over time. For, at any given now, all that one has is a person-stage. The notion of time as a tenseless sequence of events ordered according to the time relations of simultaneous, earlier, and later has a great deal of support in physical theory. It is controversial whether a person may be regarded as a spatio-temporal continuant from a point which abstracts from the passage of successive nows. The same person cannot have tenselessly incompatible properties, but this is possible with respect to tensed properties. In a tensed ontology it makes sense to say that the "present me" can have had the same properties as the "former me" had, whereas this is precluded in a tenseless ontology.[20] This suggests that a tenseless ontology precludes the possibility of strict identity over time allowed for in a tensed ontology. Branching or fusing persons seem to be genuine possibilities on a tenseless approach to personal identity, since such persons are not characterized by strict identity on the tenseless view.

Heidegger's response to such possibilities may be understood in the following way. Statements about personal identity are true in virtue of facts about human beings. These facts about human beings are distinct from facts about the dependence or continuity of mental and physical states. Facts about the continuity or similarity of mental or physical states could, at best, provide evidence for or against personal identity but never constitute the very meaning of human identity. When counterfactual cases seem to force one to give up on self-identity in favor of some weaker notion of continuity, what they in fact display is the paradoxical force of the sequential model of the self. This sequential model of the self has difficulty in accounting for

---

[20] "There aren't two you's, a present one having one set of properties, and a past one having another. It is rather that you *are* now such that you have these properties and lack those, whereas formerly, you *were* such that you had those properties and lacked these," Roderick Chisholm, *Person and Object* (La Salle: Open Court, 1976), p. 92.

an agent's responsibility for his or her actions. The problem is that a person is never, strictly speaking, the same person at different points in time. It is thus never, strictly speaking, the same individual who performs an action and is later to be held responsible for the action.

Heidegger does not simply reject the assumption that time is sequential.[21] Instead, he reconstructs temporal sequence in terms of his purportedly more basic conception of time. Heidegger's criticism of the traditional theory of personal identity thus depends, in part, on the plausibility of his own preferred conception of the relation between time and the self. At issue, then, is whether time either conceived of as a tensed sequence of nows or as a tenseless sequence of events ordered according to earlier and later is adequate to the understanding of our transactions with the particulars in the world. Heidegger argues that both of these alternative conceptions of time are, in fact, intelligible only against the background of involvements with one's spatio-temporal environment as a whole. But it is precisely from these enabling conditions that they abstract.

If one thinks of persons in a very abstract way as sequences of mental and physical states, the reductionist approach to personal identity seems to be quite plausible. But there is some question as to whether the abstract model of personal identity that the reductionist picture invokes is any longer adequate to the phenomenon it is intended to describe. While it may, in some sense, be possible for something analogous to a person to fuse or divide, it is less obvious that the thing in question would be something that we could still rightly regard as a person. The kind of thing in question is not what our common-sense conception of a person is intended to describe. This would, perhaps, be conceded by most of the new reductionists. They argue that we need to revise the common-sense conception of personal identity to make it conform to puzzle cases that seem to require us to give up the transitivity and one-to-one relation of strict

---

21 Although there is not an extensive literature which attempts to reconstruct Heidegger's theory of time, the view is prevalent that Heidegger fails to explain passage. This is certainly the view defended by William Barrett, "The Flow of Time," in Richard Gale (ed.), *The Philosophy of Time* (New Jersey: Humanities Press, 1978), pp. 364ff. William Blattner puts the point in a more non-committal way: "These two features of Dasein – the precondition that Dasein not be able to become any of its possibilities, and the nullity of its being-the-ground – arise in the context of Heidegger's discussion of authenticity and inauthenticity, yet they themselves are essential aspects of care, not phenomena of authentic Dasein alone. Once revealed they force him to do 'violence' to our everyday understanding of time, just because they are incompatible with sequentiality," "Existential Temporality in *Being and Time*," in H. Dreyfus and H. Hall (eds.), *Heidegger: A Critical Reader*, p. 122.

identity. For this, we need to know if these puzzle cases represent genuine possibilities for our existence. If they do not represent genuine possibilities, the notion of a person as a sequence of stages involves a greater revision in our concept of a person than we should accept. We should resist then such revision. On the other hand, if the puzzle cases articulate genuine possibilities for how things might be for us, the revisionist conception will have considerable plausibility.

Heidegger need not deny that there are insights to be derived from the Lockean or physicalist conception of personal identity and spatio-temporal continuity. The problem with these approaches to identity or continuity over time is that they already begin their reflections on the identity of persons at a very high level of abstraction. The level of abstraction in question is arguably too high for them to be able to address the basic concerns that we have in posing the problem of self-identity.

In the next chapter, I propose to develop a temporal conception of personal responsibility or responsibility for self on the basis of the kind of identity over time that I have argued for in this chapter. From the point of view of that theory of responsibility for self, the notion of a person as a current time-slice can be interpreted as a form of flight from taking responsibility for one's life as a whole.

CHAPTER 10

"Dasein" and the forensic notion of a person

In this chapter, I discuss Heidegger's conception of responsibility for self. The chapter has two sections. In section one, I discuss Heidegger's conception of authenticity and the manner in which it is supposed to express responsibility for self. In section two, I then discuss Heidegger's notion of our everyday conception of self based on the social roles we occupy.

According to the forensic notion of a person, a person is to be understood primarily in terms of behavior for which she may be praised or blamed. Such behavior involves actions and consequences for which an individual can be held responsible. The key to this idea of being responsible for action is that one is somehow regarded as the source of the action. Persons are the kind of agents that are capable of acting on the basis of their own deliberations. This is why the question whether a person can be held responsible for a given action is regarded as at all to the point. The extent to which one is held responsible for one's actions, the extent to which one may be praised or blamed for one's actions, reflects the spectator's evaluation of the extent to which one performed that action independently of coercion.

There is a close historical connection between the notion of a person and that of an agent who can be held accountable for his or her actions. Use of the term "person" or rather "persona" (literally: "mask" or "role") to refer to individuals actually originated in Roman law courts where it referred to individuals capable of bearing legal responsibility for their actions.[1] Legal responsibility

---

[1] Slaves were not generally regarded as persons by Roman law courts, since they did not have the privileges and responsibilities of full-fledged agents, while corporations counted as persons since they could be held responsible for their actions. However, even slaves could be regarded as persons insofar as they were taken to be potential legal subjects, see M. Kaser, "Das römische Privatrecht," in *Handbuch der Altertumswissenschaft* III, 3; also S. Schlossmann, *Persona und Prosopon im Recht und im Christlichen Dogma*, pp. 75ff. The use of "person" to refer to

was generally restricted to individuals who were free in the sense that they were not the property of other individuals. This legal notion of a person was not identical with that of a certain human life, since one could lose the status of personhood through enslavement or acquire personhood through manumission. It was thus possible for a Roman to cease to be a person and then become a person again at some later time.

The Roman notion of personal identity as legal identity became philosophically prominent through the influence of Locke. Locke argued that a person should be conceived as a locus of responsibility for action. He described this notion of personal identity based on personal responsibility as the forensic notion of a person. Locke's use of the term "forensic" is due to the importance of questions of responsibility for one's action and for one's character in the deliberations undertaken by law courts.[2] The distinction in Roman law between human existence and the identity of a legal person provided the basis for Locke's famous distinction between human and personal identity. Human identity consists, for Locke, in one's identity as a living organism, while personal identity is tied to those actions for which one is responsible. Since Locke thought that one is only responsible for actions of which one is conscious that one performed them, he concluded that the best criterion of personal identity was continuity in one's consciousness. This criterion of continuity in consciousness could lead one, in some cases, to conclude that a human being is more than one person, or not a person at all.

Heidegger does not seem to have been directly influenced by Locke, and he rejects the Roman and later Judaeo-Christian conception of individuals as persons. In rejecting talk using the vocabulary of "persons" in favor of the vocabulary of "life," and then later of "human existence," and "selfhood," he distances himself from the

all human beings has its roots in Cicero's identification of persons with human beings. Cicero took over the interpretation of "persona" in terms of "humanitas" ("humanity") from the Stoic philosopher Panaitios and gave it wide distribution. The connection between Panaitios and Cicero is discussed in Georg Picht, *Die Grundlagen der Ethik des Panaitios* (Freiburg: Ph.D. dissertation, 1943).

2 "Whenever a man finds what he calls himself, there, I think, another may say is the same person. It is a forensic term, appropriating actions and their merit; and so belongs only to intelligent agents, capable of a law, and happiness, and misery. This personality extends itself beyond present existence to what is past, only by consciousness, – whereby it becomes concerned and accountable; owns and imputes to itself past actions, just upon the same ground and for the same reason as it does the present," John Locke, *An Essay Concerning Human Understanding*, Book ii, ch. xxvii, 126, pp. 466–467.

idea that there is a significant distinction to be drawn between persons and human beings. In contrast to this Lockean notion of personal identity, and the more general metaphysical theory that selves may be reconstructed from physical or mental person-stages that exist at different clock-times, Heidegger emphasizes the unity of human existence from birth to death. But, like Locke, Heidegger thinks what is of primary interest in self-identity are the concerns that make each of us who we are. My self-identity is a matter of the way in which I take responsibility for my self and my actions. The self is thus understood primarily as the bearer of responsibility for behavior. This is very much in the spirit of the Lockean notion of a person.

Heidegger's rejection of Locke's idea that there might be instances of personal identity without human identity has its ultimate source in Heidegger's rejection of the Lockean conception of personal identity as constituted by similarity relations between states of consciousness. Heidegger is convinced that defenders of the forensic notion of a person, such as Locke, have failed correctly to understand the temporal structure of responsibility for action and therefore to understand the relation of personal identity to action. They have tended to base the notion of a person on a theory of time and consciousness that gives primacy to what is present to consciousness. Present-orientedness is the basis for Locke's notion of time as comprising "fleeting and perpetually perishing parts of succession."[3] These parts of succession are present moments that are successively real. Present-orientedness is also apparent in Locke's appeal to consciousness in the form of memory to get one beyond the present in order to establish personal identity. For Heidegger, succession is not a fundamental feature of time. The present is for him simply an abstraction from the history of a human being, or of a community of human beings.

TAKING RESPONSIBILITY FOR ONESELF

Heidegger maintains that any *Dasein*, any human being, is identical with itself in the same formal ontological sense in which any object is identical with itself. It is what it is and is not something else. But it is also true that any *"Dasein* has a distinctive sameness with itself in the

---

[3] Ibid., Book II, ch. xiv, 1, p. 238.

sense of selfhood. It is such that it in some way *belongs to* (*sich zueigen*) itself, it *has itself*, and only in this way can it *lose* itself" (*GA* 24, p. 242). To have my self in this way is to have a set of constitutive concerns that connect the various aspects of my spatio-temporal existence together in one identical self. One's competence at life involves an implicit understanding of oneself, of what it is for me to be. This self-understanding serves to structure the various capacities which one has, just as these capacities give one a distinctive sense of identity. Such "for-each-my-ownness" ("Jemeinigkeit," *SuZ*, p. 42), or understanding of oneself from a particular point of view, is constitutive of what it is to be a human being. This mineness entails "that this entity is in each instance one I and not others" (*SuZ*, p. 114). What is often referred to as the discreteness of persons is therefore a fundamental feature of human existence. Mineness involves the capacity for each of us to refer to her- or himself. But it need not involve any particular conception of who one is. In existing, each of us relates to his or her own distinctive being. What it is to be me and what it is to be mine is a matter of the particular context in which I exist. This spatio-temporal context distinguishes me from other human beings.

The kind of self-possession that is involved in the mineness of human existence provides the basis for a distinction between being oneself authentically or inauthentically (*SuZ*, pp. 43, 53). The possibility of authenticity is based on the fact that a human being must have some understanding of the truth about itself in order to exist at all. Its existence involves disclosure of what is here, there, now, and then. Inauthenticity, by contrast, is based on the inherent tendency of human beings to deceive themselves about themselves and their world, to disclose in the mode of mere semblance (*SuZ*, p. 222). To be authentic is for me to identify with the constitutive concerns that make my life distinctive. It is to know how to live out this identity of self that makes me who I am. To be inauthentic, by contrast, is for me to lose myself by failing to articulate constitutive concerns that distinguish my point of view from that of the other individuals in the world in terms of which I must come to understand myself. This loss of self, that is never quite complete, expresses itself not only in my failure to understand my existence as a project which it is up to me to live through, but also in my failure to understand the dependence of each part of that project on the project as a whole.

Heidegger's interest in the distinction between authenticity and inauthenticity is ultimately ontological. In understanding myself authentically, I understand what it is for me to be. This involves some more general understanding of being and an implicit understanding of the way being in general is different from any particular entity in the world. For my being, like being in general, transcends any and all of the entities of my world. When I understand myself inauthentically, by contrast, I understand my own being in terms of the entities that make up my world. I lose track of the distinction between being in general and the particular entities that make up the world I share with other persons.[4] This distinction between my being and anything that is simply given to me in my world expresses itself in the way human beings exist. This is why Heidegger thinks that human beings have an essential concern with the question of being.

For a human being to be, is for him or her to exist as a project, a process directed at self-determination, whose goal does not exist outside of the project itself and the things which the person cares about. "The project is the existential ontological constitution of the play [*Spielraums*] of the factic ability to be ... Understanding is as projecting the mode of being of *Dasein* in which it is its possibilities as possibilities" (*SuZ*, p. 145). This notion of projecting possibilities is linked, for Heidegger, to an unanalyzed conception of human freedom. Heidegger does not explicitly endorse either a compatibilist or incompatibilist conception of human freedom. For the purposes of his project it is probably enough to note that responsibility requires some notion of human freedom without specifying what the precise nature of this freedom must be. It is, to a certain extent, up to a person what he or she is to be. For this is just what it is for a person to be the project that he or she is. This is why we are responsible for the character that we have.

Heidegger seems to assume, controversially, that freedom will involve the possibility of choosing between alternative possibilities. He thinks of every human being, and indeed of history in general, as a complex of possibilities. These possibilities are not divided into ones which are past, present, and future as the notion of successive choices would have it. Instead, possibilities have a past, present, and

---

[4] The connection between authenticity and the question of being is stressed by Heidegger in his "Letter on Humanism," *GA* 9, pp. 332–333.

future aspect to them. Possibilities are past insofar as they determine our actions and restrict or enhance our prospects for action. This is what makes them past. These past possibilities are themselves possibilities because they circumscribe the way the self can be. Possibilities are future insofar as they express what we can do or be. Possibilities are also future only insofar as they are past, in virtue of the way we are determined by our past, just as they are also past only insofar as they circumscribe what we are to be, and thus have a futural aspect. The present is itself nothing but the way in which pastness and futurity of possibilities are mutually dependent. According to his understanding of time, past, present, and future actually coexist as different ways in which the potentialities of persons exhibit themselves. Past potentialities are past precisely in that they can be modified by the agent only in the way in which they structure future potentialities, while future potentialities are fixed for the agent only in the way in which they are modified by past potentialities. The present is just the modification of past potentialities in terms of the projects understood in terms of future potentialities.

Our initial understanding of such potentialities is based on the public persona we have on the basis of our social roles. Heidegger refers to this as the anyone-self ("das Man-selbst"). The problem with one's public persona is that it fails to treat the possibilities of human existence as genuine possibilities. For my public persona who I am is a matter of facts about what I have to do given the roles that I have taken on. This leads Heidegger to look to my *resolve* to take responsibility for my actions for a full expression of my identity as a person: "In terms of care the *constancy of the self*, as the supposed persistence of the *subjectum*, gets clarified ... Existentially, 'self-constancy' signifies nothing other than anticipatory resoluteness" (*SuZ*, p. 322). Resolute decision is decision that bears responsibility for the whole of my existence. This resolve is thus an expression of the way the self is when it is authentically itself. Indeed, Heidegger regards resoluteness as the "most original truth because the *authentic* truth of *Dasein*" (*SuZ*, p. 297). It involves a process of working through the tendency to resist genuine understanding of who one is in favor of some self-image that one has taken from one's interactions with others: "When *Dasein* discloses and brings the world closer on its own ('eigens'), when it discloses its authentic being to itself, then this discovery of 'world' and disclosure of *Dasein* always takes place as a clearing away of covering overs and obscurations, as a breaking up of distortions with which *Dasein* closes itself off from itself" (*SuZ*, p. 129). This struggle with the distortions about myself provided by everyday existence and the "anyone-self" with which it provides me should lead to behavior that expresses a more adequate, a truer conception of myself (*SuZ*, pp. 256–257). This truer conception of myself is a conception that can genuinely express the unity of my life.

Resolution takes into consideration not what you or I momentarily "intend" to be, but how any mode of behavior is to be a part of the ground project of your or my life as a whole. It thus anticipates the structure that my life will have as a whole. In doing so, it expresses a recognition of the fact that I must take responsibility for the choices that I make and their consequences, even though those choices are not completely in my power (*SuZ*, pp. 284–285). If the tendency toward absorption in the present that comes with the various social roles one has is to be avoided, the connection between the way one achieves a certain project, in particular the ground project of one's own existence, and the project itself, must be so intimate that one cannot lose sight of the overall project in the pursuit of its realization.

Once human identity is understood in terms of the constitutive concerns of one's ground project, it is no longer possible to view a person as a construct out of independent temporal phases. The concerns of a human being can no more be constituted out of momentary states than the general well-being of a person can be agglomerated from the well-being of that individual over particular moments of his or her life. The particular position which events have in a person's life as a whole affects the way in which those events are to be factored into an evaluation of that person's identity and overall welfare.[5] Thus the import of past decisions as well as present decisions is alterable through future decisions which themselves have their particular significance for the individual as a result of the way in which they are linked to past and present decisions.

This way in which the way the past is understood is structured by its relation to what it is to be, and the present is understood from the way things have been and will be, is what Heidegger refers to as authentic temporality. This is the form of temporality that supposedly truly expresses what it is to be a human being. Most conceptions of the way time structures human experience take the primary

---

[5] A subtle defense of this claim may be found in J. D. Velleman, "Well Being and Time," *The Pacific Philosophical Quarterly* 72 (1992), 48–77.

phenomenon to be the replacement of the present by new states that come to be present. Such everyday conceptions of time are thus largely structured by the relation of the present to what is and has become past. This notion of passage is, for Heidegger, a function of the present-orientedness of everyday temporality. This experience of time as passage is genuine for Heidegger, although not fundamental. Temporal experience is more fundamentally a process in which one understands the present through information from the past which one interprets against the background of the constitutive set of projects that determine what one takes to be significant. This gives the future primacy. The future is a "letting-oneself-come-at-oneself" (*SuZ*, p. 325). It is the way in which we come to terms with the way in which the projects that make up our lives develop into what they are. In this way, my life is understood to be a spatio-temporal unity that precedes any of the individual moments of my existence and that is also essentially connected to the spatio-temporal world in which we exist together.

In authentic temporality, the self understands itself and the world in terms of its ground project of determining itself to be a certain human being. Such temporal experience expresses each of our own distinctive senses of self and the responsibility that we take for our lives as a whole. Heidegger distinguishes three forms of authentic temporality: (1) repetition, (2) blink of an eye, and (3) anticipation, corresponding to what has been (the past), what is present, and what is to be (future) (*SuZ*, pp. 336–339). My appropriation of the past, and confrontation with the present, are structured by my understanding of the ground project of being me with all its constitutive goals. The past is repetition for me because I appropriate it with a concern for what I can make of it for my own ground project. The term "repetition" is misleading to the extent that it suggests the idea of reproducing states that no longer exist. Repetition also has the meaning of re-evaluating what is already there. Heidegger understands it as coming to terms with who one is to be through who and what has formed one into who one is.

Repetition involves an appropriation of possibilities as ones which belong to the way one is situated in the world.[6] It is supposed to

---

[6] This theme finds expression in a remark of Kierkegaard's pseudonym who is appropriately called Constantin Constantius: "Repetition is a decisive expression for what recollection was for the Greeks. Just as they taught that all knowledge is a recollection, so will modern philosophy teach that the whole of life is a repetition," S. Kierkegaard, *Repetition* (Princeton

reflect the situatedness of one's moods, but it expresses our situated-ness as it is understood by us in terms of our ground projects. Heidegger insists that repetition consists in choosing a hero from one's tradition as a role model, although one is not supposed to copy that hero, but rather to use his or her actions as a way of coming to understand and deal with what is unique about one's own historical situation (*SuZ*, pp. 385–386). This involves the future and an anticipatory determination of self in relation to an ideal of what one is to be even in the way in which the past is appropriated.

The present is the manifestation of one's ground project and one's situatedness in particular actions. The present is a blink of the eye because it is the way I manifest my appropriation of the past in determining who I am to be. The term "blink of an eye" is again misleading, since it suggests the notion of a now which distinguishes a past that is no longer and a future that is not yet. The "blink of an eye" should, however, be understood as the way in which one comes to terms with information about the way things have been in order to determine how one is to engage with one's environment in the realization of one's constitutive projects. The future is anticipation not in the sense of waiting for something to happen. It expresses my understanding that who I am is not something fixed. I am something whose nature, although circumscribed by my past, is always to some extent up to me to determine. Both the past and the future are involved in present action. Actions are thus not really detachable from the whole context of significance to which they give expression. The "blink of an eye" of presence is thus sunk into the past and the future in a manner which involves a rather radical revision of our common-sense intuitions about the present, since the present is absorbed by the past and the future.[7]

University Press, 1941), p. 33. In formulating his notions of blink of an eye and repetition, Kierkegaard tends to fall back on the concepts of Greek ontology according to Heidegger (see *SuZ*, pp. 235n, 338n). Kierkegaard sees his notion of repetition as that which explains the relation between the atemporal being championed by the Eleatics and the becoming upon which Heraclitus insists. However, Kierkegaard (p. 53) insists that metaphysics founders upon this relationship. He also insists that Greek ontology, with its commitment to a cyclical conception of time, is oriented towards the past, while his own Christian conception of time is future oriented. In the blink of an eye one is supposed to make a commitment which is also a timeless or eternal choice. A commitment is a choice made not for the moment but for eternity. Heidegger attempts to incorporate this idea of a choice made at a certain time which involves a commitment throughout one's life into his own position without appealing to the notion of the eternal or timeless.

[7] In using these terms, Heidegger seems to be appealing to the Kierkegaardian theme of the "purity of heart" which is to will one unifying thing in one's life. Dreyfus and Rubin put the

Heidegger draws here on Kierkegaard's reconstruction of the process of human life as a continuous anxious confrontation with death:[8] "We wish to know how the conception of death will transform a man's entire life, when in order to think its uncertainty he has to think it in every moment, so as to prepare himself for it."[9] Indeed, Kierkegaard develops much of the conception of temporality that Heidegger works with. The terms "blink of an eye," and "repetition" are Kierkegaardian terms that he uses to describe the future directedness of the Christian conception of time and experience. Kierkegaard contrasts the past directedness of Greek thought with its notion of eternal recurrence with the future directedness of Christian thought: "For freedom, the possible is the future, and the future is for time the possible. To both of these corresponds anxiety in the individual life."[10]

The anxiety that we face with respect to the future has to do with our mortality and the limitations which that mortality imposes on our capacity for choice.[11] The theological context of Kierkegaard's thought is undeniable. Thus, Kierkegaard insists that time is a

point nicely in their discussion of Heidegger's appropriation of Kierkegaard: "Heidegger wants to say that, viewed from the perspective of everyday temporality, Dasein's facing the truth about its being occurs at a certain datable time. But, since what Dasein discovers is what Dasein is (i.e., always has been and always will be), this truth, although not created at the moment of discovery as in Kierkegaard, crucially affects all Dasein's future acts as well as its interpretation of the past," Dreyfus, *Being-in-the-World*, p. 322.

[8] There is also a Lutheran dimension to the idea of a human being as a potentiality that Heidegger was aware of through his study of Martin Luther, *Lectures on Romans* (1515–1516) in *Luther's Works* (Philadelphia: Fortress Press, 1955). According to Luther "a human being is always in privation, always in becoming or in potentiality, in matter, and always in action." Aristotle philosophizes about such matters, and he does it well, but he is not understood in this sense. I am indebted here to the discussion of Heidegger's appropriation of the young Luther in John van Buren, *The Young Heidegger* (Bloomington: University of Indiana Press, 1994), p. 200. The best discussion of Heidegger's appropriation of Paul on whose lectures Luther comments is, however, still that in Karl Lehmann, "Christliche Geschichtserfahrung und ontologische Frage beim jungen Heidegger," *Philosophisches Jahrbuch* 74 (1966), pp. 126–153.

[9] Ibid., pp. 150–151. Kierkegaard especially emphasizes the importance of death in human existence in his "At a Graveside," in *Three Discourses on Imagined Occasions*, trans. V. Hong and E. Hong (Princeton University Press, 1993), pp. 69–102.

[10] Søren Kierkegaard, *The Concept of Anxiety*, R. Thomte and A. Anderson trans. (Princeton University Press, 1980), p. 91.

[11] Heidegger maintains that care is constitutive of temporality and hence of intentionality. Concerning his idea that care is essential to being human, Heidegger notes in *Being and Time* that "the way in which 'care' is viewed in the foregoing analysis of *Dasein* is one which has grown upon the author in connection with his attempts to interpret the Augustinian (i.e., Helleno-Christian) anthropology with regard to the principal foundations arrived at in the ontology of Aristotle," p. 264. The role that Heidegger assigns to care is already to some degree anticipated and thus influenced by Kierkegaard. Kierkegaard insists, in his "Speech at the Grave," that care (Danish: "Bekymryng"; German, "Bekümmerung") directed at

process or succession in which there is no past, or future, because there is no present. There is no present because the present must exclude the past and the future and thus reduces to a punctual moment that cannot itself be a part of time. The only way that Kierkegaard sees of rescuing time as tense is by invoking the eternal, in which succession or process is "annulled."[12] While Heidegger agrees with Kierkegaard that succession is not a freestanding notion, he rejects Kierkegaard's appeal to the eternal in order to make sense of time. Such an appeal is not necessary for Heidegger, since he maintains that one need not think of time as connected together by copresent experiences.

Heidegger agrees with Kierkegaard that resoluteness involves a unity of what has been and will be. This unity of the past and the future in a moment of decision suggests a conception of the self as a succession of time-slices that might need to be connected by some notion of copresence (to, for instance, a God's-eye point of view, as Kierkegaard would have it). But these momentary situations are not independent constituents out of which the "continuous span" of time between birth and death is built up. Any particular choice which a person makes is a function of its relation to all the other choices which that person has or will make in his or her lifetime. The actions of an individual may be assigned a certain position and order in time. One may even assume that there are basic actions into which all actions may be decomposed. But even these basic actions are what they are only because of the specific role they play in the ground project of being a person. They are the choices they are only through the way they express the whole of a person's ground project. Nor are the momentary situations which may be distinguished within that span to be thought of as undergoing successive replacement. We must, then, think of the whole of time and action as presupposed by any particular action.

The inherent unity of the span between one's birth and death as experienced in resoluteness is what makes one's personal identity an all or nothing kind of thing for Heidegger. As resolute, one decides what to do based on the import of that potential action for the meaning of one's mortal life as a whole. It is this meaning that Heidegger considers to be constitutive of one's true or authentic

our whole existence is crucial to the kind of earnestness that the confrontation with the certainty that we will die and the uncertainty of when we will die demands of us.

[12] Kierkegaard, *The Concept of Anxiety*, pp. 85–87.

personal identity. However, this authentic selfhood itself presupposes some underlying self-identity which it can express authentically. This is just my existence as a particular human being from my birth through my death. The authenticity of this existence is a function of my success in living this life from birth to death in a way which is uniquely my own.

RESPONSIBILITY AND EVERYDAY SELF-IDENTITY

One's initial understanding of one's identity as a self comes, for Heidegger, from the transactions that one has with one's environment and from the social roles and involvements that one has. These involvements presuppose a distinct person who is able to carry out the commitments they entail. But it is through the tasks set by social roles that the individual comes to understand her own responsibility for what she does. The everyday interpretation of what it is to be a self is based on a public and, hence, shared world of institutional and natural involvements.

It is a significant feature of our experience that the public or anyone-self bears responsibility for what anyone does as one who has certain social roles to perform. These social roles have a normative dimension to them. One can succeed or fail to live up to the demands of these roles. One can expect praise for success in satisfying such demands, and blame in failure to satisfy these demands. Thus one comes to recognize that one is accountable *for* how one does what one does. This accountability *to* "the others" makes for a distinctive reciprocal distance ("Abständigkeit") between me and the others as we do what any one of us is supposed to do (*SuZ*, p. 126). One treats oneself like one treats the others with whom one has dealings. In this way, the differences between us are averaged out. In being accountable to "the others" I am accountable to myself, but I am accountable to myself in the same way that I am accountable to persons who are distinct from me. In having an "anyone-self" ("ein 'Man-selbst'") one does not have a group mind in which one's own distinctness as a person is lost. But it is, as Heidegger points out, characteristic of this anyone-self that it makes constant references to "the others" in order to hide the fact that one belongs oneself to these others (*SuZ*, p. 126). This effort to distance oneself from others is, indeed, a fundamental aspect of the anyone-self. This distancing of oneself from others is the flip-side of the levelling and averaging out of substantive distinctions between individual persons. "Anyone" understands oneself as others do, but one still has an understanding of oneself as a distinct individual.

What we do is laid out for us in everyday existence by social conventions and the environment in which we move. As a person with a particular job description, one has a certain identity. This identity consists in the responsibilities which devolve on one as a result of that job description. It is this social role that is given responsibility for what one does. There is a certain "constancy" ("Ständigkeit") to the self in its social roles, but the self is also "inconstant" or "non-independent" ("unselbständig") because it has nothing but these social roles to give it a sense of identity and responsibility (*SuZ*, p. 128). Heidegger avoids talk of personal identity in favor of talk of the constancy ("Ständigkeit") or self-sufficiency ("Selbstständigkeit") of the self (*SuZ*, pp. 316ff. and 375). In part, this reflects his reservations about identifying the self with a certain persona. It also reflects his tendency to assimilate genuine self-identity with independence or autonomy. The persona that I have on the basis of a certain role I have gives a certain constancy to my life: "*Dasein* speaks about itself, it sees itself as thus and such, and yet it is a mere *mask*, that it puts in front of itself in order not to be frightened by itself. Defense against anxiety... in this mask of public interpretedness *Dasein* presents itself as the *highest vivacity* (that is, of business)" (*GA* 63, p. 32). This anxiety is a result of the fact that we do not have control over the conditions that govern our own existence. Doing what is expected of "anyone" helps us to hide our lack of control from ourselves. But each of us has to work through the mask or persona provided by the one in order to become who each of us truly is.

It seems that the masks or roles that one has in everyday life cannot be all there is to personal identity, for I can give up old roles and take up new ones and still remain the same person, or self. This view can, however, be challenged by those who identify selfhood and personality with social roles.[13] Here there is clearly a notion of responsibility, but the person-neutral nature of my responsibilities discourages me from taking responsibility for my own life in what is

---

[13] In Balinese culture, for instance, the human being seems to be regarded as almost exhausted by his or her social role. Status titles, birth order names, and kinship terms are the only names that are of any significance; see Clifford Geertz, *Person, Time and Conduct* (New Haven: Yale University Press, 1966).

distinctive about it, for it tends to suppress the development of just this distinctive sense of self: "Since the one prescribes all judgment and decision, it takes over responsibility from each *Dasein*" (*SuZ*, p. 127). Thus one must say that *"first of all* 'I' 'am'" not in the sense of my own self, but rather the others in the mode of the anyone" (*SuZ*, p. 129). I am not truly me or independent to the extent that I simply identify with the roles that I take on through my interaction with others.

Heidegger takes the possibility that one might have an understanding of oneself that is quite divided very seriously. This is a central theme in his concern with the endemic character of inauthenticity in human existence. He sees human existence as a constant struggle against self-fragmentation. But he argues that the problem of personal identity as it has been traditionally understood, and continues to be understood, especially in the neo-Lockean tradition, is based on one's tendency in everyday existence to disperse oneself in the various tasks and roles that one has. In fulfilling the individual tasks connected with these roles, one comes to understand oneself in terms of the failure or success of these tasks, rather than in terms of the human existence that links these roles together. This generates the question of how these various events can be connected together in one persistent self (*SuZ*, p. 390). This problem is exacerbated by the tendency to think of the self as an object or rather sequence of objects that corresponds to statements about events occurring at various clock-times.

Heidegger insists against this conception of a person as a construction from different person-stages that the notion of a person-stage is itself parasitic on the notion of a human being with an essentially extended spatio-temporal existence. He thus does not take seriously the possibility that one's identity as a human being might be different from the ultimate basis for one's identity as a self.[14] He takes our

[14] Michael Haar, *Heidegger and the Essence of Man* (Buffalo: State University of New York Press, 1993), pp. 77ff., suggests that Heidegger tends to see an opposition between the importance of language and truth in human existence and the animality of human beings. This would reinstate a form of the very notion of human beings as rational animals that Heidegger wants to reject. It seems to me that Heidegger's concern is rather to emphasize both the difference and the continuity between even the most primitive living creature's sensitivity to its environment and human understanding of its world. This is the force of the contrast between animals that are "world-poor," and human beings as "world-bound" in *Die Grundbegriffe der Metaphysik. Welt-Endlichkeit-Einsamkeit* (1929–1930), *GA* 29–30, pp. 272–396. Animals have some sensitivity to their environment, but lack the full-blooded articulated understanding of their environment that humans have. Our understanding of our

everyday pre-theoretical understanding of the self and time as his starting-point. This conception of time takes spatial and temporal intervals belonging to a publicly shared space and time in which we pursue our various engagements as a given. These engagements are an expression of the involvements that we have in virtue of our various roles in society. Our everyday identity as persons is, indeed, determined, for Heidegger, by the responsibility that we have for the social roles that we occupy. The future expresses itself for us in the form of our expectations concerning the success or failure of these tasks set for us by our social roles. Heidegger maintains that this leads to a particular forgetfulness of self, as one does not concern oneself with what it is to be who one is with the history that one has, but rather with one's success or failure in the social role that one has.

Heidegger takes authentic existence and the authentic conception of time that is supposed to go with it to be the ultimate basis for understanding the persistence of the self (*SuZ*, p. 322). We are authentic just when we understand and interpret our whole existence in terms of an underlying theme that distinguishes me or you from all other human beings. Still, authenticity presupposes but does not itself constitute the unity of a human existence. Human existence is authentic to the extent to which it understands itself as an inherent unity. My understanding of my existence in terms of a certain meaning that I give to my life must include my commitment to live out this way of giving sense to how I am to live. This conception of the self as the bearer of responsibility for one's whole existence thus contrasts with the notion of a self as the short-term satisfaction or failure to satisfy the demands of a certain social role in everyday life, as well as with the even more abstract notion of a self as a sequence of states of consciousness. Heidegger is able to provide a rather plausible reconstruction of the notion of personal identity in terms of the way each of us must take responsibility for our existence as human beings. This notion of responsibility is itself an expression of the way we understand our essentially spatial and temporal existence as human beings.

environment also circumscribes the ways in which we can understand ourselves and everything else. There is a helpful discussion of the distinction between world-poor and world bound in F. Olafson, *Heidegger and the Philosophy of Mind*, pp. 236ff.

Select bibliography

WORKS OF HUSSERL

Husserl, E., "Bewußtsein und Sinn – Sinn und Noema," (1920) in: *Analysen Zur Passiven Synthesis (1918–1926)*, *Husserliana: Edmund Husserls Gesammelte Werke* (The Hague: Martinus Nijhoff, 1966), vol. 11.

Cartesianische Meditationen und Pariser Vorträge, *Husserliana: Edmund Husserls Gesammelte Werke* (The Hague: Martinus Nijhoff, 1950), vol. 1. English: *Cartesian Meditations*, trans. Dorian Cairns (The Hague: Martinus Nijhoff, 1973).

"Kritische Diskussion von K. Twardowski, *Zur Lehre vom Inhalt und Gegenstand der Vorstellungen. Eine Psychologische Untersuchung* (Wien, 1894)," in: *Aufsätze und Rezensionen, (1890–1910)*, *Husserliana: Edmund Husserls Gesammelte Werke* (The Hague: Martinus Nijhoff, 1979), vol. 22. English: "A Critical Discussion of K. Twardowski, *On the Doctrine of Content and the Objects of Presentation. A Psychological Investigation* (Vienna, 1984)" in: Willard D. (ed.), *Edmund Husserl: Early Writings in the Philosophy of Logic and Mathematics* (Dordrecht: Kluwer, 1994).

Ding und Raum. Vorlesungen 1907, *Husserliana: Edmund Husserls Gesammelte Werke* (The Hague: Martinus Nijhoff, 1973), vol. 16.

Edmund Husserl Briefwechsel (Dordrecht: Kluwer, 1990).

Erfahrung und Urteil (Hamburg: Meiner, 1975). English: *Experience and Judgement*, trans. J. S. Churchill and K. Ameriks (London: Routledge and Kegan Paul, 1973).

Erste Philosophie, *Husserliana: Edmund Husserls Gesammelte Werke* (The Hague: Martinus Nijhoff, 1956, 1959.), vol. 7–8.

Formale und Transzendentale Logik, *Husserliana: Edmund Husserls Gesammelte Werke* (The Hague: Martinus Nijhoff, 1974), vol. 17. English: *Formal and Transcendental Logic*, trans. D. Cairns (The Hague: Martinus Nijhoff, 1969).

Ideen zu einer reinen Phänomenologie und phänomenologischen Philosophie. Erstes Buch, *Husserliana: Edmund Husserls Gesammelte Werke* (The Hague: Martinus Nijhoff, 1950), vol. 3. English: *Ideas Pertaining to a Pure Phenomenology and to a Phenomenological Philosophy*, trans. F. Kersten (The Hague: Nijhoff, 1982).

242

Ideen zu einer reinen Phänomenologie und phänomenologischen Philosophie. Zweites Buch, Husserliana: Edmund Husserls Gesammelte Werke (The Hague: Martinus Nijhoff, 1952), vol. 4. English: *Ideas Pertaining to a Pure Phenomenology and to a Phenomenological Philosophy, 2nd Book*, trans. R. Rojcewicz and A. Schuwer (Dordrecht: Kluwer, 1989).

"Intentionale Gegenstände," in: *Aufsätze und Rezensionen, (1990–1910), Husserliana: Edmund Husserls Gesammelte Werke* (The Hague: Martinus Nijhoff, 1979), vol. 22, and *Brentano-Studien* 3 (1990–1991), 137–176. English: "Intentional Objects," in: Willard D. (ed.), *Edmund Husserl: Early Writings in the Philosophy of Logic and Mathematics* (Dordrecht: Kluwer, 1994).

Die Krisis der Europäischen Wissenschaften und die Phänomenologie, Husserliana: Edmund Husserls Gesammelte Werke (The Hague: Martinus Nijhoff, 1954), vol. 6. English: *The Crisis of European Sciences and Phenomenology*, David Carr trans. (Evanston: Northwestern University Press, 1970).

Logische Untersuchungen, Husserliana: Edmund Husserls Gesammelte Werke (The Hague: Martinus Nijhoff, 1984), vols. 18–19. English: *Logical Investigations*, trans. J. N. Findlay (New York: Humanities Press, 1970).

Phänomenologische Psychologie. Vorlesungen Sommersemester 1925, Husserliana: Edmund Husserls Gesammelte Werke (The Hague: Martinus Nijhoff, 1962), vol. 9. English: *Phenomenological Psychology. Lectures of Summer semester 1925.*

Phantasie, Bildbewußtsein,Erinnerung. Zur Phänomenologie der anschaulichen Vergegenwärtigungen, Husserliana: Edmund Husserls Gesammelte Werke (The Hague: Martinus Nijhoff, 1980), vol. 23.

"Philosophie als Strenge Wissenschaft," in: *Aufsätze und Rezensionen, (1890–1910), Husserliana: Edmund Husserls Gesammelte Werke* (The Hague: Martinus Nijhoff, 1979), vol. 22. English: "Philosophy as Rigorous Science," in: Q. Lauer trans. *Phenomenology and the Crisis of Philosophy* (New York: Harper, 1969), pp. 71–147.

Philosophie der Arithmetik. Mit ergänzenden Texten (1890– 1901), Husserliana: Edmund Husserls Gesammelte Werke (The Hague: Martinus Nijhoff, 1970), vol. 12.

"Psychologische Studien zur elementaren Logik," in: *Aufsätze und Rezensionen, (1890–1910), Husserliana: Edmund Husserls Gesammelte Werke* (The Hague: Martinus Nijhoff, 1987), vol. 22. English: "Psychological Studies for Elementary Logic," in: P. McCormick and F. Elliston (eds.), *Husserl: Shorter Works* (University of Notre Dame Press, 1981), and in: Willard D. (ed.), *Edmund Husserl: Early Writings in the Philosophy of Logic and Mathematics* (Dordrecht: Kluwer, 1994).

"A Reply to a Critic of my Refutation of Logical Psychologism," in: J. N. Mohanty (ed.), *Readings on Edmund Husserl's Logical Investigations* (The Hague: Martinus Nijhoff, 1977).

Vorlesungen über Bedeutungslehre Sommersemester 1908, Husserliana: Edmund Husserls Gesammelte Werke (The Hague: Martinus Nijhoff, 1987.), vol. 26.

Zur Phänomenologie der Intersubjektivität: Husserliana: Edmund Husserls Gesammelte Werke (The Hague: Martinus Nijhoff, 1973), vol. 13–15.
Zur Phänomenologie des inneren Zeitbewußtseins, Husserliana: Edmund Husserls Gesammelte Werke (The Hague: Martinus Nijhoff, 1966), vol. 10. English: *On the Phenomenology of the Consciousness of Internal Time (1893–1917)*, trans. J. Brough (Dordrecht: Kluwer, 1990).

WORKS OF HEIDEGGER

Heidegger, M., *Aus der Erfahrung des Denken, Martin Heidegger: Gesamtausgabe* (Frankfurt: Vittorio Klostermann, 1983), vol. 13.
"Brief über den Humanismus," in: *Wegmarken (1919–1961), Martin Heidegger: Gesamtausgabe* (Frankfurt: Vittorio Klostermann, 1976), vol. 9. English: "Letter on Humanism," *Martin Heidegger: Basic Writings* (New York: Harper and Row, 1977).
"Das Ende der Philosophie und die Aufgabe des Denkens," in: *Zur Sache des Denkens* (Tübingen: Niemeyer, 1969). English: *Heidegger on Time and Being*, trans. Joan Stambaugh (New York: Harper, 1972).
Grundbegriffe der antiken Philosophie, Martin Heidegger: Gesamtausgabe (Frankfurt: Klostermann, 1993), vol. 22.
Grundbegriffe der Metaphysik. Welt-Endlichkeit-Einsamkeit, Martin Heidegger: Gesamtausgabe (Frankfurt: Klostermann, 1983), vols. 29–30. English: *The Fundamental Problems of Metaphysics: World, Finitude, Solitude*, trans. William McNeill and Nicholas Walker (Bloomington: Indiana University Press, 1995).
Die Grundprobleme der Phänomenologie, Martin Heidegger: Gesamtausgabe (Frankfurt: Klostermann, 1975), vol. 24. English: *The Basic Problems of Phenomenology*, trans. Albert Hofstadter (Bloomington: University of Indiana Press, 1982).
History of The Concept of Time, English–German edition (Oxford: Blackwell, 1992).
Kant und das Problem der Metaphysik, Martin Heidegger: Gesamtausgabe (Frankfurt: Vittorio Klostermann, 1991), vol. 3. English: *Kant and the Problem of Metaphysics*, trans. Richard Taft (Bloomington: Indiana University Press, 1990).
Die Kategorien- und Bedeutungslehre des Duns Scotus, Martin Heidegger: Gesamtausgabe (Frankfurt: Vittorio Klostermann, 1978), vol. 1.
Logik. Die Frage nach der Wahrheit, Martin Heidegger: Gesamtausgabe (Frankfurt: Vittorio Klostermann, 1976), vol. 21.
Martin Heidegger/Karl Jaspers: Briefwechsel 1920–1963 (Frankfurt: Klostermann, 1990).
Die Metaphysik des Deutschen Idealismus, Martin Heidegger: Gesamtausgabe (Frankfurt: Vittorio Klostermann, 1991), vol. 49.
Metaphysische Anfangsgründe im Ausgang von Leibniz, Martin Heidegger: Gesamtausgabe (Frankfurt: Vittorio Klostermann, 1990), vol. 26. English:

Metaphysical Foundations of Logic Starting from Leibniz, trans. Michael Haim, (Bloomington: Indiana University Press, 1984).

"Neuere Forschungen in der Logik (1912)," in: *Frühe Schriften, Martin Heidegger: Gesamtausgabe* (Frankfurt: Vittorio Klostermann, 1978), vol. 1.

Ontologie (Hermeneutik der Faktizität), Martin Heidegger: Gesamtausgabe (Frankfurt: Vittorio Klostermann, 1988), vol. 63. English: *Ontology (Hermeneutics of Facticity)*, trans. John van Buren (Bloomington: Indiana University Press, 1995).

"Phänomenologische Interpretation zu Aristoteles (Anzeige der hermeneutischen Situation)," *Dilthey Jahrbuch für Philosophie und Geschichte der Geisteswissenschaften* 6 (1989), 228–274. English: "Phenomenological Interpretations of Aristotle (Indication of the Hermeneutical Situation)," trans. Michael Bauer, *Man and World* 25 (1992), 358–393.

Phänomenologische Interpretationen zu Aristoteles. Einführung in die phänomenologische Forschung, Martin Heidegger: Gesamtausgabe (Frankfurt: Vittorio Klostermann, 1985), vol. 61.

Phänomenologische Interpretation von Kants Kritik der reinen Vernunft, Martin Heidegger: Gesamtausgabe (Frankfurt: Vittorio Klostermann, 1987), vol. 25. English: *Phenomenological Interpretation of Kant's Critique of Pure Reason*, trans. Parvis Emad and Kenneth Maly (Bloomington: Indiana University Press, 1997).

Platon: Sophistes, Martin Heidegger: Gesamtausgabe (Frankfurt: Vittorio Klostermann, 1992), vol. 19.

Prolegomena zur Geschichte des Zeitbegriffs, Martin Heidegger: Gesamtausgabe (Frankfurt: Vittorio Klostermann, 1978), vol. 20. English: *The History of the Concept of Time*, trans. Theodore Kisiel (Bloomington: Indiana University Press, 1985).

Sein und Zeit, in: *Martin Heidegger: Gesamtausgabe* (Frankfurt: Vittorio Klostermann, 1977), vol. 2. English: *Being and Time*, trans. Macquarrie and Robinson (New York: Harper and Row, 1962), and trans. Joan Stambaugh (Stoneybrook: State University of New York Press, 1996).

Seminare (1951–73), *Martin Heidegger: Gesamtausgabe* (Frankfurt: Vittorio Klostermann, 1986), vol. 15.

"Summary of a Seminar on the lecture on 'Time and Being,'" *On Time and Being* (New York: Harper and Row, 1972).

Vom Wesen der Wahrheit: Zu Platons Höhlengleichnis und Theätet (1931–2), *Martin Heidegger: Gesamtausgabe* (Frankfurt: Vittorio Klostermann, 1988), vol. 34.

"Was ist Metaphysik," in: *Wegmarken Martin Heidegger: Gesamtausgabe* (Frankfurt: Vittorio Klostermann, 1976), vol. 9. English: "What is Metaphysics?," *Martin Heidegger: Basic Writings* (New York: Harper and Row, 1977).

"Wilhelm Diltheys Forschungsarbeit und die historische Weltanschauung," *Dilthey Jahrbuch für Philosophie und Geschichte der Geisteswissenschaften* 8 (1993), 144–177.

Zur Bestimmung der Philosophie, Martin Heidegger: Gesamtausgabe (Frankfurt: Vittorio Klostermann, 1988), vol. 56–57.

Zur Sache des Denkens (Tübingen: Max Niemeyer, 1969). English: *On Time and Being* (New York: Harper and Row, 1972).

"Die Zeit des Weltbildes," in: *Holzwege, Martin Heidegger: Gesamtausgabe* (Frankfurt: Vittorio Klostermann, 1977), vol. 5. English: "The Age of the World Picture," in: *The Question Concerning Technology and other Essays* (New York: Harper and Row, 1960).

"Der Zeitbegriff in der Geisteswissenschaft," in: *Frühe Schriften, Martin Heidegger: Gesamtausgabe* (Frankfurt: Vittorio Klostermann, 1978), vol. 1, pp. 413–434.

SELECT SECONDARY LITERATURE

Anscombe, Elizabeth, *Intention* (Oxford: Blackwell, 1957).

"The Intentionality of Sensation: A Grammatical Feature," in: R. J. Butler (ed.), *Analytical Philosophy*, second series (Oxford: Blackwell, 1965), pp. 158–180.

Apel, Karl-Otto, "Wittgenstein und Heidegger. Die Frage nach dem Sinn von Sein und der Sinnlosigkeitsverdacht gegen alle Metaphysik," in: Otto Pöggeler (ed.) *Heidegger* (Königstein: Athenäum, 1984), 358–396.

Aquila, Richard, *Intentionality: A Study of Mental Acts* (University Park: Pennsylvania State University Press, 1977).

Aristotle, "De Memoria et Reminiscentia," trans. in Richard Sorabji, *Aristotle on Memory* (London: Duckworth, 1972).

On the Soul, Parva Naturalia, On Breath (Cambridge, Mass.: Harvard University Press, 1936).

Metaphysics (Cambridge, Mass.: Harvard University Press, 1935).

Atwell, John, "Husserl on Signification and Object," *American Philosophical Quarterly* 6 (1967).

Barrett, William, "The Flow of Time," in: Richard Gale (ed.), *The Philosophy of Time* (New Jersey: Humanities Press, 1978).

Bell, David, *Husserl* (London: Routledge, 1990).

Benacerraf, Paul, "Mathematical Truth," *Journal of Philosophy* 70 (1973), 661–679.

Bergson, Henri, *Essai sur les données immédiates de la conscience, Oeuvres* (Paris: Presses universitaires de France, 1963). English: *Time and Free Will* (New York: Harper, 1960).

Matière et mémoire. Essai sur la relation du corps avec l'esprit, Oeuvres (Paris: Presses universitaires de France, 1963). English: *Matter and Memory* (New York: Doubleday, 1911).

Bernet, Rudolf, Iso Kern, Eduard Marbach, *Edmund Husserl: An Exposition of his Thought* (Bloomington: Indiana University Press, 1994).

"Is the Present Ever Present? Phenomenology and the Metaphysics of Presence," *Research in Phenomenology* 12 (1982), 85–112.

La vie du sujet: Recherches sur l'interprétation de Husserl dans la phénoménologie (Paris: Presses universitaires de France, 1994).

"Transcendence et intentionalité: Heidegger et Husserl sur les prolégomènes d'une ontologie phénoménologique," in: F. Volpi et al. (eds.), *Heidegger et l'idée de la phénoménologie* (Dordrecht: Kluwer, 1988), pp. 195–216.

Binswanger, Ludwig, "The Case of Lola Voss," in: *Being-in-the-World* (New York: Basic Books, 1963).

Blattner, William, "Existential Temporality in *Being and Time*," in: H. Dreyfus and H. Hall (eds.), *Heidegger: A Critical Reader* (Oxford: Blackwell, 1992).

Bolzano, Bernard, *Wissenschaftslehre* (Sulzbach: Seidel, 1837). English: *Theory of Science*, trans. Rolf George (Oxford: Blackwell, 1972).

Brandom, Robert, "Heidegger's Categories in *Being and Time*," in Dreyfus and Hall (eds.), *Heidegger: A Critical Reader* (Oxford: Blackwell, 1992).

Making It Explicit: Reasoning, Representing, and Discursive Commitment (Cambridge, Mass.: Harvard University Press, 1994).

Brentano, Franz, *Abkehr vom Nichtrealen* (Hamburg: Meiner Verlag, 1966).

Kategorienlehre, Alfred Kastil (ed.) (Hamburg: Meiner Verlag, 1933). English: *The Theory of the Categories*, trans. R. M. Chisholm and N. Guterman (The Hague: Martinus Nijhoff, 1981).

Von der mannigfachen Bedeutung des Seienden nach Aristoteles (Freiburg: Herder, 1862). English: *On the Several Senses of Being in Aristotle*, trans. Rolf George (Berkeley: University of California Press, 1975).

Psychologie vom empirischen Standpunkt, Oskar Kraus (ed.) (Hamburg: Meiner, 1924). English: *Psychology from an Empirical Standpoint*, trans. L. L. McAlister (London: Routledge and Kegan Paul, 1973).

Die Psychologie des Aristoteles insbesondere seine Lehre vom nous poietikos (Darmstadt: Wissenschaftliche Buchgesellschaft, 1967). English: *The Psychology of Aristotle*, trans. Rolf George (Berkeley: University of California Press, 1977).

Wahrheit und Evidenz, Oskar Kraus (ed.) (Hamburg: Meiner, 1930). English: *The True and the Evident*, trans. R. Chisholm and E. Politzer (London: Routledge and Kegan Paul, 1966).

Brentano, Franz and F. Mayer-Hillerbrand (ed.), *Grundzüge der Ästhetik* (Bern: Francke, 1959).

Broad, C. D., *An Examination of McTaggart's Philosophy* (Cambridge: Cambridge University Press, 1938).

Bronstein, M. and L. Landau, *Soviet Physics* 4 (1933).

Brough, John, "The Emergence of Absolute Consciousness in Husserl's Early Writings on Time-Consciousness," *Husserl: Expositions and Appraisals*, pp. 83–100.

"Husserl on Memory," *Monist* 59 (1975), 40–62.

"Husserl's Phenomenology of Time-Consciousness," in: J. N. Mohanty and W. R. McKenna (eds.), *Husserl's Phenomenology: A Textbook* (Washington, DC: University Press of America, 1989).

Burnyeat, Myles, "Is Aristotelian Philosophy of Mind Still Credible? A Draft," in: Martha Nussbaum and Amélie Rorty (eds.), *Essays on Aristotle's De Anima* (New York: Oxford University Press, 1992), pp. 15–26.

"Idealism and Greek Philosophy: What Descartes Saw and Berkeley Missed," in: G. Vesey (ed.), *Idealism Past and Present* (Cambridge University Press, 1982).

Carman, Taylor, "On Being Social: A Reply to Olafson," *Inquiry* 37 (1994), 203–223.

Carr, David, *Interpreting Husserl* (Dordrecht: Martinus Nijhoff, 1987).

Carrol, Lewis, *Through the Looking Glass* (London: Macmillan, 1872).

Casey, Edward, "Imagination and the Phenomenological Method," in: F. Elliston and P. McCormick (eds.), *Husserl. Expositions and Appraisals* (University of Notre Dame Press, 1977), pp. 70–82.

Cassirer, Ernst, *Substance and Function and Einstein's Theory of Relativity*, trans. W. and Marie Swabey (New York: Dover, 1923).

Chisholm, Roderick M., "Brentano on Descriptive Psychology and the Intentional," in: Harold Morick (ed.), *Introduction to the Philosophy of Mind* (Glenview: Scott Foresman and Co., 1970).

Perceiving: A Philosophical Study (Ithaca, N.Y.: Cornell University Press, 1957).

Person and Object (La Salle: Open Court, 1976).

Chisholm, Roderick M. and Wilfried Sellars, "Intentionality and the Mental," in: H. Feigl, M. Scriven, and G. Maxwell (eds.), *Concepts, Theories, and the Mind–Body Problem* (Minneapolis, Minn.: University of Minnesota Press, 1958), pp. 507–539.

Chomsky, Noam, "Contributions to the Theory of Innate Ideas," *Synthese* 17 (1967).

Claesges, Ulrich, *Edmund Husserl's Theorie der Raumkonstitution* (The Hague: Martinus Nijhoff, 1964).

Cohen, L. Jonathan, "Criteria of Intentionality," *Aristotelian Society Supplementary Volume* 42 (1968), 123–142.

Cohen, Sheldon M, "Thomas Aquinas on the Immaterial Reception of Sensible Forms," *Philosophical Review* 91 (1982), 193–209.

Conant, James, "The Search for Logically Alien Thought: Descartes, Kant, Frege, and the *Tractatus*," *Philosophical Topics* 20 (1991), 115–180.

Cramer, Konrad, "Erlebnis: Thesen zu Hegels Theorie des Selbstbewußtseins mit Rücksicht auf die Aporien eines Grundbegriffs nachhegelscher Philosophie," *Hegel-Studien*, 11 (1974), 537–603.

Dastur, Françoise, *Dire le temps* (Fougères: Editions encre marine, 1994).

Heidegger et la question du temps (Paris: Presses universitaires de France, 1990). English: *Heidegger and the Question of Time* (Atlantic Highlands: Humanities Press, 1998).

"Heidegger und die Logischen Untersuchungen," *Heidegger Studies* 7 (1991), 37–52.

"La constitution ekstatique-horizontale de la temporalité chez Heidegger," *Heidegger Studies* 2 (1984), 97–110. English: "The ecstatic-horizonal constitution of temporality in Heidegger," in: Christopher Macann (ed.), *Critical Heidegger* (London: Routledge, 1996).

Dennett, Daniel, *The Intentional Stance* (Boston: MIT Press, 1987).

Derrida, Jacques, *La voix et le phénomène* (Paris: Presses universitaires de France, 1967). English: *Speech and Phenomena*, trans. D. Allison (Evanston: Northwestern University Press, 1973).

Descartes, René, *Oeuvres de Descartes*, C. Adam and P. Tannery (eds.), (Paris: Leopold Cerf, 1987–1913).

Diemer, Alwin, *Edmund Husserl* (Maisenheim: Hain, 1965).

Dostal, Robert J., "Time and Phenomenology in Husserl and Heidegger," in: Charles Guignon (ed.), *The Cambridge Companion to Heidegger*, pp. 141–169.

Dreyfus, Hubert, *Being-in-the-World* (Cambridge, Mass.: MIT Press, 1991).

"The Perceptual Noema," in: H. Dreyfus (ed.), *Husserl, Intentionality, and Cognitive Science* (Boston: MIT Press, 1984), pp. 135–170.

Dreyfus, Hubert and Harrison Hall (eds.), *Heidegger: A Critical Reader* (Oxford: Blackwell, 1992).

Dreyfus, Hubert and John Haugeland, "Husserl and Heidegger: Philosophy's Last Stand," in: M. Murray (ed.), *Heidegger and Modern Philosophy* (New Haven: Yale University Press, 1978).

Drummond, John, *Husserlian Intentionality and Non-Foundational Realism: Noema and Object* (Dordrecht: Kluwer, 1990).

Drummond, John and Lester Embree (eds.), *The Phenomenology of the Noema* (Dordrecht: Kluwer, 1992).

"Realism versus Antirealism: A Husserlian Contribution," in: R. Sokolowski, *Edmund Husserl and the Phenomenological Tradition* (Washington: Catholic University of America Press, 1988), pp. 87–106.

Dummett, Michael, "A Defense of McTaggart's Proof of the Unreality of Time," *Truth and Other Enigmas* (Cambridge, Mass.: Harvard University Press, 1978), pp. 351–357.

Origins of Analytical Philosophy (Cambridge: Harvard University Press, 1993).

Edwards, Paul, *Heidegger and Death* (La Salle: Open Court, 1979).

Elliston, Frederick and Peter McCormick (eds.), *Husserl. Expositions and Appraisals* (University of Notre Dame Press, 1977).

Evans, Gareth, John McDowell (ed.), *The Varieties of Reference* (Oxford University Press, 1982).

Evans, J. Claude, *Strategies of Deconstruction: Derrida and the Myth of the Voice* (Minneapolis: University of Minnesota Press, 1991).

Fell, Joseph, *Heidegger and Sartre: An Essay on Being and Place* (New York: Columbia University Press, 1979).

Figal, Günther, *Martin Heidegger: Phänomenologie der Freiheit* (Frankfurt: Suhrkamp, 1988).

Findlay, John N., "Husserl's Analysis of the Inner Time-Consciousness," *Monist* 59 (1975).

Fink, Eugen, *Die Phänomenologische Philosophie Edmund Husserl in der gegenwärtigen Kritik* (Berlin: Pan, 1934).

Fleischer, Margot, *Die Zeitanalysen in Heideggers "Sein und Zeit": Aporien, Probleme, und ein Ausblick* (Würzburg: Königsberg und Neumann, 1991).

Føllesdal, Dagfinn, *Husserl und Frege* (Oslo: Aschehoug, 1958).

"Husserl on Evidence and Justification," in: R. Sokolowski (ed.), *Husserl and the Phenomenological Tradition* (Washington, DC: Catholic University of America Press, 1988).

"Husserl's Notion of Noema," *The Journal of Philosophy* 66 (1969), 680–687.

Frede, Dorothea, "Heidegger and the Scandal of Philosophy," in: A. Donagan, A Perovich, and M. Wedin (eds.), *Human Nature and Natural Knowledge* (Dordrecht: Reidel, 1986).

Frege, Gottlob, *The Basic Laws of Arithmetic*, M. Furth trans. (Berkeley: University of California Press, 1964).

Philosophical and Mathematical Correspondence (Oxford: Blackwell, 1980).

"Review of E. Husserl's *Philosophie der Arithmetik*," E. Kluge trans., in: F. Elliston and P. McCormick (eds.), *Husserl: Expositions and Appraisals* (Notre Dame: University of Notre Dame Press, 1977), pp. 314–324.

Friedman, Michael, "Overcoming Metaphysics: Carnap and Heidegger," *Minnesota Studies in the Philosophy of Science* 26 (1996), 45–79.

Gadamer, Hans-Georg, *Wahrheit und Methode* (Tübingen: Mohr, 1960). English: *Truth and Method* (New York: Continuum, 1989).

Geach, Peter T. *Logic Matters* (Oxford: Blackwell, 1972).

Mental Acts (London: Routledge and Kegan Paul, 1957).

Geertz, Clifford, *Person, Time and Conduct* (New Haven: Yale University Press, 1966).

Geuss, Raymond, *Persons and Principles* (New York: Columbia University Ph.D. thesis, 1971).

Gibbs, J. Willard, *Elementary Principles in Statistical Mechanics* (New York: Dover Publications, 1960).

Guignon, Charles (ed.), *The Cambridge Companion to Heidegger* (New York: Cambridge University Press, 1993).

Heidegger and the Problem of Knowledge (Indianapolis: Hackett, 1983).

Gurwitsch, Aron, "On the Intentionality of Consciousness," *Studies in Phenomenological Psychology* (Evanston: Northwestern University Press, 1966).

Haar, Michael, *Heidegger et l'essence de l'homme* (Grenoble: Jerome Millon, 1990). English: *Heidegger and the Essence of Man* (Buffalo: State University of New York Press, 1993).

Habermas, Jürgen, *Der Philosophische Diskurs der Modernität* (Frankfurt: Suhr kamp, 1983). English: *The Philosophical Discourse of Modernity: Twelve Lectures*, trans. Frederick Lawrence (Boston: MIT Press, 1987).

Haddock, Guillermo, "On Husserl's Distinction between State of Affairs (Sachverhalt) and Situation of Affairs (Sachlage)," in: T. Seebohm, D. Føllesdal, and J. Mohanty (eds.), *Phenomenology and the Formal Sciences* (Dordrecht: Kluwer, 1991), pp. 35–48.

Harries, Karsten, "Fundamental Ontology and the Search for Man's Place," in Michael Murray, (ed.), *Heidegger and Modern Philosophy: Critical Essays* (New Haven: Yale University Press, 1978), pp. 65–79.

"Truth and Freedom," in: Robert Sokolowski (ed.), *Edmund Husserl and the Phenomenological Tradition* (Washington, DC: Catholic University of America Press, 1988).

"Wittgenstein and Heidegger: The Relation of Philosophy to Language," *The Journal of Value Inquiry* 2 (1968), 281–291.

Hart, W. D., "The Epistemology of Abstract Objects," *Aristotelian Society Supplementary Volume* 53 (1979).

Hartmann, Klaus, "The Logic of Deficient and Eminent Modes in Heidegger," *Journal of the British Society for Phenomenology* 5 (1974), 118–134

Haugeland, John, "Dasein's Disclosedness," in: Dreyfus, Hubert and Harrison Hall (eds.), *Heidegger: A Critical Reader* (Oxford: Blackwell, 1992), pp. 39–49.

"Heidegger on Being a Person," *Nous* 16 (1982), 15–26.

Hegel, Georg Wilhelm Friedrich, *Die Phenomenologie des Geistes* (Hamburg: Meiner). English: *The Phenomenology of Spirit*, trans. A. Miller (New York: Oxford University Press, 1977).

Heinz, Marion, *Zeitlichkeit und Temporalität im Frühwerk Martin Heideggers* (Würzburg: Königshausen and Neumann, 1982).

Held, Klaus, *Lebendige Gegenwart* (The Hague: Martinus Nijhoff, 1966).

"Phänomenologie der Zeit nach Husserl," *Perspektiven der Philosophie* 7 (1981).

Hoffman, Paul, "The Unity of Descartes' Man," *The Philosophical Review* (1983).

Hoffman, Piotr, "Death, Time, and History: Division II of *Being and Time*," in: Charles Guignon (ed.), *The Cambridge Companion to Heidegger* (New York: Cambridge University Press, 1993), pp. 195–214.

Hopkins, Burt, *Intentionality in Husserl and Heidegger* (Dordrecht: Kluwer, 1993).

Horwich, Paul, *Asymmetries in Time: Problems in the Philosophy of Science* (Cambridge, Mass.: MIT Press, 1987).

Hoy, David, "History, Historicity, and Historiography in *Being and Time*," in: Michael Murray (ed.), *Heidegger and Modern Philosophy: Critical Essays* (New Haven: Yale University Press, 1978), pp. 329–353.

Hume, David, *A Treatise of Human Nature*, Selby-Bigge (ed.) (New York: Oxford University Press, 1978).

James, William, *Principles of Psychology* (New York: Henry Holt, 1890).

Kaplan, David, "On Demonstratives" in: J. Almog, R. Perry and H. Wettstein (eds.), *Themes from Kaplan* (University of Notre Dame Press, 1989).

Kaser, M., "Das römische Privatrecht," in: *Handbuch der Altertumswissenschaft* III, (Munich: Beck, 1996), p. 3.

Katz, Jerrold, "An Outline of Platonist Grammar," *The Philosophy of Linguistics* (New York: Oxford University Press, 1985), pp. 172–203.

Keller, Pierre, "Critique of the Vulgar Notion of Time," *International Journal of Philosophical Studies* 4, 1 (1996), 43–66.

Kelsen, Hans, *General Theory of Law and the State* (New York: Russell and Russell, 1946).

Kenny, Anthony, *Action, Emotion, and the Will* (London: Routledge and Kegan Paul, 1963).

Kern, Iso, "The Three Ways to the Transcendental Phenomenological Reduction in the Philosophy of Edmund Husserl," in: F. Elliston and P. McCormick (eds.), *Husserl: Expositions and Appraisals* (University of Notre Dame Press, 1977), pp. 126–149.

Kierkegaard, Søren, *The Concept of Anxiety*, R. Thomte and A. Anderson trans. (Princeton: Princeton University Press, 1980).

Concluding Unscientific Postscript: to the Philosophical Fragments, trans. V. Hong and E. Hong (Princeton University Press, 1992) and trans. David Swenson and Walter Lowrie (Princeton University Press, 1941).

Repetition (Princeton University Press, 1941).

"At a Graveside," in: *Three Discourses on Imagined Occasions*, trans. V. Hong and E. Hong (Princeton University Press, 1993), pp. 69–102.

Kisiel, Theodore, *The Genesis of Heidegger's Being and Time* (Berkeley and Los Angeles: University of California Press, 1993).

Kneale, William and Kneale, Martha, *The Development of Logic* (Oxford University Press, 1966).

"Intentionality and Intensionality," *Aristotelian Society Supplementary Volume* 42 (1968), 73–90.

Kraus, Oskar, "Die 'kopernikanische Wendung,' in Brentanos Erkenntnis- und Wertlehre," *Philosophische Hefte* 3 (1929).

Kripke, Saul, "A Puzzle About Belief," in: A. Margalit (ed.), *Meaning and Use* (Dordrecht: Reidel, 1979).

Kuspit, Donald, "Fiction and Phenomenology," *Philosophy and Phenomenological Research* 29 (1968), 16–33.

Landgrebe, Ludwig, *Faktizität und Individuation: Studien zur Grundlage der Phänomenologie* (Hamburg: Meiner Verlag, 1982).

Phänomenologie und Metaphysik (Hamburg: Meiner Verlag, 1949).

"The Phenomenological Concept of Experience," *Philosophy and Phenomenological Research* 34 (1973), 1–13.

Lehmann, Karl, "Christliche Geschichtserfahrung und ontologische Frage beim jungen Heidegger," *Philosophisches Jahrbuch* 74 (1966), 126–153.

Levin, David, *Reason and Evidence in Husserl's Phenomenology* (Evanston: Northwestern University Press, 1970).

"Introduction to Husserl's Theory of Eidetic Variation," *Philosophy and Phenomenological Research* 29 (1968), 1–15.

Locke, John, *An Essay Concerning Human Understanding* (New York: Dover, 1959).

Löwith, Karl, *Das Individuum in der Rolle des Mitmenschen* (Munich: Mohn, 1928).

Luther, Martin, *Lectures on Romans* (1515–1516) in: *Luther's Works* (Philadelphia: Fortress Press, 1955).

Macann, Christopher (ed.), *Critical Heidegger* (London: Routledge, 1996).

Marion, Jean Luc, "Heidegger et Descartes." English: "Heidegger and Descartes," in: Christopher Macann (ed.), *Critical Heidegger* (London: Routledge, 1996), pp. 67–96.

McAlister, Linda, "Chisholm and Brentano on Intentionality," *The Review of Metaphysics* 28 (1978), 328–338.

McDowell, John, "De Re Senses," in: C. Wright (ed.), *Frege: Tradition and Influence* (Oxford: Blackwell), pp. 98–108.

"Intentionality *De Re*," in E. LePore and R. van Gulick (eds.), *John Searle And His Critics* (Oxford: Blackwell, 1991), pp. 215–226.

McGinn, Colin, *Wittgenstein* (London: Blackwell, 1987).

McInerney, Peter, *Time and Experience* (Philadelphia: Temple University Press, 1991).

McTaggart, J. M. E., *The Nature of Existence*, vol. 2 (Cambridge University Press, 1927).

"The Unreality of Time," reprinted in: his *Philosophical Studies* (London: Edward Arnold Press, 1934).

Meinong, Alexius, "Beiträge zur Theorie der psychischen Analyse," *Zeitschrift für Psychologie und Physiologie der Sinnesorgane* 6 (1893).

"Über die Stellung der Gegenstandstheorie im System der Wissenschaften," *Zeitschrift für Psychologie und Physiologie der Sinnesorgane* 129–130 (1906–1907).

"Über Gegenstandstheorie," in: *Untersuchungen zur Gegenstandstheorie und Psychologie* (Leipzig: Barth, 1904). English: "The Theory of Objects," in: R. Chisholm (ed.), *Realism and the Background of Phenomenology* (New York: The Free Press, 1960), pp. 76–117.

"Über Gegenstände höherer Ordnung und deren Verhältnis zur inneren Wahrnehmung," *Zeitschrift für Psychologie und Physiologie der Sinnesorgane* 21 (1899), 182–272.

Mellor, Hugh, *Real Time* (Cambridge University Press, 1981).

Merker, Barbara, *Selbsttäuschung und Selbsterkenntnis: zu Heideggers Transformation der Phänomenologie Husserls* (Frankfurt: Suhrkamp, 1988).

Michalski, Krysztof, *Logic and Time: An Essay on Husserl's Theory of Meaning* (Dordrecht: Kluwer, 1997).

Miller, Izchak, *Husserl's Theory of Perception* (Cambridge, Mass.: MIT Press, 1988).

Misch, Georg, *Lebensphilosophie und Phänomenologie* (Darmstadt: Wissenschaftliche Buchgesellschaft, 1967).

Mohanty, J. N., "Husserl and Frege: A new look at their relationship," in: J. N. Mohanty (ed.), *Readings on Edmund Husserl's Logical Investigations* (The Hague: Martinus Nijhoff, 1977), pp. 22–32.

"Husserl's theory of meaning," in: F. Elliston and P. McCormick (eds.), *Husserl. Expositions and Appraisals* (University of Notre Dame Press, 1977).

"The Development of Husserl's Thought," in: B. Smith and D. Smith (eds.), *The Cambridge Companion to Husserl* (New York: Cambridge University Press, 1995).

Murray, Michael, *Heidegger and Modern Philosophy: Critical Essays* (New Haven: Yale University Press, 1978).

Oaklander, L. and Smith, Quentin (eds.), *The New Theory of Time* (New Haven: Yale University Press, 1994).

Okrent, Mark, *Heidegger's Pragmatism* (Ithaca: Cornell, 1988).

Olafson, Frederick, *Heidegger and the Philosophy of Mind* (New Haven: Yale University Press, 1987).

What is a Human Being?: A Heideggerian View (New York: Cambridge, 1995).

"Heidegger *à la* Wittgenstein or 'Coping' with Professor Dreyfus," *Inquiry* 37 (1994), pp. 45–64.

"Individualism, Subjectivity, and Presence: A Response to Taylor Carman," *Inquiry* 37 (1994), 331–337.

Parfit, Derek, *Reasons and Persons* (New York: Oxford University Press, 1984).

"Personal Identity," *Philosophical Review* 80 (1971), 3–27.

Parsons, Charles, "Husserl and the Linguistic Turn," in: Juliet Floyd and Sanford Shieh (eds.), *Future Pasts: Reflections on the History and Nature of Analytic Philosophy* (Cambridge, Mass.: Harvard University Press, 1999).

"A Plea for Substitutional Quantification," in: *Mathematics in Philosophy* (Ithaca: Cornell University Press, 1983).

Patzig, Günther, "Kritische Bemerkungen zu Husserls Thesen über das Verhältnis von Wahrheit und Evidenz," *Neue Hefte für Philosophie* 1 (1971), 12–32. English: "Husserl on Truth and Evidence," in J. Mohanty (ed.), *Readings on E. Husserl's Logical Investigations*" (The Hague: Martinus Nijhoff, 1977), pp. 179–196.

Picht, Georg, *Die Grundlagen der Ethik des Panaitios* (Freiburg: Ph.D. dissertation, 1943).

Pöggeler, Otto, *Der Denkweg Martin Heidegger* (Neske, Pfullingen: 1963). English: *Martin Heidegger's Path of Thinking* (The Hague: Martinus Nijhoff, 1987).

"Heidegger und das Problem der Zeit," *L'héritage de Kant* (Paris: Bibliothèque des Archives de philosophie, 1982), pp. 287–307.

Price, Huw, *Time's Arrow and Archimedes' Point* (New York: Oxford University Press, 1996).

Putnam, Hilary, "Time and Physical Geometry," *Journal of Philosophy* 64 (1967), 240–247.

"The Meaning of Meaning," *Mind, Language, and Reality: Philosophical Papers* 2 (New York: Cambridge University Press, 1981).

Radner, Daisie, "Descartes' Notion of the Union of Mind and Body," *Journal of the History of Philosophy* 9 (1971), 159–170.

Richardson, John, *Existential Epistemology: A Heideggerian Critique of the Cartesian Project* (New York: Oxford University Press, 1986).

Richardson, Robert, "Brentano on Intentional Inexistence and the Distinction Between Mental and Physical Phenomena," *Archiv für Geschichte der Philosophie* 65 (1983), 250–282.

Richardson, William, *Heidegger from Phenomenology to Thought* (The Hague: Martinus Nijhoff, 1963).

Ricketts, Thomas, "Objectivity and Objecthood: Frege's Metaphysics of Judgment," in: L. Haaparanta and J. Hintikka (eds.), *Frege Synthesized* (Dordrecht: Reidel, 1986).

Rietdijk, C. W., "A Rigorous Proof of Determinism Derived from the Special Theory of Relativity," *Philosophy of Science* 33 (1966), 341–344.

Rorty, Richard, "Heidegger, Contingency, and Pragmatism," in: Dreyfus and Hall (eds.), *Heidegger: A Critical Reader* (Oxford: Blackwell, 1992), pp. 209–230.

Russell, Bertrand, "Knowledge by Acquaintance and Knowledge by Description," *Mysticism and Logic* (London: Allen and Unwin, 1917), pp. 152–167.

The Problems of Philosophy (Oxford University Press, 1973).

Scheler, Max, *Wesen und Formen der Sympathie, Gesammelte Werke* 7 (Bern: Francke, 1973, original 1913).

Schmitz, Hermann, *Husserl und Heidegger* (Bonn: Bouvier, 1996).

Schuhmann, Karl, "Husserls doppelter Vorstellungsbegriff: Die Texte von 1893," *Brentano-Studien* 3 (1990–1901), pp. 119–136.

Schutz, Alfred, "The Problem of Transcendental Intersubjectivity in Husserl," in: *Collected Paper: Studies in Phenomenological Philosophy* 3, (The Hague: Martinus Nijhoff, 1966), pp. 51–91.

Searle, John R., *Intentionality: an Essay in the Philosophy of Mind* (New York: Cambridge University Press, 1983).

Shoemaker, Sidney, "Persons and their Pasts," *American Philosophical Quarterly* 7 (1970).

Sklar, Lawrence, *Space, Time, and Spacetime* (Berkeley: University of California Press, 1974), pp. 272–275.

Sluga, Hans, *Frege* (London: Routledge and Kegan Paul, 1980).

Smith, Barry, *Austrian Philosophy: The Legacy of Franz Brentano* (La Salle: Open Court, 1994).

Smith, Barry and D. Smith (eds.), *The Cambridge Companion to Husserl* (New York: Cambridge University Press, 1995).

Smith, David Woodruff, "Husserl on Demonstrative Reference and Perception," in: H. Dreyfus (ed.), *Husserl, Intentionality, and Cognitive Science* (Boston: MIT Press, 1982).

"On Situations and States of Affairs," in: T. Seebohm, D. Føllesdal, and J. Mohanty (eds.), *Phenomenology and the Formal Sciences* (Dordrecht: Kluwer, 1991), pp. 49–58.

Smith, David Woodruff and Ronald McIntyre, *Husserl and Intentionality* (Dordrecht: Reidel, 1982).

"Theory of Intentionality," in: J. N. Mohanty and R. McKenna (eds.), *Husserl's Phenomenology: A Textbook* (Washington: University Press of America, 1989), pp. 147–180.

Sokolowski, Robert, "Intentional Analysis and the Noema," *Dialectica* 38 (1984), 113–139.

Solomon, Robert, "Husserl's Concept of the Noema," in: F. Elliston and McCormick (eds.), *Husserl: Expositions and Appraisals* (University of Notre Dame Press, 1977), pp. 168–181.

Sorabji, Richard, "Intentionality and Physiological Processes," in: Martha Nussbaum and Amélie Rorty (eds.), *Essays on Aristotle's De Anima* (New York: Oxford University Press, 1992), pp. 195–225.

"From Aristotle to Brentano: The Development of the Concept of Intentionality," *Oxford Studies in Ancient Philosophy*, Supplementary Volume 9 (1991), 227–259.

Spiegelberg, Herbert, " 'Intention' and 'Intentionality' in the Scholastics, Brentano, and Husserl," trans. L. McAlister and M. Schättle, in: L. McAlister (ed.), *The Philosophy of Brentano* (London: Duckworth, 1976),

Stein, Howard, "Minkowski Space-Time," *Journal of Philosophy* 65 (1968), 5–23.

Stich, Stephen, *Deconstructing the Mind* (New York: Oxford University Press, 1996).

From Folk Psychology to Cognitive Science: The Case Against Belief (Cambridge, Mass.: MIT Press, 1983).

Strawson, P. F., "Freedom and Resentment," in: *Freedom and Resentment and Other Essays* (London: Methuen, 1974).

Individuals: An Essay in Descriptive Metaphysics (London: Methuen, 1959).

Ströker, Elizabeth, *Husserl's Transcendental Phenomenology* (Palo Alto: Stanford University Press, 1993).

"Zeit und Geschichte in Husserls Phänomenologie. Zur Frage ihres Zusammenhangs," *Zeit und Zeitlichkeit bei Husserl und Heidegger*, pp. 111–137.

Stump, Eleanore and Norman Kretzmann, "Eternity," *Journal of Philosophy* 78 (1981), 429–458.

Suessbauer, Alfons, *Intentionalität, Sachverhalt, Noema* (Freiburg: Karl Alber, 1995).

Taminiaux, Jacques, "Remarques sur Heidegger et les *Recherches Logiques* de Husserl," in: *Le regard et l'excédent* (The Hague: Martinus Nijhoff, 1977).

Theunissen, Michael, *The Other: Studies in the Social Ontology of Husserl, Heidegger, Sartre, Buber*, trans. C. Macann (Boston: MIT Press, 1984).

Thomas Aquinas, *Summa Theologica* (New York: Benzinger Brothers, 1952).

Tieszen, Richard, *Mathematical Intuition: Phenomenology and Mathematical Knowledge* (Dordrecht: Kluwer, 1989).

Tugendhat, Ernst, *Vorlesungen zur Einleitung in die sprachanalytische Philosophie* (Frankfurt: Suhrkamp, 1974).

Der Wahrheitsbegriff bei Husserl und Heidegger (Berlin: de Gruyter, 1967).

"Heidegger's Idee von Wahrheit," in: Otto Pöggeler (ed.), *Heidegger: Perspektiven zur Deutung seines Werkes* (Köln: Neue Wissenschaftliche Bibliothek, 1969). English: "Heidegger's idea of truth," in: Christopher Macann (ed.) *Critical Heidegger* (London: Routledge, 1996).

"Philosophy and Linguistic Analysis," in: F. Elliston and P. McCormick, *Husserl. Expositions and Appraisals* (University of Notre Dame Press, 1977).

Twardowski, Kasimir, *Zur Lehre vom Inhalt und Gegenstand der Vorstellungen: Eine psychologische Untersuchung* (Munich: Philosophia, 1982). English: *On the Content and Object of Presentations*, trans. R. Grossman (The Hague: Martinus Nijhoff, 1977).

Überweg-Geyer, *Geschichte der Philosophie*, vol. 2 (1928).

Van Buren, John, *The Young Heidegger* (Bloomington: University of Indiana Press, 1994).

Velleman, J. D., "Well Being and Time," *The Pacific Philosophical Quarterly* 72 (1992), 48–77.

Volpi, Franco, et al. (eds.), *Heidegger et l'idée de la phénoménologie* (Dordrecht: Kluwer, 1988).

"Heidegger in Marburg: Die Auseinandersetzung mit Aristoteles," *Philosophischer Literaturanzeiger* 37 (1984), 172–188.

"Heidegger in Marburg: Die Auseinandersetzung mit Husserl," *Philosophischer Literaturanzeiger* 37 (1984), 48–69.

Von Weizsäcker, Carl Friedrich, *Aufbau der Physik* (Hamburg: Hanser, 1985).

"The Second Law and the Difference between Past and Future," in: *The Unity of Nature* (New York: Farrar, Strauss, Giroux, 1980), pp. 138–146.

Wilkes, Kathleen, *Real People* (Oxford: Clarendon, 1988).

Willard, Dallas, *Logic and the Objectivity of Knowledge. A Study of Husserl's Early Philosophy* (Athens: Ohio University Press, 1984).

"The Paradox of Logical Psychologism: Husserl's Way Out," *American Philosophical Quarterly* 9 (1972), reprinted in: J. N. Mohanty (ed.), *Readings on Edmund Husserl's Logical Investigations* (The Hague: Martinus Nijhoff, 1977), pp. 43–54.

Zaner, Richard M., "The Art of Free-Phantasy in Rigorous Phenomenological Science," in: F. Kersten and R. Zaner (eds.), *Phenomenology: Continuation and Criticism* (The Hague: Martinus Nijhoff, 1972), pp. 192–219.

"Examples and Possibles: A Criticism of Husserl's Theory of Free-Phantasy Variation," *Research in Phenomenology* 3 (1973), 29–43.

Index

absolute time-consciousness, 80–82
abstract objects, 91
anthropologism and anthropomorphism,
   108–111
Aristotle
  life and the soul, 93
  on authenticity, and truth, 103
  on memory, 74 and 74n
  on noetic and practical insight, 94
  on time 30, 66–68
  on truth 94
  the scholastic interpretation of, 84–85
Augustine
  on time, 30
authenticity and inauthenticity, 230–238,
   241–242

Beaufret, Jean
  Heidegger and the phenomenological
    reduction, 145n
being, 88, 91
being-in-the-world, 127–128, 152–153
Bernet, Rudolf
  phenomenological reduction, 145n
  time-consciousness, 66n, 89n
Binswanger, Ludwig
  self-loss, 219n
Blattner, William
  sequentiality, 225n
Brand, Gerd
  punctual moment, 66n
Brandom, Robert
  social objects, 150n
Brentano, Franz
  and descriptive psychology, 86
  and Heidegger, 84, 84n, 85
  time 64–68, 70
Broad, C. D.
  on McTaggart's paradox, 81n
Brough, John
  time-consciousness, 65n, 74n, 83n

care, structure of, 174–177, 187–188
Carman, Taylor
  being social, 160, 165–166
Carr, David
  horizonal character of intentionality, 116n
Cartesianism, 128, 170n, 173, 218
categories, 89, 91
categorial intuition, 88–91
Chisholm, Roderick
  temporal identity, 224
Clarke, Samuel
  on space and time, 63
commissurotomy, 214–215
Cramer, Konrad
  on experience, 88n

Dasein
  and *Existenz*, 99
  and indexical expressions, 100
  as a distinctive mode of being, 121–123
Dastur, Françoise
  on temporal transcendence, 188–189n
  on time, 88–89
deconstruction, 107
demonstratives, 193–197
Derrida, Jacques
  presence, 65n
  vulgar time, 205n
Descartes, René
  and world, 218
  unity of mind and body, 218
Dewey, John
  pragmatism, 156–157
Diemer, Alwin
  Husserl, 108n
Dilthey, Wilhelm
  descriptive psychology, 86
  life, 85
disclosure, 92
  truth, 97
  and intelligibility, 174

discourse, 134–139
attunement and know-how, 179
dispositions, 122–123
Dostal, Robert
intelligibility, 150n
Dreyfus, Hubert
and Rubin on Kierkegaard, 236–237n
intelligibility, 159–167
meaning, 167–174
Dun Scotus, 85
duration, 63

Edwards, Paul
temporal stretch, 189
eidos, 122
eidetic reduction, 119
embodiment, 213–214
essence, 118
and existence, 121
of consciousness, 121
existence, 86
experiences, 59–60, 86, 88, 186
explanation, 150–153
Evidenz
and Heidegger, 98–99, 104
and truth, 92
of temporal succession, 62

Fell, Joseph
on groundlessness, 170n
on nature, 147n
Findlay, John N.
retention, 71
Føllesdal, Dagfinn
antifoundationalism, 115
Frede, Dorothea
intelligibility, 152
Frege, Gottfried
logic, 113n
Friedman, Michael
pure consciousness, 121

Gadamer, Hans Georg
Husserl, Heidegger and historicity, 107n
Geertz, Clifford
social roles, 239
Gibbs, J. Willard
probabilities, 192
Gödel, Kurt
circular time, 200n
Guignon, Charles
das Man, 158–159
discourse and intelligibility, 136–138

Haar, Michael
animality and language use, 240

Harries, Karsten
worldless things, 204n
Hartmann, Klaus
definient and eminent modes, 161n
Haugeland, John
self as institution, 209–211
Hawking, Stephen
models of the universe, 200n
Held, Klaus
retention, 121n
Hopkins, Burt
horizonal intentionality, 116n
Horwich, Paul
temporal asymmetries, 191
Hume, David
bundle theory, 222
Husserl, Edmund
personalistic psychology, 87
Philosophy of Arithmetic, 89–90

image
in memory, 74–75
intelligibility
and *das Man*, 158–174
and discourse, 136–138
and temporality, 174–181
intentionality, 84
and temporality, 179–183
externalist conception of, 100
horizonal, 60, 72, 114
referential 60, 72, 98
intuition and truth, 99

James, William
primary and secondary memory, 73
specious present, 63
Jaspers, Karl
existence 86, 99

Kant, Immanuel, 61
Anticipations of Perceptions, 63
conception of a person, 87–88, 122
on Schematism, 90
Refutation of Idealism, 101, 218
things in themselves, 76
Transcendental Aesthetic, 63
Transcendental Deduction, 76
Kaser, M.
Roman notion of a person, 227n
Kierkegaard, Søren, 86
critique of pure consciousness, 118
life as anxious confrontation with death, 236–237
on Aristotle on the process of life, 93
truth, subjectivist notion of, 95

Kisiel, Theodor
  indexicals, 194
  life and *Dasein*, 86n
Kraus, Oskar
  Brentano, 68
Kretzmann, Norman and Eleanore Stump
  eternity, 202n

Landgrebe, Ludwig
  theoretical, 129n
Lange, Friedrich Ernst
  number, 89
language, 134, 144
  and communication, 148–149
Lehmann, Karl
  Paul, 236n
Leibniz, Gottfried Wilhelm Friedrich, 63
level metaphysics (Schichtenmetaphysik),
  126
life
  Aristotle, 93
  Aristotle and Dilthey, 86
  Marcuse and Hegel, 86n
Locke, John
  memory, 220–221
  perpetual perishing, 229
  person, 216–219
Luria, Alexander
  mnemotics, 220
Luther, Martin
  human existence, 236n

Man, das, 157–167
Marcuse, Herbert
  life in Hegel, 86n
McInerney, Peter
  passage, 197
McTaggart, J. Ellis
  alternative time-series, 198
  unreality of time, 76–79, 81
Meinong, Alexius
  duration, 68–69
memory
  factual, 76
  personal, 76
  primary, 73–76
  realist theory of, 74
  representative theory of, 74–75
  secondary, 73–76
Merleau-Ponty, Maurice
  perceptual presence, 130, 130n
Miller, Izchak
  present, 65, 69 and 69n, 70
moment, punctual, 63
monothetic acts, 99

mood, 134
  of anxiety, 152

narrow and wide content, 111–113
natural attitude, 124
naturalistic attitude, 125
noema, 94–95
normativity, 154

Okrent, Mark, 134
objectivity
  and truth, 104
Olafson, Frederick
  being as presence, 205
  perceptual presence, 130
  social, 160–162, 171n
  world, 241n
ontology, 88

Parfit, Derek
  self, 207
passage, 81
  myth of, 193
perception
  and truth, 130–131
personalistic psychology, 87
persons
  as annexes, 124–126
  identity of, 224–226, 240–241
phenomenological reduction 61, 129, 144–154
Picht, Georg
  Cicero, 228n
Platonism, 91, 113, 119
Pöggeler, Otto
  historical phenomenology, 107n
pragmatism, 134
presence, 103
protention, 72, 80
proteraisthesis, 68n
Price, Hew
  temporal asymmetry, 191n
Putnam, Hilary
  externalism, 111
  special relativity and becoming, 198n

relativity
  general theory of, 199–200
  special theory of, 197–199
retention, 72, 80
Ricoeur, Paul
  historical time, 203
  real time, 83, 83n

Scheler, Max
  Husserl as Platonist, 119

personalistic psychology, 87–88
Schematism, 90n
Schmitz, Hermann, 87n
Shoemaker, Sidney
  quasi-memories, 217
Sklar, Lawrence
  becoming and relativity, 198n
Stein, Howard
  relativity and becoming, 198n
Searle, John R.
  intentionality, 112n
sensations, 59–62
  of zero durations, 71
  original sensations, 71
  sensation and the lived body, 124
significance, 132
  breakdown of context of, 144–154
  holistic context of, 141–144
Sigwart, Heinrich
  on anthropocentric truth, 104–105
specious present, 65
Stenzel, Julius
  and Husserl's purported Platonism, 119
Ströker, Elizabeth
  sensations, 124

Taminiaux, Jacques
  categorial intuition, 90n
thermodynamics, second law of, 190–191
time
  A-series, 76–79
  absolute and relational, 199–200
  B-series, 76–79
  direction of, 190–193
  sequential, 225

source of intelligibility, 174–183
  vulgar conception of, 184, 193–197
Thomas Aquinas, 85
Thomas of Erfurt, 85
tools
  in Husserl, 127
  their use and breakdown, 153
Trendelenburg, Adolf
  and Aristotelianism, 86
  importance of process, 93
transcendence, and truth, 98
transcendental idealism, 80, 153–154
truth, 88, 91, 93
  and pragmatism, 134
  as correspondence, 149–150
  as disclosure 100–103
  as discovery, 104–107
  contextualization of, 106–108
  eternal truths, 105
Tugendhat, Ernst
  on truth, 97
  on being human, 122n

Velleman, J. D.
  well-being, 233
von Weizsäcker, Carl Friedrich Freiherr
  second law and tenses, 192

Weberman, David
  das Man, 156
Wilkes, Kathleen
  brain bisection, 215
Wittgenstein, Ludwig
  everyday practices, 156
  Robinson Crusoe, 157n